The Struggle for Racial Equality

The Struggle for Racial Equality

A Documentary Record

Selected and Edited by

Henry Steele Commager

Harper Torchbooks ▼ The Academy Library
Harper & Row, Publishers
NEW YORK

To
Evan

THE STRUGGLE FOR RACIAL EQUALITY

Printed in the United States of America.

This book was originally published as Part Four, Chapter 14, of *Living Ideas in America* (New, Enlarged Edition), copyright © 1951, 1964 by Henry Steele Commager. It has been revised and greatly expanded for the Torchbook edition.

First HARPER TORCHBOOK edition published 1967 by Harper & Row, Publishers, Incorporated, New York, N.Y. 10016.

Library of Congress Catalog Card Number: 67–15626.

Designed by Darlene Starr Carbone

Sources and Acknowledgments

Chapter 1. AN AMERICAN DILEMMA. Gunnar Myrdal et al., *An American Dilemma.* Two vols. New York: Harper & Row, 1944, pp. li–lii. Copyright 1944 by Harper & Row, Publishers. Reprinted by permission.
Chapter 2. THE CIVIL WAR AMENDMENTS, 1868–70. Constitution of the United States.
Chapter 3. THE FREEDMAN'S CASE. George Washington Cable, "The Freedman's Case in Equity," *Century* Magazine, January 1885.
Chapter 4. FREDERICK DOUGLASS CALLS ON THE FREEDMEN TO ORGANIZE FOR SELF-PROTECTION. Frederick Douglass, "Why a Colored Convention?" in *Three Addresses on the Relations Sub-*

sisting Between White and Colored People of the United States. Washington, 1886, pp. 3–23.
Chapter 5. "The Agitation of Questions of Social Equality is the Extremist Folly." Booker T. Washington, Address at the Cotton States' Exposition in Atlanta, Georgia, 1895, in Carter G. Woodson, ed., *Negro Orators and Their Orations.* Washington, 1925, pp. 580–3.
Chapter 6. "Mr. Washington Represents the Old Attitude of Submission." W. E. B. DuBois, "Of Booker T. Washington," in *The Souls of Black Folk.* Chicago, 1903.
Chapter 7. "Separate But Equal." Opinion of Henry Billings Brown and John Marshall Harlan in Plessy *v.* Ferguson, 163 U.S. 537 (1896).
Chapter 8. "To Secure These Rights." A. Executive Order 9908, December 5, 1946, Harry S. Truman, in *To Secure These Rights.* Washington, 1947, pp. viii–ix. B. The Report of the President's Committee on Civil Rights, in *To Secure These Rights.* Washington, 1947, pp. 62–7.
Chapter 9. Equality in the Armed Services, 1948. Executive Order 9981, July 26, 1948, Harry S. Truman, in *Freedom to Serve.* Washington, 1950, pp. xi–xii.
Chapter 10. Equal Opportunities for All: Truman's Civil Rights Program. Civil Rights Message, February 2, 1948, Harry S. Truman, in U. S. House Documents, no. 516, 80th Congress, 2nd Session.
Chapter 11. "Separate Educational Facilities are Inherently Unequal." Opinion of Chief Justice Earl Warren in Brown *v.* Topeka 347 U.S. 483 (1954).
Chapter 12. "Brown *v.* Topeka is a Naked Exercise of Judicial Power." Southern Declaration on Integration. *The New York Times,* March 12, 1956.
Chapter 13. An Argument that the Negro is Inherently Inferior. Carleton Putnam, *Race and Reason: A Yankee View.* Washington: Public Affairs Press, 1961, pp. 21–9. Reprinted by permission.
Chapter 14. Southern Extremists Deplore "Black Monday," 1954. Tom P. Brady, *Black Monday.* Jackson, Miss.: The Citizens' Council of America, 1955, pp. 41–4, 60–3. Reprinted by permission.
Chapter 15. The White Citizens' Council Lets Loose the Winds of Fear. James Graham Cook, *The Segregationists.* New York: Appleton-Century-Crofts, 1962, pp. 34–43. Copyright © 1962 by James Graham Cook. Reprinted by permission.
Chapter 16. Crisis in Little Rock. A. The Eisenhower Address on Little Rock, September 24, 1957. *Public Papers of the Presidents: D. D. Eisenhower,* 1957, No. 198. B. Cooper *v.* Aaron 358 U.S. 1 (1958).
Chapter 17. The Court Vindicates the NAACP, 1958. Opinion of John Marshall Harlan in NAACP *v.* Alabama 357 U.S. 449 (1958).
Chapter 18. Crisis in Montgomery. Martin Luther King, Jr., "Where do we go from Here?" in *Stride Toward Freedom.* New York: Harper & Row, 1958, pp. 189–95, 196, 211, 212–3, 213–6. Copyright © 1958 by Martin Luther King, Jr. Reprinted by permission of Harper & Row, Publishers.
Chapter 19. Justice Douglas Vindicates the Negro Sit-ins, 1961. Opinion of William Douglas in Garner *v.* Louisiana 368 U.S. 157 (1961).
Chapter 20. Policy and Reality in Negro Employment. William Peters, *The Southern Temper.* Garden City, New York: Doubleday & Co., 1959, pp. 242–62, *passim.* Copyright 1958 and 1959 by William Peters; copyright 1958 by McCall Corporation. Reprinted by permission of Curtis Brown Ltd.
Chapter 21. A Southern Student is Loyal to the Traditions of the Old South. Margaret Long, "A Southern Teenager Speaks his Mind," in *The New York Times,* November 19, 1963. © 1963 by The New York Times Company. Reprinted by permission.
Chapter 22. Equal Rights: The Unending Struggle. A. Opinion of Earl Warren in Wright *v.* Georgia 373 U.S. 284 (1963). B. Opinion of Earl Warren in Peterson *v.* Greenville 373 U.S. 244 (1963).
Chapter 23. A Night of Terror in Plaquemine, Louisiana, 1963. James J. Farmer, *Freedom—When?* New York: Random House, 1965, pp. 4–16. © copyright 1963 by The Congress of Racial Equality. Reprinted by permission of Random House, Inc.
Chapter 24. The Reverend Dr. Martin Luther King, Jr. Writes a Letter From the Birmingham Jail. Martin Luther King, Jr., *Why We Can't Wait.* New York: Harper & Row, 1964, pp. 76–95. Copyright © 1963 by Martin Luther King, Jr. Reprinted by permission of Harper & Row, Publishers.

Chapter 25. "We Face a Moral Crisis," June, 1963. President John F. Kennedy, Address, June 11, 1963, in *The New York Times,* June 12, 1963.
Chapter 26. Tragedy in Birmingham. James Reston, "Birmingham," in *The New York Times,* September 20, 1963. © 1963 by The New York Times Company. Reprinted by permission.
Chapter 27. Official Lawlessness in the South. Anthony Lewis and *The New York Times, Portrait of a Decade.* New York: Random House, 1964, pp. 284–93. © 1964 by The New York Times Company. Reprinted by permission of Random House, Inc.
Chapter 28. Official Lawlessness: A Documentary Record. Margaret Long, ed., *New South* (June 1964), journal of The Southern Regional Council, Atlanta, Georgia. Reprinted by permission.
Chapter 29. A Student Crusade to Mississippi, 1964. Elizabeth Sutherland, ed., *Letters from Mississippi.* New York: McGraw-Hill, 1965, *passim.* Copyright © 1965 by McGraw-Hill, Inc. Used by permission of McGraw-Hill Book Company.
Chapter 30. The End of the Poll-Tax: The Twenty-Fourth Amendment, 1964. The Constitution of the United States.
Chapter 31. The Civil Rights Act of 1964. Public Law 88–352, 88th Congress, 2nd Session, July 2, 1964.
Chapter 32. President Johnson Asks Congress to Redeem the Fifteenth Amendment, 1965. President Lyndon B. Johnson, Address before joint session of Congress, March 15, 1965. A White House Release.
Chapter 33. The Voting Rights Act of 1965. Appendix to South Carolina *v.* Katzenbach 86 S. Ct. Rep. 803, August 6, 1965.
Chapter 34. The Right to Vote: The Unending Struggle. A. Opinion of Tom Clark in Anderson *v.* Martin 375 U.S. 399 (1964). B. Opinion of Hugo Black in Louisiana *v.* the United States 380 U.S. 145 (1965). C. Opinion of Earl Warren in South Carolina *v.* Katzenbach 86 S. Ct. Rep. 803 (1966).
Chapter 35. The Dark Ghetto of Harlem. Kenneth B. Clark, *Dark Ghetto.* New York: Harper & Row, 1965, pp. 111–5. Copyright © 1965 by Kenneth B. Clark. Reprinted by permission of Harper & Row, Publishers.
Chapter 36. Watts. Arna Bontemps and Jack Conroy, *Anyplace but Here.* New York: Hill & Wang, 1966, pp. 269–77. Originally published as *They Seek a City.* Copyright © 1945, 1966 by Arna Bontemps and Jack Conroy. Reprinted by permission of Hill & Wang, Inc. Reprinted by permission of Harold Ober Associates, Inc.
Chapter 37. "The Barriers to Freedom are Tumbling Down." President Lyndon B. Johnson, Address on Civil Rights at Howard University, June 4, 1965. A White House Release.
Chapter 38. The Emergence of Black Power. Stokely Carmichael, "What We Want," in *The New York Review of Books,* September 22, 1966. Reprinted by permission of the Student Non-violent Coordinating Committee.

Contents

Preface

IN HIS PEORIA speech of 1854 Abraham Lincoln asserted that "slavery deprives our republican example of its just influence in the world; enables the enemies of free institutions with plausibility to taunt us as hypocrites; causes the real friends of freedom to doubt our sincerity; and forces so many good men among ourselves into an open war with the very fundamental principles of civil liberty." The denial of equal rights to Negroes during the Second World War, and the world-wide revolution which ensued, had much the same effect. It enabled our enemies once again to taunt us with hypocrisy, and to assert that though we proclaimed equality we practiced racism. A time when the colored peoples of Africa and Asia were bursting their century-old bonds, and when some two score African and Asian nations moved resolutely onto the historical stage, was not an auspicious one for the maintenance of racial discrimination in a nation which was making a bid for political and moral leadership of the free world.

As the centenary of the Civil War, emancipation, and the Reconstruction Amendments approached, Negroes in the South, and in many parts of the North too, were still second-class citizens. Negro children were fobbed off with schools that were not only segregated but materially and academically inferior, and Negro youths were denied entrance to State universities for whose support they were taxed. When Negroes traveled they were forced to sit in segregated waiting rooms, ride in segregated sections of buses and trains, to eat in segregated dining rooms. They were condemned to segregation in most public places as well—playgrounds, swimming pools, theaters, and even churches. And half a century after Booker T. Washington's Atlanta Speech calling for economic partnership between Negroes and whites, Southern Negroes were still tenant farmers and Northern Negroes still largely unskilled workers. North and South alike, urban Negroes—and by 1960 that meant most of them—lived in slums that would have been called ghettos had they been in Warsaw or Prague. Their right to vote and to hold office—guaranteed them by the Constitution itself—was flouted and even their most elementary rights were denied, rights presumably sacred: freedom of speech, freedom of assembly, freedom of association, and a fair trial.

The great Swedish sociologist, Gunnar Myrdal, called all this the American Dilemma, and it was. The Dilemma, wrote Myrdal, "is the ever-raging conflict between, on the one hand, the valuations preserved on the general plane which we . . . call 'the American creed,' where the American thinks, talks, and acts under the influence of high national and Christian precepts, and, on the other hand, the valuation on specific planes of individual and group living, where personal and local interests, economic, social, and sectional jealousies; considerations of community prestige and conformity; group prejudice against particular persons or types of people; and all sorts of miscellaneous wants, impulses, and habits, dominate his outlook" (*An American Dilemma*, I, xliii). That dilemma weighed heavily on the conscience of most Northerners, and of many Southerners too, though most Southerners had learned to live with it and even to ignore it. They contrasted the position of the free Negro not with their own but with that of the slave, and concluded that the Negro was, after all, making great progress, and should be content with that progress. They knew that there was a "Negro problem," just as their grandfathers had known that there was a slavery problem, but they persuaded themselves that the problem would somehow work itself out, all in good time, and concluded that nothing was to be gained and much was to be lost by rushing things. They knew that evolution was better than revolution, and they knew too that evolution was a slow process, and they did not understand why Negroes should not take the same satisfaction in gradual evolution as they did. Basic to their attitude was one explicit and one implicit assumption. The explicit assumption was that Southerners knew best—the Southern white, that is—and that race relations would take care of themselves if only outsiders, e.g., Northerners, would leave the South alone. The implicit assumption—which was explicit enough under pressure—was that the Negro was after all inferior to the white, and that he should not therefore expect genuine equality, political, economic, or social. The Southern solution to the Negro problem was, then, at its best merely ameliorative.

It was the New Deal, and the Second World War, which made the first real dent in this façade of complacency and intransigence; the New Deal by leveling up the economic condition of the Negro and by some rather ineffectual gestures toward desegregation, and the war by ending segregation in some elements of the armed forces and in defense industries, and by giving to Negroes themselves a new experience and a new dimension of hope and expectation. With the coming of peace many Negroes who had seen and even experienced equality in Europe were unwilling to go back to their old position of inferiority in their own country. Many, too, returned not to their old homes in the South, but to Northern cities, and the movement of Negroes from South to North accelerated sharply in the decades until 1964, when the majority of Negroes lived in the North; New York had the largest Negro population of any State, and New York City, Washington, Philadelphia, and Detroit were the largest Negro cities. This meant new economic and educational opportunities for hundreds of thousands of Negroes. It meant, too, that the Negroes were now a power to be reckoned with politically, for though they could not vote in the South, they could and did vote in the North. As it was not practicable to deny economic and social rights to those who held political power, the contrast between the condition of Negroes in the North and in the South sharpened with every year.

The new attitude toward the Negro was dramatized by a series of State and Federal laws, and Executive Orders, forbidding racial discrimination in employment and in the civil service—orders often dishonored or evaded by local authorities. It was dramatized even more effectively by a series of Supreme Court decisions chipping away at the walls of discrimination which had been erected by the South. One series of decisions looked to the implementation of the requirements of due process of law. Another required political parties to act as public, not private, organizations, and to admit Negroes to primaries. A third series announced the beginning of the end of discrimination in public facilities such as housing and transportation. The climax of this judicial assault on the doctrine and practice of white supremacy came with the historic school desegregation case of 1954—Brown *versus* Board of Education of Topeka—which reversed the fifty-year-old Plessy *versus* Ferguson decision, vindicated Justice Harlan's dissenting opinion in that memorable case, and overthrew the "separate but equal" doctrine with the simple proposition that what was separate was not equal.

Brown *versus* Topeka called for desegregation of public schools "with all deliberate speed," and thus inaugurated more than a decade of turmoil and struggle. For Southerners saw clearly enough the implications of this doctrine: what today applied to schools would apply tomorrow to all other public facilities and accommodations. They resisted therefore with a kind of desperation, resisted at first by subterfuge and evasion and delay, and then by outright violence. In the border States—except in parts of Virginia and Tennessee—there was reluctant aquiescence, but the "Deep" South was intransigent, and ten years after the judicial fiat there were no Negro children in the schools of South Carolina, Alabama, or Mississippi and only token desegregation in other States.

As so often in the past—and not in the South alone—defiance took on a cloak of legality. After the first shock, Southerners gathered their intellectual as well as their physical resources for resistance. While White Citizens' Councils—a kind of respectable Ku Klux Klan—were resorting to force and intimidation, over ninety Southern Congressmen issued a statement denouncing the Supreme Court decision as a usurpation of power, and calling on the South for resistance.

Perhaps the most important development in the long struggle for Negro rights was not in the Courts or in the Congress, but in the ranks of the Negroes themselves. Under Booker T. Washington Negro leadership had been cooperative and acquiescent; under W. E. B. DuBois it was defiant but highly intellectual. Now under men like Philip Randolph, Thurgood Marshall, James Farmer, and the Reverend Martin Luther King, Jr., the Negroes took affairs pretty much into their own hands. They embarked upon vigorous programs of publicity, political campaigns, sit-in demonstrations, orderly marches to city halls and to schools, and eventually a grand march on the city of Washington itself. Along with all this, Negroes employed the tactic of the economic boycott—as in the campaign for desegregated buses in Montgomery—and in this they had the support of important segments of Northern consumers, white and Negro alike. Southern authorities responded to these measures—the demonstration, the sit-in, the boycott—with wholesale arrests, but with almost monotonous regularity Federal Courts voided these arrests and asserted the constitutional right of Negroes to agitate peacefully for their constitutional rights.

Meantime the issue of civil rights moved back into the halls of Congress, where it had troubled the surface of the political waters during the Reconstruction years, and occasionally thereafter. Every President after Franklin Roosevelt insisted on the necessity of Federal action, but little action materialized. A civil rights bill was passed early in Eisenhower's second administration, but it proved almost wholly ineffective. President Kennedy made an eloquent plea for the enactment of a broad civil rights program embracing political, economic, and social rights. The Congress did not reject his arguments, but ignored them. His tragic death did not end the matter; on the contrary it provided a kind of dramatic and romantic argument for carrying this program to fulfilment. By good fortune, too, President Johnson was just as determined as President Kennedy to guarantee that equality so long promised and so long denied. In mid-summer 1964, after prolonged parliamentary maneuvers and filibusters, Congress enacted a sweeping civil rights bill. This was followed by a Voting Rights Bill the next year. Stimulated by this new legislation, by energetic support from the Attorney-General and the federal Courts, by a massive campaign for civic education and registration undertaken by various civil rights groups, Negro registration in the South soared to unprecedented heights. By 1966 it was clear that the battle for equality at the polls had been won; only a few mopping-up operations remained. Already the center of gravity had shifted to the intractable areas of education, housing, and employment. And it was finally clear that these were not regional but national problems. But impatience with the slow actual progress in these fields led to the emergence of a philosophy of Black Power, which alarmed large segments of the white community and probably contributed to the defeat of the 1966 Civil Rights Bill. But the most persuasive and moderate case for Black Power was made by a new group of leaders, most prominently by Stokely Carmichael, whose essay, "What We Want," is the final entry in this book.

1. An American Dilemma

Gunnar Myrdal

EDITORIAL NOTE: *For three quarters of a century after Appomattox—and in some quarters for an even longer time—the American people indulged themselves in the habit of talking about the "Negro problem." It was the great Swedish economist Gunnar Myrdal who, more than anyone else, made it clear that what confronted Americans was not a Negro problem but a white problem, that what confronted them was not, fundamentally, a sociological but a moral problem. Invited by the Carnegie Corporation to make a fresh study of American race relations, Myrdal came to the United States in 1938 and devoted four years to an extensive and intensive study of all aspects of Negro-white relationships. The result was a classic in social literature:* An American Dilemma. *In his introduction to this study Myrdal concluded that "not since Reconstruction has there been more reason to anticipate fundamental changes in American race relations, changes which will involve a development toward the American ideals." We take from Myrdal's introductory chapter this admonition to the American people.*

IN THEIR BASIC traits the Negroes are inherently not much different from other people. Neither are, incidentally, the white Americans. But Negroes and whites in the United States live in singular human relations with each other. All the circumstances of life—the "environmental" conditions in the broadest meaning of that term—diverge more from the "normal" for the Negroes than for the whites, if only because of the statistical fact that the Negroes are the smaller group. The average Negro must experience many times more of the "abnormal" interracial relations than the average white man in America. The more important fact, however, is that practically all the economic, social, and political power is held by whites. The Negroes do not by far have anything approaching a tenth of the things worth having in America.

It is thus the white majority group that naturally determines the Negro's "place." All our attempts to reach scientific explanations of why the Negroes are what they are and why they live as they do have regularly led to determinants on the white side of the race line. In the practical and political struggles of effecting changes, the views and attitudes of the white Americans are likewise strategic. The Negro's entire life, and, consequently, also his opinions on the Negro problem, are, in the main, to be considered as secondary reactions to more primary pressures from the side of the dominant white majority.

The Negro was brought to America for the sake of the white man's profit. He was kept in slavery for generations in the same interest. A civil war was fought between two regional groups of white Americans. For two years no one wanted Negroes involved in the fighting. Later on some two hundred thousand Negro soldiers fought in the Northern army, in addition to all the Negro laborers, servants, spies, and helpers in both armies. But it was not the Negroes' war. As a result of the war, which took a toll of some half million killed and many more wounded, the four million Negro slaves were liberated. Since then the Negro's "place" in American society has been precarious, uncertain and changing; he was no longer so necessary and profitable to the white man as in slavery before the Civil War. In the main, however, the conflicting and vacillating valuations of the white majority have been decisive, whether the issue was segregation in the schools, discrimination with reference to public facilities, equal justice and protection under the laws, enjoyment of the franchise, or the freedom to enter a vocation and earn an honest living. The Negro, as a minority, and a poor and suppressed minority at that, in the final analysis, has had little other strategy open to him than to play on the conflicting values held in the white majority group. In so doing, he has been able to identify his cause with broader issues in American politics and social life and with moral principles held dear by the white Americans. This is the situation even today and will remain so in the foreseeable future. In that sense, "this is a white man's country."

—Gunnar Myrdal, *An American Dilemma*, 1944

2. The Civil War Amendments, 1868–70

EDITORIAL NOTE: *The so-called Civil War Amendments—numbers Thirteen, Fourteen, and Fifteen—were designed to guarantee not only freedom but civil rights to the Negro. The Thirteenth needs no explanation. The Fourteenth was originally formulated to assure validity to the civil rights bill of 1866, whose constitutionality was in question. In the course of its Congressional career, new and somewhat irrelevant sections were added; we give here only those sections addressed to the position of the freedman. The Fifteenth Amendment, designed to assure the vote to freedmen, was couched in language so ambiguous that it invited evasion. Though both Amendments provided for Congressional enforcement the Congress failed until very recently to implement the provisions of these Amendments by appropriate legislation.*

SEC. 1. NEITHER slavery nor involuntary servitude, except as a punishment for crime whereof the party shall have been duly convicted, shall exist within the United States, or any place subject to their jurisdiction.
Sec. 2. Congress shall have power to enforce this article by appropriate legislation.

—The Thirteenth Amendment, December 18, 1865

Sec. 1. All persons born or naturalized in the United States, and subject to the jurisdiction thereof, are citizens of the United States and of the State wherein they reside. No State shall make or enforce any law which shall abridge the privileges or immunities of citizens of the United States; nor shall any State deprive any person of life, liberty, or property, without due process of law; nor deny to any person within its jurisdiction the equal protection of the laws.

Sec. 2. Representatives shall be apportioned among the several States according to their respective numbers, counting the whole number of persons in each State, excluding Indians not taxed. But when the right to vote at any election for the choice of electors for President and Vice President of the United States, Representatives in Congress, the Executive and Judicial officers of a State, or the members of the Legislature thereof, is denied to any of the male inhabitants of such State, being twenty-one years of age, and citizens of the United States, or in any way abridged, except for participation in rebellion, or other crime, the basis of representation therein shall be reduced in the proportion which the number of such male citizens shall bear to the whole number of male citizens twenty-one years of age in such State. . . .

—The Fourteenth Amendment, July 28, 1868

Sec. 1. The right of citizens of the United States to vote shall not be denied or abridged by the United States or by any State on account of race, color, or previous condition of servitude—

Sec. 2. The Congress shall have power to enforce this article by appropriate legislation—

—The Fifteenth Amendment, March 30, 1870

3. The Freedman's Case

George Washington Cable

EDITORIAL NOTE: *George Washington Cable was the most distinguished Southern writer during the Reconstruction era. Though he fought in the Confederate Army he did not share the Southern view of the war, Reconstruction, or the Negro. He first achieved literary fame with* The Great South, *a series of essays on the postwar South, published in* Scribner's Magazine. *A few years later came his most famous book,* Old Creole Days, *a group of stories which rejected the romantic view of the Creoles. With* The Silent South, *from which this essay is drawn, Cable broke sharply with the Southern view of the freedman. His book earned him such hostility in his own section that in 1885 he moved to Northampton, Massachusetts. For the rest of his life he devoted himself to writing and lecturing about the South and the Negro.*

THE NATION'S ATTITUDE

THE GREATEST SOCIAL problem before the American people today is, as it has been for a hundred years, the presence among us of the Negro.

No comparable entanglement was ever drawn round itself by any other modern nation with so serene a disregard of its ultimate issue, or with a more distinct national responsibility. The African slave was brought here by cruel force, and with everybody's consent except his own. Everywhere the practice was favored as a measure of common aggrandizement. When a few men and women protested, they were mobbed in the public interest, with the public consent.

There rests, therefore, a moral responsibility on the whole nation never to lose sight of the results of African-American slavery until they cease to work mischief and injustice. . . .

WHAT THE WAR LEFT

The old alien relation might have given way if we could only, while letting that pass, have held fast by the other old ideas. But they were all bound together. See our embarrassment. For more than a hundred years we had made these sentiments the absolute essentials to our self-respect. And yet if we clung to them, how could we meet the Freedman on equal terms in the political field? Even to lead would not compensate us; for the fundamental profession of American politics is that the leader is servant to his followers. It was too much. The ex-master and ex-slave—the quarter-deck and the forecastle, as it were—could not come together. But neither could the American mind tolerate a continuance of martial law. The agonies of Reconstruction followed.

The vote, after all, was a secondary point, and the robbery and bribery on one side, and whipping and killing on the other were but huge accidents of the situation. The two main questions were really these: on the Freedman's side, how to establish republican state government under the same recognition of his rights that the rest of Christendom accorded him; and on the former master's side, how to get back to the old semblance of republican state government, and—allowing that the Freedman was *de facto* a voter—still to maintain a purely arbitrary superiority of all whites over all blacks, and a purely arbitrary equality of all blacks among themselves as an alien, menial, and dangerous class.

Exceptionally here and there some one in the master caste did throw off the old and accept the new ideas, and, if he would allow it, was instantly claimed as a leader by the newly liberated thousands around him. But just as promptly the old master race branded him also an alien reprobate, and in ninety-nine cases out of a hundred, if he had not already done so, he soon began to confirm by his actions the brand on his cheek. However, we need give no history here of the dreadful episode of Reconstruction. Under an experimentative truce its issues rest today upon the pledge of the wiser leaders of the master class: Let us but remove the hireling demagogue, and we will see to it that the Freedman is accorded a practical, complete, and cordial recognition of his equality with the white man before the law. As far as there has been any understanding at all, it is not that the originally desired ends of Reconstruction have been abandoned, but that the men of North and South have agreed upon a new, gentle, and peaceable method for reaching them; that, without change as to the ends in view, compulsory Reconstruction has been set aside and a voluntary Reconstruction is on trial.

It is the fashion to say we paused to let the "feelings engendered by the war" pass away, and that they are passing. But let not these truths lead us into error. The sentiments we have been analyzing, and upon which we saw the old compulsory Reconstruction go hard aground—these are not the "feelings engendered by the war." We must disentangle them from the "feelings engendered by the war," and by Reconstruction. They are older than either. But for them slavery would have perished of itself, and emancipation and Reconstruction been peaceful revolutions.

Indeed, as between master and slave, the "feelings engendered by the war" are too trivial, or at least were too short-lived, to demand our present notice. One relation and feeling the war destroyed: the patriarchal tie and its often really tender and benevolent sentiment of dependence and protection. When the slave became a Freedman, the sentiment of alienism became for the first time complete. The abandonment of this relation was not one-sided; the slave, even before the master, renounced it. Countless times, since Reconstruction began, the master has tried, in what he believed to be everybody's interest, to play on that old sentiment. But he found it a harp without strings. The Freedman could not formulate, but he could see, all our old ideas of autocracy and subserviency, of master and menial, of an arbitrarily fixed class to guide and rule, and another to be guided and ruled. He rejected the overture. The old master, his well-meant condescensions slighted, turned away estranged, and justified himself in passively withholding that simpler protection without patronage which any one American citizen, however exalted, owes to any other, however humble. Could the Freedman in the bitterest of those days have consented to throw himself upon just that one old relation, he could have found a physical security for himself and his house such as could not, after years of effort, be given him by constitutional amendments, Congress, United States marshals, regiments of regulars, and ships of war. But he could not; the very nobility of the civilization that had held him in slavery had made him too much a man to go back to that shelter; and by his manly neglect to do so he has proved to us who once ruled over him that, be his relative standing among the races of men what it may, he is worthy to be free.

FREED—NOT FREE

To be a free man is his [the Negro's] still distant goal. Twice he has been a Freedman. In the days of compulsory Reconstruction he was freed in the presence of his master by that master's victorious foe. In these days of voluntary Reconstruction he is virtually freed by the consent of his master, but the master retaining the exclusive right to define the bounds of his freedom. Many everywhere have taken up the idea that this state of affairs is the end to be desired and the end actually sought in Reconstruction as handed over to the state. I do not charge such folly to the best intelligence of any American community; but I cannot ignore my own knowledge that the average thought of some regions rises to no better idea of the issue. The belief is all too common that the nation, having aimed at a wrong result and missed, has left us of the Southern states to get now such other result as we think best. I say this belief is not universal. There are those among us who see that America has no room for a state of society which makes its lower classes harmless by abridging their liberties, or, as one of the favored class lately said to me, has "got 'em so they don't give no trouble." There is a growing number who see that the one thing we cannot afford to tolerate at large is a class of people less than citizens; and that every interest in the land demands that the Freedman be free to become in all things, as far as his own personal gifts will lift and sustain him, the same sort of American citizen he would be if, with the same intellectual and moral caliber, he were white.

Thus we reach the ultimate question of fact. Are the Freedman's liberties suffering any real abridgement? The answer is easy. The letter of the laws, with a few exceptions, recognizes him as entitled to every right of an American citizen; and to some it may seem unimportant that there is scarcely one public relation of life in the South where he is not arbitrarily and unlawfully compelled to hold toward the white man the attitude of an alien, a menial, and a probable reprobate, by reason of his race and color. One of the marvels of future history will be that it was counted a small matter, by a majority of our nation, for six millions of people within it, made by its own decree a component part of it, to be subjected to a system of oppression so rank that nothing could make it seem small except the fact that they had already been ground under it for a century and a half.

Examine it. It proffers to the Freedman a certain security of life and property, and then holds the respect of the community, that dearest of earthly boons, beyond his attainment. It gives him certain guarantees against thieves and robbers, and then holds him under the unearned contumely of the mass of good men and women. It acknowledges in constitutions and statutes his title to an American's freedom and aspirations, and then in daily practice heaps upon him in every public place the most odious distinctions, without giving ear to the humblest plea concerning mental or moral character. It spurns his ambition, tramples upon his languishing self-respect, and indignantly refuses to let him either buy with money, or earn by any excellence of inner life or outward behavior, the most momentary immunity from these public indignities even for his wife and daughters. Need we cram these pages with facts in evidence, as if these were charges denied and requiring to be proven? They are simply the present avowed and defended state of affairs peeled of its exteriors.

Nothing but the habit, generations old, of enduring it could make it endurable by men not in actual slavery. Were we whites of the South to remain every way as we are, and our six million blacks to give place to any sort of whites exactly their equals, man for man, in mind, morals, and wealth, provided only that they had tasted two years of American freedom, and were this same system of tyrannies attempted upon them, there would be as bloody an uprising as this continent has ever seen. We can say this quietly. There is not a scruple's weight of present danger. These six million Freedmen are dominated by nine million whites immeasureably stronger than they, backed by the virtual consent of thirty-odd millions more. Indeed, nothing but the habit of oppression could make such oppression possible to a people of the intelligence and virtue of our Southern whites, and the invitation to practice it on millions of any other than the children of their former slaves would be spurned with a noble indignation.

Suppose, for a moment, the tables turned. Suppose the courts of our Southern states, while changing no laws requiring the impaneling of jurymen without distinction as to race, etc., should suddenly begin to draw their thousands of jurymen all black, and well-nigh every one of them counting, not only himself, but all his race, better than any white man. Assuming that their average of intelligence and morals should be not below that of jurymen as now drawn, would a white man, for all that, choose to be tried in one of those courts? Would he suspect nothing? Could one persuade him that his chances of even justice were all they should be, or all they would be were the court not evading the law in order to sustain an outrageous distinction against him because of the accidents of his birth? Yet only read white man for black man, and black man for white man, and that—I speak as an eyewitness—has been the practice for years, and is still so today; an actual emasculation, in the case of six million people both as plaintiff and defendant, of the right of trial by jury.

In this and other practices the outrage falls upon the Freedman. Does it stop there? Far from it. It is the first premise of American principles that whatever elevates the lower stratum of the people lifts all the rest, and whatever holds it down holds all down. For twenty years, therefore, the nation has been working to elevate the Freedman. It counts this one of the great necessities of the hour. It has poured out its wealth publicly and privately for this purpose. It is confidently hoped that it will soon bestow a royal gift of millions for the reduction of the illiteracy so largely shared by the blacks. Our Southern states are, and for twenty years have been, taxing themselves for the same end. The private charities alone of the other states have given twenty millions in the same good cause. Their colored seminaries, colleges, and normal schools dot our whole Southern country, and furnish our public colored schools with a large part of their teachers. All this and much more has been or is being done in order that, for the good of himself and everybody else in the land, the colored man may be elevated as quickly as possible from all the debasements of slavery and semi-slavery to the full stature and integrity of citizenship. And it is in the face of all this that the adherent of the old regime stands in the way to every public privilege and place—steamer landing, railway platform, theater, concert hall, art display, public library, public school, courthouse, church, everything—flourishing the hot branding iron of ignominious distinctions. He forbids the Freedman to go into the water until *he* is satisfied that he knows how to swim and, for fear he should learn, hangs millstones about his neck. This is what we are told is a small matter that will settle itself. Yes, like a roosting curse, until the outraged intelligence of the South lifts its indignant protest against this stupid firing into our own ranks.

—George Washington Cable, "The Freedman's Case in Equity," 1885

4. Frederick Douglass Calls on the Freedman to Organize for Self-Protection

Frederick Douglass

EDITORIAL NOTE: *Frederick Douglass, the greatest Negro leader of the Civil War generation, was born in slavery, but escaped to freedom as early as 1838. Almost at once he attached himself to the Abolitionist cause and for twenty years worked ceaselessly with Garrison, Phillips, and other leaders of that cause. During the Civil War he helped recruit Negro soldiers for the Union Army and advised Lincoln on problems of race relationships and the future of the Negro. He early saw what Booker T. Washington was to insist upon, the importance of economic equality for the Negro. By the 1880's—when young Booker T. Washington emerged on the scene—Douglass was the patriarch of the Negro race, speaking with an authority that no other Negro could command. This speech was delivered at a Negro convention in Louisville, Kentucky, in 1883.*

IT IS OUR lot to live among a people whose laws, traditions, and prejudices have been against us for centuries, and from these they are not yet free. To assume that they are free from these evils simply because they have changed their laws is to assume what is utterly unreasonable and contrary to facts. Large bodies move slowly. Individuals may be converted on the instant and change their whole course of life. Nations never. Time and events are required for the conversion of nations. Not even the character of a great political organization can be changed by a new platform. It will be the same old snake though in a new skin. Though we have had war, reconstruction and abolition as a nation, we still linger in the shadow and blight of an extinct institution. Though the colored man is no longer subject to be bought and sold, he is still surrounded by an adverse sentiment which fetters all his movements. In his downward course he meets with no resistance, but his course upward is resented and resisted at every step of his progress. If he comes in ignorance, rags and wretchedness, he conforms to the popular belief of his character, and in that character he is welcome. But if he shall come as a gentleman, a scholar, and a statesman, he is hailed as a contradiction to the national faith concerning his race, and his coming is resented as impudence. In the one case he may provoke contempt and derision, but in the other he is an affront to pride, and provokes malice. Let him do what he will, there is at present, therefore, no escape for him. The color line meets him everywhere, and in a measure shuts him out from all respectable and profitable trades and callings. In spite of all your religion and laws he is a rejected man.

He is rejected by trade unions, of every trade, and refused work while he lives, and burial when he dies, and yet he is asked to forget his color, and forget that which everybody else remembers. If he offers himself to a builder as a mechanic, to a client as a lawyer, to a patient as a physician, to a college as a professor, to a firm as a clerk; to a Government Department as an agent, or an officer, he is sternly met on the color line, and his claim to consideration in some way is disputed on the ground of color.

Not even our churches, whose members profess to follow the despised Nazarene, whose home, when on earth, was among the lowly and despised, have yet conquered this feeling of color madness, and what is true of our churches is also true of our courts of law. Neither is free from this all-pervading atmosphere of color hate. The one describes the Deity as impartial, no respecter of persons, and the other the Goddess of Justice as blindfolded, with sword by her side and scales in her hand held evenly between high and low, rich and poor, white and black, but both are the images of American imagination, rather than American practices.

Taking advantage of the general disposition in this country to impute crime to color, white men *color* their faces to commit crime and wash off the hated color to escape punishment. In many places where the commission of crime is alleged against one of our color, the ordinary processes of the law are set aside as too slow for the impetuous justice of the infuriated populace. They take the law into their own bloody hands and proceed to whip, stab, shoot, hang, or burn the alleged culprit, without the intervention of courts, counsel, judges, juries, and witnesses. In such cases it is not the business of the accusers to prove guilt, but it is for the accused to prove his innocence, a thing hard for any man to do, even in a court of law, and utterly impossible for him to do in these infernal Lynch courts. A man accused, surprised, frightened and captured by a motley crowd, dragged with a rope around his neck in midnight-darkness to the nearest tree, and told in the coarsest terms of profanity to prepare for death, would be more than human if he did not, in his terror-stricken appearance, more confirm suspicion of guilt than the contrary. Worse still, in the presence of such hell-black outrages, the pulpit is usually dumb and the press in the neighborhood is silent or openly takes sides with the mob. There are occasional cases in which white men are lynched, but one sparrow does not make a summer. Every one knows that what is called Lynch law is peculiarly the law for colored people and for nobody else. If there were no other grievance than this horrible and barbarous Lynch law custom, we should be justified in assembling, as we have now done, to expose and denounce it. But this is not all. Even now, after twenty years of so-called emancipation, we are subject to lawless raids of midnight riders, who, with blackened faces, invade our homes and perpetrate the foulest of crimes upon us and our families. This condition of things is too flagrant and notorious to require specifications or proof. Thus in all the relations of life and death we are met by the color line. We cannot ignore it if we would, and ought not if we could. It hunts us at midnight, it denies us accommodations in hotels and justice in the courts; excludes our children from schools, refuses our sons the chance to learn trades, and compels us to pursue only such labor as will bring the least reward. While we recognize the color line as a hurtful force, a mountain barrier to our progress, wounding our bleeding feet with its flinty rocks at every step, we do not despair. We are a hopeful people.

This convention is a proof of our faith in you, in reason, in truth, and justice—our belief that prejudice, with all its malign accompaniments, may yet be removed by peaceful means; that, assisted by time and events and the growing enlightenment of both races, the color line will ultimately become harmless. When this shall come it will then only be used, as it should be, to distinguish one variety of the human family from another. It will cease to have any civil, political, or moral significance, and colored conventions will then be dispensed with as anachronisms, wholly out of place, but not till then. . . .

If the six millions of colored people of this country, armed with the Constitution of the United States, with a million votes of their own to lean upon, and millions of white men at their back, whose hearts are responsive to the claims of humanity, have not sufficient spirit and wisdom to organize and combine to defend themselves from outrage, discrimination, and oppression, it will be idle for them to expect that the Republican party or any other political party will organize and combine for them or care what becomes of them. Men may combine to prevent cruelty to animals, for they are dumb and cannot speak for themselves; but we are men and must speak for ourselves, or we shall not be spoken for at all. We have conventions in America for Ireland, but we should have none if Ireland did not speak for herself. It is because she makes a noise and keeps her cause before the people that other people go to her help. It was the sword of Washington and of Lafayette that gave us Independence. In conclusion upon this color objection, we have to say that we meet here in open daylight. There is nothing sinister about us. The eyes of the nation are upon us. Ten thousand newspapers may tell if they choose of whatever is said and done here. They may commend our wisdom or condemn our folly, precisely as we shall be wise or foolish.

We put ourselves before them as honest men, and ask their judgment upon our work. . . .

—Frederick Douglass, "Why a Colored Convention?" 1883

5. "The Agitation of Questions of Social Equality is the Extremest Folly"

Booker T. Washington

EDITORIAL NOTE: *By the 1890's Booker T. Washington was widely recognized as the spokesman for his race. It was as such that he was invited to deliver the address at the Cotton States' Exposition in Atlanta, Georgia, in September, 1895. In this address, which aroused greater enthusiasm among whites than among Negroes, he proclaimed that the two races could be as separate as the fingers in all things purely social, yet one as the hand in all things essential to progress. This acquiescence—strategic rather than fundamental—in social inequality aroused widespread exasperation among Northern Negro leaders.*

ONE-THIRD OF THE population of the South is of the Negro race. No enterprise seeking the material, civil, or moral welfare of this section can disregard this element of our population and reach the highest success. I but convey to you, Mr. President and Directors, the sentiment of the masses of my race when I say that in no way have the value and manhood of the American Negro been more fittingly and generously recognized than by the managers of this magnificent Exposition at every stage of its progress. It is a recognition that will do more to cement the friendship of the two races than any occurrence since the dawn of freedom.

Not only this, but the opportunity here afforded will awaken among us a new era of industrial progress. Ignorant and inexperienced, it is not strange that in the first years of our new life we began at the top instead of at the bottom; that a seat in Congress or the State Legislature was more sought than real estate or industrial skill; that the political convention or stump speaking had more attractions than starting a dairy farm or truck garden.

A ship lost at sea for many days suddenly sighted a friendly vessel. From the mast of the unfortunate vessel was seen a signal: "Water, water; we die of thirst!" The answer from the friendly vessel at once came back: "Cast down your bucket where you are." A second time the signal, "Water, water; send us water!" ran up from the distressed vessel, and was answered: "Cast down your bucket where you are." The captain of the distressed vessel, at last heeding the injunction, cast down his bucket, and it came up full of fresh, sparkling water from the mouth of the Amazon River. To those of my race who depend upon bettering their condition in a foreign land, or who underestimate the importance of cultivating friendly relations with the Southern white man, who is his next door neighbor, I would say: "Cast down your bucket where you are"—cast it down in making friends in every manly way of the people of all races by whom we are surrounded.

Cast it down in agriculture, mechanics, in commerce, in domestic service, and in the professions. And in this connection it is well to bear in mind that whatever other sins the South may be called to bear, when it comes to business, pure and simple, it is in the South that the Negro is given a man's chance in the commercial world, and in nothing is this Exposition more eloquent than in emphasizing this chance. Our greatest danger is that in the great leap from slavery to freedom we may overlook the fact that the masses of us are to live by the productions of our hands, and fail to keep in mind that we shall prosper in proportion as we learn to dignify and glorify common labor, and put brains and skill into the common occupations of life; shall prosper in proportion as we learn to draw the line between the superficial and the substantial, the ornamental gewgaws of life and the useful. No race can prosper till it learns that there is as much dignity in tilling a field as in writing a poem. It is at the bottom of life we must begin, and not at the top. Nor should we permit our grievances to overshadow our opportunities.

To those of the white race who look to the incoming of those of foreign birth and strange tongue and habits for the prosperity of the South, were I permitted I would repeat what I say to my own race, "Cast down your bucket where you are." Cast it down among the 8,000,000 Negroes whose habits you know, whose fidelity and love you have tested in days when to have proved treacherous meant the ruin of your firesides. Cast down your bucket among these people who have, without strikes and labor wars, tilled your fields, cleared your forests, builded your railroads and cities, and brought forth treasures from the bowels of the earth, and helped make possible this magnificent representation of the progress of the South. Casting down your bucket among my people, helping and encouraging them as you are doing on these grounds, and, with education of head, hand and heart, you will find that they will buy your surplus land, make blossom the waste places in your fields, and run your factories. While doing this, you can be sure in the future, as in the past, that you and your families will be surrounded by the most patient, faithful, law-abiding, and unresentful people that the world has seen. As we have proved our loyalty to you in the past, in nursing your children, watching by the sick bed of your mothers and fathers, and often following them with tear-dimmed eyes to their graves, so in the future, in our humble way, we shall stand by you with a devotion that no foreigner can approach, ready to lay down our lives, if need be, in defense of yours, interlacing our industrial, commercial, civil, and religious life with yours in a way that shall make the interests of both races one. In all things that are purely social we can be as separate as the fingers, yet one as the hand in all things essential to mutual progress.

There is no defense or security for any of us except in the highest intelligence and development of all. If anywhere there are efforts tending to curtail the fullest growth of the Negro, let these efforts be turned into stimulating, encouraging, and making him the most useful and intelligent citizen. Effort or means so invested will pay a thousand per cent interest. These efforts will be twice blessed—blessing him that gives and him that takes.

There is no escape through law of man or God from the inevitable:

> The laws of changeless justice bind
> Oppressor with oppressed;
> And close as sin and suffering joined
> We march to fate abreast.

Nearly sixteen millions of hands will aid you in pulling the load upwards, or they will pull against you the load downwards. We shall constitute one-third and more of the ignorance and crime of the South, or one-third its intelligence and progress; we shall contribute one-third to the business and industrial prosperity of the South, or we shall prove a veritable body of death, stagnating, depressing, retarding every effort to advance the body politic.

Gentlemen of the Exposition, as we present to you our humble effort at an exhibition of our progress, you must not expect overmuch. Starting thirty years ago with ownership here and there in a few quilts and pumpkins and chickens (gathered from miscellaneous sources), remember the path that has led from these to the invention and production of agricultural implements, buggies, steam engines, newspapers, books, statuary, carving, paintings, the management of drug stores and banks has not been trodden without contact with thorns and thistles. While we take pride in what we exhibit as a result of our independent efforts, we do not for a moment forget that our part in this exhibition would fall short of your expectations but for the constant help that has come to our educational life, not only from the Southern States, but especially from Northern philanthropists, who have made their gifts a constant stream of blessing and encouragement.

The wisest among my race understand that the agitation of questions of social equality is the extremest folly, and that progress in the enjoyment of all the privileges that will come to us must be the result of severe and constant struggle rather than of artificial forcing. No race that has anything to contribute to the markets of the world is long in any degree ostracized. It is important and right that all privileges of the law be ours, but it is vastly more important that we be prepared for the exercise of those privileges. The opportunity to earn a dollar in a factory just now is worth infinitely more than the opportunity to spend a dollar in an opera house.

In conclusion, may I repeat that nothing in thirty years has given us more hope and encouragement, and drawn us so near to you of the white race, as this opportunity offered by the Exposition; and here bending, as it were, over the altar that represents the results of the struggles of your race and mine, both starting practically empty-handed three decades ago, I pledge that, in your effort to work out the great and intricate problem which God has laid at the doors of the South, you shall have at all times the patient, sympathetic help of my race; only let this be constantly in mind that, while from representations in these buildings of the products of field, of forest, of mine, of factory, letters, and art, much good will come, yet far above and beyond material benefits will be the higher good, that let us pray God will come, in a blotting out of sectional differences and racial animosities and suspicions, in a determination to administer absolute justice, in a willing obedience among all classes to the mandates of law. This, coupled with our material prosperity, will bring into our beloved South a new heaven and a new earth.

—Booker T. Washington, "The Atlanta Address," 1895

6. "Mr. Washington Represents the Old Attitude of Submission"

W. E. B. DuBois

EDITORIAL NOTE: *At the beginning of the century the young W. E. B. DuBois, trained at Harvard and Berlin, challenged the Washingtonian program of compromise and concession. It was folly, said DuBois, to suppose that Negroes could ever win either economic security or social equality or achieve self-respect through that program. DuBois first attacked Washington openly in an essay which appeared in* The Souls of Black Folk *in 1903. Two years later DuBois and his followers met at Niagara Falls to inaugurate what came to be called the Niagara Movement. "We want the Constitution of the country enforced," said the Niagara platform. "We want the Fourteenth Amendment carried out to the letter." Four years later the Niagara group with the aid of many liberals like John Dewey and Jane Addams founded the National Association for the Advancement of Colored People.*

EASILY THE MOST striking thing in the history of the American Negro since 1876 is the ascendancy of Mr. Booker T. Washington. It began at the time when war memories and ideals were rapidly passing; a day of astonishing commercial development was dawning; a sense of doubt and hesitation overtook the freedmen's sons,—then it was that his leading began. Mr. Washington came, with a single definite programme, at the psychological moment when the nation was a little ashamed of having bestowed so much sentiment on Negroes, and was concentrating its energies on Dollars. His programe of industrial education, conciliation of the South, and submission and silence as to civil and political rights, was not wholly original; the Free Negroes from 1830 up to war-time had striven to build industrial schools, and the American Missionary Association had from the first taught various trades; and Price and others had sought a way of honorable alliance with the best of the Southerners. But Mr. Washington first indissolubly linked these things; he put enthusiasm, unlimited energy, and perfect faith into this programme, and changed it from a by-path into a veritable Way of Life. And the tale of the methods by which he did this is a fascinating study of human life.

It startled the nation to hear a Negro advocating such a programme after many decades of bitter complaint; it startled and won the applause of the South, it interested and won the admiration of the North; and after a confused murmur of protest, it silenced if it did not convert the Negroes themselves.

To gain the sympathy and cooperation of the various elements comprising the white South was Mr. Washington's first task; and this, at the time Tuskegee was founded, seemed, for a black man, well-nigh impossible. And yet ten years later it was done in the word spoken at Atlanta: "In all things purely social we can be as separate as the five fingers, and yet one as the hand in all things essential to mutual progress." This "Atlanta Compromise" is by all odds the most notable thing in Mr. Washington's career. The South interpreted it in different ways: the radicals received it as a complete surrender of the demand for civil and political equality; the conservatives, as a generously conceived working basis for mutual understanding. So both approved it, and to-day its author is certainly the most distinguished Southerner since Jefferson Davis, and the one with the largest personal following.

Next to this achievement comes Mr. Washington's work in gaining place and consideration in the North. Others less shrewd and tactful had formerly essayed to sit on these two stools and had fallen between them; but as Mr. Washington knew the heart of the South from birth and training, so by singular insight he intuitively grasped the spirit of the age which was dominating the North. And so thoroughly did he learn the speech and thought of triumphant commercialism, and the ideals of material prosperity, that the picture of a lone black boy poring over a French grammar amid the weeds and dirt of a neglected home soon seemed to him the acme of absurdities. One wonders what Socrates and St. Francis of Assisi would say to this.

And yet this very singleness of vision and thorough oneness with his age is a mark of the successful man. It is as though Nature must needs make men narrow in order to give them force. So Mr. Washington's cult has gained unquestioning followers, his work has wonderfully prospered, his friends are legion, and his enemies are confounded. To-day he stands as the one recognized spokesman of his ten million fellows, and one of the most notable figures in a nation of seventy millions. One hesitates, therefore, to criticise a life which, beginning with so little, has done so much. And yet the time is come when one may speak in all sincerity and utter courtesy of the mistakes and shortcomings of Mr. Washington's career, as well as of his triumphs, without being thought captious or envious, and without forgetting that it is easier to do ill than well in the world.

The criticism that has hitherto met Mr. Washington has not always been of this broad character. In the South especially has he had to walk warily to avoid the harshest judgments,—and naturally so, for he is dealing with the one subject of deepest sensitiveness to that section. Twice—once when at the Chicago celebration of the Spanish-American War he alluded to the color-prejudice that is "eating away the vitals of the South," and once when he dined with President Roosevelt—has the resulting Southern criticism been violent enough to threaten seriously his popularity. In the North the feeling has several times forced itself into words, that Mr. Washington's counsels of submission overlooked certain elements of true manhood, and that his educational programme was unnecessarily narrow. Usually, however, such criticism has not found open expression, although, too, the spiritual sons of the Abolitionists have not been prepared to acknowledge that the schools founded before Tuskegee, by men of broad ideals and self-sacrificing spirit, were wholly failures or worthy of ridicule. While, then, criticism has not failed to follow Mr. Washington, yet the prevailing public opinion of the land has been but too willing to deliver the solution of a wearisome problem into his hands, and say, "If that is all you and your race ask, take it."

Among his own people, however, Mr. Washington has encountered the strongest and most lasting opposition, amounting at times to bitterness, and even to-day continuing strong and insistent even though largely silenced in outward expression by the public opinion of the nation. Some of this opposition is, of course, mere envy; the disappointment of displaced demagogues and the spite of narrow minds. But aside from this, there is among educated and thoughtful colored men in all parts of the land a feeling of deep regret, sorrow, and apprehension at the wide currency and ascendancy which some of Mr. Washington's theories have gained. These same men admire his sincerity of purpose, and are willing to forgive much to honest endeavor which is doing something worth the doing. They cooperate with Mr. Washington as far as they conscientiously can; and, indeed, it is no ordinary tribute to this man's tact and power that, steering as he must between so many diverse interests and opinions, he so largely retains the respect of all.

But the hushing of the criticism of honest opponents is a dangerous thing. It leads some of the best of the critics to unfortunate silence and paralysis of effort, and others to burst into speech so passionately and intemperately as to lose listeners. Honest and earnest criticism from those whose interests are most nearly touched,—criticism of writers by readers, of government by those governed, of leaders by those led,—this is the soul of democracy and the safeguard of modern society. If the best of the American Negroes receive by outer pressure a leader whom they had not recognized before, manifestly there is here a certain palpable gain. Yet there is also irreparable loss,—a loss of that peculiarly valuable education which a group receives when by search and criticism it finds and commissions its own leaders. The way in which this is done is at once the most elementary and the nicest problem of social growth. History is but the record of such group-leadership; and yet how infinitely changeful is its type and character! And of all types and kinds, what can be more instructive than the leadership of a group within a group?—that curious double movement where real progress may be negative and actual advance be relative retrogression. All this is the social student's inspiration and despair.

Now in the past the American Negro has had instructive experience in the choosing of group leaders, founding thus a peculiar dynasty which in the light of present conditions is worth while studying. When sticks and stones and beasts form the sole environment of a people, their attitude is largely one of determined opposition to and conquest of natural forces. But when to earth and brute is added an environment of men and ideas, then the attitude of the imprisoned group may take three main forms,—a feeling of revolt and revenge; an attempt to adjust all thought and action to the will of the greater group; or, finally, a determined effort at self-realization and self-development despite environing opinion. The influence of all of these attitudes at various times can be traced in the history of the American Negro, and in the evolution of his successive leaders. . . .

Then came the Revolution of 1876, the suppression of the Negro votes, the changing and shifting of ideals, and the seeking of new lights in the great night. Douglass, in his old age, still bravely stood for the ideals of his early manhood,—ultimate assimilation *through* self-assertion, and on no other terms. For a time Price arose as a new leader, destined, it seemed, not to give up, but to re-state the old ideals in a form less repugnant to the white South. But he passed away in his prime. Then came the new leader. Nearly all the former ones had become leaders by the silent suffrage of their fellows, had sought to lead their own people alone, and were usually, save Douglass, little known outside their race. But Booker T. Washington arose as essentially the leader not of one race but of two,—a compromiser between the South, the North, and the Negro. Naturally the Negroes resented, at first bitterly, signs of compromise which surrendered their civil and political rights, even though this was to be exchanged for larger chances of economic development. The rich and dominating North, however, was not only weary of the race problem, but was investing largely in Southern enterprises, and welcomed any method of peaceful cooperation. Thus, by national opinion, the Negroes began to recognize Mr. Washington's leadership; and the voice of criticism was hushed.

Mr. Washington represents in Negro thought the old attitude of adjustment and submission; but adjustment at such a peculiar time as to make his programme unique. This is an age of unusual economic development, and Mr. Washington's programme naturally takes an economic cast, becoming a gospel of Work and Money to such an extent as apparently almost completely to overshadow the higher aims of life. Moreover, this is an age when the more advanced races are coming in closer contact with the less developed races, and the race-feeling is therefore intensified; and Mr. Washington's programme practically accepts the alleged inferiority of the Negro races. Again, in our own land, the reaction from the sentiment of war time has given impetus to race-prejudice against Negroes, and Mr. Washington withdraws many of the high demands of Negroes as men and American citizens. In other periods of intensified prejudice all the Negro's tendency to self-assertion has been called forth; at this period a policy of submission is advocated. In the history of nearly all other races and peoples the doctrine preached at such crises has been that manly self-respect is worth more than lands and houses. and that a people who voluntarily surrender such respect, or cease striving for it, are not worth civilizing.

In answer to this, it has been claimed that the Negro can survive only through submission. Mr. Washington distinctly asks that black people give up, at least for the present, three things,—

First, political power,

Second, insistence on civil rights,

Third, higher education of Negro youth,—

and concentrate all their energies on industrial education, the accumulation of wealth, and the conciliation of the South. This policy has been courageously and insistently advocated for over fifteen years, and has been triumphant for perhaps ten years. As a result of this tender of the palm-branch, what has been the return? In these years there have occurred:

1. The disfranchisement of the Negro.

2. The legal creation of a distinct status of civil inferiority for the Negro.

3. The steady withdrawal of aid from institutions for the higher training of the Negro.

These movements are not, to be sure, direct results of Mr. Washington's teachings; but his propaganda has, without a shadow of doubt, helped their speedier accomplishment. The question then comes: Is it possible, and probable, that nine millions of men can make effective progress in economic lines if they are deprived of political rights, made a servile caste, and allowed only the most meagre chance for developing their exceptional men? If history and reason give any distinct answer to these questions, it is an emphatic *No*. And Mr. Washington thus faces the triple paradox of his career:

1. He is striving nobly to make Negro artisans business men and property-owners; but it is utterly impossible, under modern competitive methods, for workingmen and property-owners to defend their rights and exist without the right of suffrage.

2. He insists on thrift and self-respect, but at the same time counsels a silent submission to civic inferiority such as is bound to sap the manhood of any race in the long run.

3. He advocates common-school and industrial training, and depreciates institutions of higher learning; but neither the Negro common-schools, nor Tuskegee itself, could remain open a day were it not for teachers trained in Negro colleges, or trained by their graduates.

—W. E. B. DuBois, *The Souls of Black Folk*, 1903

7. "Separate But Equal"

Henry Billings Brown & John Marshall Harlan

EDITORIAL NOTE: *The case of Plessy* versus *Ferguson in 1896 wrote finis to the Congressional program designed to guarantee equal rights to Negroes. By accepting—or inventing—the doctrine of separate but equal accommodations, it threw the mantle of judicial approval over segregation. Almost sixty years later it was to be reversed in the famous case of Brown* versus *Topeka. We give here not only the decision of Justice Brown but the historic dissenting opinion by Justice Harlan.*

BROWN, J.: THIS CASE TURNS upon the constitutionality of an act of the general assembly of the state of Louisiana, passed in 1890, providing for separate railway carriages for the white and colored races. . . .

The constitutionality of this act is attacked upon the ground that it conflicts both with the 13th Amendment of the Constitution, abolishing slavery, and the 14th Amendment, which prohibits certain restrictive legislation on the part of the states.

1. That it does not conflict with the 13th Amendment, which abolished slavery and involuntary servitude, except as a punishment for crime, is too clear for argument. . . .

A statute which implies merely a legal distinction between the white and colored races—a distinction which is founded in the color of the two races, and which must always exist so long as white men are distinguished from the other race by color—has no tendency to destroy the legal equality of the two races, or re-establish a state of involuntary servitude. Indeed, we do not understand that the 13th Amendment is strenuously relied upon by the plaintiff in error in this connection. . . .

The object of the amendment was undoubtedly to enforce the absolute equality of the two races before the law, but in the nature of things it could not have been intended to abolish distinctions based upon color, or to enforce social, as distinguished from political, equality, or a commingling of the two races upon terms unsatisfactory to either. Laws permitting, and even requiring, their separation in places where they are liable to be brought into contact do not necessarily imply the inferiority of either race to the other, and have been generally, if not universally, recognized as within the competency of the state legislatures in the exercise of their police power. The most common instance of this is connected with the establishment of separate schools for white and colored children, which have been held to be a valid exercise of the legislative power even by courts of states where the political rights of the colored race have been longest and most earnestly enforced. . . .

It is claimed by the plaintiff in error that, in any mixed community, the reputation of belonging to the dominant race, in this instance the white race, is *property*, in the same sense that a right of action, or of inheritance, is property. Conceding this to be so, for the purposes of this case, we are unable to see how this statute deprives him of, or in any way affects his right to, such property. If he be a white man and assigned to a colored coach, he may have his action for damages against the company for being deprived of his so-called property. Upon the other hand, if he be a colored man and be so assigned, he has been deprived of no property, since he is not lawfully entitled to the reputation of being a white man. . . .

So far, then, as a conflict with the 14th Amendment is concerned, the case reduces itself to the question whether the statute of Louisiana is a reasonable regulation, and with respect to this there must necessarily be a large discretion on the part of the legislature. In determining the question of reasonableness it is at liberty to act with reference to the established usages, customs, and traditions of the people, and with a view to the promotion of their comfort, and the preservation of the public peace and good order. Gauged by this standard, we cannot say that a law which authorizes or even requires the separation of the two races in public conveyances is unreasonable or more obnoxious to the 14th Amendment than the acts of Congress requiring separate schools for colored children in the District of Columbia, the constitutionality of which does not seem to have been questioned, or the corresponding acts of state legislatures.

We consider the underlying fallacy of the plaintiff's argument to consist in the assumption that the enforced separation of the two races stamps the colored race with a badge of inferiority. If this be so, it is not by reason of anything found in the act, but solely because the colored race chooses to put that construction upon it. The argument necessarily assumes that if, as has been more than once the case, and is not unlikely to be so again, the colored race should become the dominant power in the state legislature, and should enact a law in precisely similar terms, it would thereby relegate the white race to an inferior position. We imagine that the white race, at least, would not acquiesce in this assumption. The argument also assumes that social prejudice may be overcome by legislation, and that equal rights cannot be secured to the Negro except by an enforced commingling of the two races. We cannot accept this proposition. If the two races are to meet on terms of social equality, it must be the result of natural affinities, a mutual appreciation of each other's merits and a voluntary consent of individuals. . . . Legislation is powerless to eradicate racial instincts or to abolish distinctions based upon physical differences, and the attempt to do so can only result in accentuating the difficulties of the present situation. If the civil and political rights of both races be equal, one cannot be inferior to the other civilly or politically. If one race be inferior to the other socially, the Constitution of the United States cannot put them upon the same plane.

HARLAN, J., dissenting. . . . IN RESPECT OF civil rights, common to all citizens, the Constitution of the United States does not, I think, permit any public authority to know the race of those entitled to be protected in the enjoyment of such rights. Every true man has pride of race, and under appropriate circumstances, when the rights of others, his equals before the law, are not to be affected, it is his privilege to express such pride and to take such action based upon it as to him seems proper. But I deny that any legislative body or judicial tribunal may have regard to the race of citizens when the civil rights of those citizens are involved. Indeed such legislation as that here in question is inconsistent, not only with that equality of rights which pertains to citizenship, national and state, but with the personal liberty enjoyed by everyone within the United States. . . .

In my opinion, the judgment this day rendered will, in time, prove to be quite as pernicious as the decision made by this tribunal in the Dred Scott Case. It was adjudged in that case that the descendants of Africans who were imported into this country and sold as slaves were not included nor intended to be included under the word "citizens" in the Constitution, and could not claim any of the rights and privileges which that instrument provided for and secured to citizens of the United States; that at the time of the adoption of the Constitution they were "considered as a subordinate and inferior class of beings, who had been subjugated by the dominant race, and, whether emancipated or not, yet remained subject to their authority, and had no rights or privileges but such as those who held the power and the government might choose to grant them." The recent amendments of the Constitution, it was supposed, had eradicated these principles from our institutions. But it seems that we have yet, in some of the states, a dominant race, a superior class of citizens, which assumes to regulate the enjoyment of civil rights, common to all citizens, upon the basis of race. The present decision, it may well be apprehended, will not only stimulate aggressions, more or less brutal and irritating, upon the admitted rights of colored citizens, but will encourage the belief that it is possible, by means of state enactments, to defeat the beneficient purposes which the people of the United States had in view when they adopted the recent amendments of the Constitution, by one of which the blacks of this country were made citizens of the United States and of the states in which they respectively reside and whose privileges and immunities, as citizens, the states are forbidden to abridge. Sixty millions of whites are in no danger from the presence here of eight millions of blacks. The destinies of the two races in this country are indissolubly linked together, and the interests of both require that the common government of all shall not permit the seeds of race hate to be planted under the sanction of law. What can more certainly arouse race hate, what more certainly create and perpetuate a feeling of distrust between these races, than state enactments which in fact proceed on the ground that colored citizens are so inferior and degraded that they cannot be allowed to sit in public coaches occupied by white citizens? That, as all will admit, is the real meaning of such legislation as was enacted in Louisiana. . . .

If evils will result from the commingling of the two races upon public highways established for the benefit of all, they will be infinitely less than those that will surely come from state legislation regulating the enjoyment of civil rights upon the basis of race. We boast of the freedom enjoyed by our people above all other peoples. But it is difficult to reconcile that boast with a state of the law which, practically, puts the brand of servitude and degradation upon a large class of our fellow citizens, our equals before the law. The thin disguise of "equal" accommodations for passengers in railroad coaches will not mislead anyone, or atone for the wrong this day done. . . .

I am of opinion that the statute of Louisiana is inconsistent with the personal liberty of citizens, white and black, in that state, and hostile to both the spirit and letter of the Constitution of the United States. If laws of like character should be enacted in the several states of the Union, the effect would be in the highest degree mischievous. Slavery as an institution tolerated by law would, it is true, have disappeared from our country, but there would remain a power in the states, by sinister legislation, to interfere with the full enjoyment of the blessings of freedom; to regulate civil rights, common to all citizens, upon the basis of race; and to place in a condition of legal inferiority a large body of American citizens, now constituting a part of the political community, called the people of the United States, for whom and by whom, through representatives, our government is administered. Such a system is inconsistent with the guarantee given by the Constitution to each state of a republican form of government, and may be stricken down by Congressional action, or by the courts in the discharge of their solemn duty to maintain the supreme law of the land, anything in the Constitution or laws of any state to the contrary notwithstanding.

For the reasons stated, I am constrained to withhold my assent from the opinion and judgment of the majority.

—Opinions of Henry Billings Brown and John Marshall Harlan, Plessy *v.* Ferguson, 1896.

8. "To Secure These Rights"

Harry S. Truman

EDITORIAL NOTE: *Although born and raised in a border State, President Truman showed himself more concerned with the problem of civil rights for Negroes than any of his predecessors. In 1946 he established a committee on civil rights with a mandate to undertake a full-scale investigation of the civil rights situation and report its findings and recommendations to the President and Congress. We give here the Executive Order and an excerpt from the general introduction describing vividly the persistent denial of Negro rights.*

A. *Executive Order 9908, December 5, 1946*

WHEREAS THE PRESERVATION of civil rights guaranteed by the Constitution is essential to domestic tranquility, national security, the general welfare, and the continued existence of our free institutions, and

Whereas the action of individuals who take the law into their own hands and inflict summary punishment and wreak personal vengeance is subversive of our democratic system of law enforcement and public criminal justice, and gravely threatens our form of government; and

Whereas it is essential that all possible steps be taken to safeguard our civil rights:

Now, Therefore, by virtue of the authority vested in me as President of the United States by the Constitution and the statutes of the United States, it is hereby ordered as follows:

1. There is hereby created a committee to be known as the President's Committee on Civil Rights, which shall be composed of the following-named members, who shall serve without compensation. . . .

2. The Committee is authorized on behalf of the President to inquire into and to determine whether and in what respect current law-enforcement measures and the authority and means possessed by Federal, State, and local governments may be strengthened and improved to safeguard the civil rights of the people.

3. All executive departments and agencies of the Federal Government are authorized and directed to cooperate with the Committee in its work, and to furnish the Committee such information or the services of such persons as the Committee may require in the performance of its duties.

4. When requested by the Committee to do so, persons employed in any of the executive departments and agencies of the Federal Government shall testify before the Committee and shall make available for the use of the Committee such documents and other information as the Committee may require.

5. The Committee shall make a report of its studies to the President in writing, and shall in particular make recommendations with respect to the adoption or establishment, by legislation or otherwise, of more adequate and effective means and procedures for the protection of the civil rights of the people of the United States.

6. Upon rendition of its report to the President, the Committee shall cease to exist, unless otherwise determined by further Executive Order.

—Harry S. Truman, "To Secure These Rights," 1947

B. *The Report of the President's Committee on Civil Rights*

The United States has made remarkable progress toward the goal of universal education for its people. The number and variety of its schools and colleges are greater than ever before. Student bodies have become increasingly representative of all the different peoples who make up our population. Yet we have not finally eliminated prejudice and discrimination from the operation of either our public or our private schools and colleges. Two inadequacies are extremely serious. We have failed to provide Negroes and, to a lesser extent, other minority group members with equality of educational opportunities in our public institutions, particularly at the elementary and secondary school levels. We have allowed discrimination in the operation of many of our private institutions of higher education, particularly in the North with respect to Jewish students.

Discrimination in public schools.—The failure to give Negroes equal educational opportunities is naturally most acute in the South, where approximately 10 million Negroes live. The South is one of the poorer sections of the country and has at best only limited funds to spend on its schools. With 34.5 percent of the country's population, 17 southern states and the District of Columbia have 39.4 percent of our school children. Yet the South has only one-fifth of the taxpaying wealth of the nation. Actually, on a percentage basis, the South spends a greater share of its income on education than do the wealthier states in other parts of the country. For example, Mississippi, which has the lowest expenditure per school child of any state, is ninth in percentage of income devoted to education. A recent study showed Mississippi spending 3.41 percent of its income for education as against New York's figure of only 2.61 percent. But this meant $400 per classroom unit in Mississippi, and $4,100 in New York. Negro and white school children both suffer because of the South's basic inability to match the level of educational opportunity provided in other sections of the nation.

But it is the South's segregated school system which most directly discriminates against the Negro. This segregation is found today in 17 southern states and the District of Columbia. Poverty-stricken though it was after the close of the Civil War, the South chose to maintain two sets of public schools, one for whites and one for Negroes. With respect to education, as well as to other public services, the Committee believes that the "separate but equal" rule has not been obeyed in practice. There is a marked difference in quality between the educational opportunities offered white children and Negro children in the separate schools. Whatever test is used—expenditure per pupil, teachers' salaries, the number of pupils per teacher, transportation of students, adequacy of school buildings and educational equipment, length of school term, extent of curriculum—Negro students are invariably at a disadvantage. Opportunities for Negroes in public institutions of higher education in the South—particularly at the professional graduate school level—are severely limited.

Statistics in support of these conclusions are available. Figures provided by the United States Office of Education for the school year, 1943–44, show that the average length of the school term in the areas having separate schools was 173.5 days for whites and 164 for Negroes; the number of pupils per teacher was 28 for white and 34 for Negroes; and the average annual salary for Negro teachers was lower than that for white teachers in all but three of the 18 areas. Salary figures are as follows:

State or District of Columbia	Average annual salary of principals, supervisors, and teachers in schools for—	
	Whites	Negroes
Alabama	$1,158	$661
Arkansas	924	555
Delaware	1,953	1,814
Florida	3,530	970
Georgia	1,123	515
Louisiana	1,683	828
Maryland	2,085	2,002
Mississippi	1,107	342
Missouri	1,397	[1]1,590
North Carolina	1,380	1,249
Oklahoma	1,428	1,438
South Carolina	1,203	615
Tennessee	1,071	1,010
Texas	1,395	946
Virginia	1,364	1,129
District of Columbia	2,610	2,610

[1] Higher salaries due to the fact that most Negro schools are located in cities where all salaries are higher.

The South has made considerable progress in the last decade in narrowing the gap between educational opportunities afforded the white children and that afforded Negro children. For example, the gap between the length of the school year for whites and the shorter one for Negroes has been narrowed from 14.8 days in 1939–40 to 9.5 days in 1943–44. Similarly, the gap in student load per teacher in white and Negro schools has dropped from 8.5 students in 1939–40 to six students in 1943–44.

In spite of the improvement which is undoubtedly taking place, the Committee is convinced that the gap between white and Negro schools can never be completely eliminated by means of state funds alone. The cost of maintaining separate, but truly equal, school systems would seem to be utterly prohibitive in many of the southern states. It seems probable that the only means by which such a goal can finally be won will be through federal financial assistance. The extension of the federal grant-in-aid for educational purposes, already available to the land-grant colleges and, for vocational education, to the secondary school field, seems both imminent and desirable.

Whether the federal grant-in-aid should be used to support the maintenance of separate schools is an issue that the country must soon face.

In the North, segregation in education is not formal, and in some states is prohibited. Nevertheless, the existence of residential restrictions in many northern cities has had discriminatory effects on Negro education. In Chicago, for example, the schools which are most crowded and employ double shift schedules are practically all in Negro neighborhoods.

Other minorities encounter discrimination. Occasionally Indian children attending public schools in the western states are assigned to separate classrooms. Many Texas schools segregate Mexican American children in separate schools. In California segregation of Mexican American children was also practiced until recently. The combined effect of a federal court ruling, and legislative action repealing the statute under which school boards claimed authority to segregate, seems to have ended this pattern of discrimination in California schools.

Discrimination in private schools.—The second inadequacy in our present educational practices in America is the religious and racial discrimination that exists in the operation of some private educational institutions, both with respect to the admission of students and the treatment of them after admission.

The Committee is absolutely convinced of the importance of the private educational institution in a free society. It does not question the right of groups of private citizens to establish such institutions, determine their character and policies, and operate them. But it does believe that such schools immediately acquire a public character and importance. Invariably they enjoy government support, if only in the form of exemption from taxation and in the privilege of income-tax deduction extended to their benefactors. Inevitably, they render public service by training our young people for life in a democratic society. Consequently, they are possessed of a public responsibility from which there is no escape.

Leading educators assert that a careful selection in admissions practices may be necessary to insure a representative and diversified student body. Liberal arts colleges, in particular, have used this reasoning to limit the number of students enrolled from any one race or religion, as well as from any geographical section, preparatory school, or socio-economic background.

Nevertheless it is clear that there is much discrimination, based on prejudice, in admission of students to private colleges, vocational schools, and graduate schools. Since accurate statistical data is almost impossible to obtain this is difficult to prove. But competent observers are agreed that existence of this condition is widespread. Application blanks of many American colleges and universities include questions pertaining to the candidate's racial origin, religious preference, parents' birthplace, etc. In many of our northern educational institutions enrollment of Jewish students seems never to exceed certain fixed points and there is never more than a token enrollment of Negroes.

The impact of discriminatory practices in private education is illustrated by the situation in New York City. The students of the city colleges of New York are predominantly Jewish, resulting in part from the discrimination practiced by some local private institutions. These colleges have high academic standards, but graduates from them with excellent records have been repeatedly denied admission to private and nonsectarian professional schools. A Special Investigating Committee of the Council of the City of New York, recently established to examine this situation, found convincing evidence of discrimination against graduates of the city colleges by the medical schools in the city in violation of the Civil Rights Act of New York. The Investigating Committee, after questioning witnesses and examining application blanks, concluded that various professional schools tried to get information about applicants which would indicate their race, religion, or national origin for "a purpose other than judging their qualifications for admission." Jews are not alone in being affected by these practices. One witness, a member of a medical school's admission committee, admitted to a prejudice against Irish Catholics which affected his judgment. The number of Negroes attending these medical schools has been extremely low; less than 50 have been graduated from them in 25 years.

Certainly the public cannot long tolerate practices by private educational institutions which are in serious conflict with patterns of democratic life, sanctioned by the overwhelming majority of our people. By the closing of the door through bigotry and prejudice to equality of educational opportunity, the public is denied the manifold social and economic benefits that the talented individual might otherwise contribute to our society.

—"To Secure These Rights," 1947

9. Equality in the Armed Services, 1948

Harry S. Truman

EDITORIAL NOTE: *In 1941 President Roosevelt had banned racial discrimination in defense industries. Discrimination and segregation, however, persisted in the armed services except on bases and in small units and ships. The heroic participation of many Negroes in the war and their experience with equality in European countries made this situation intolerable. In 1948, under pressure from A. Philip Randolph, who threatened a mass civil disobedience campaign against the draft, President Truman launched a new attack on discrimination in the armed services. This proved only partially successful.*

WHEREAS IT IS essential that there be maintained in the armed services of the United States the highest standards of democracy, with equality of treatment and opportunity for all those who serve in our country's defense:

Now, therefore, by virtue of the authority vested in me as President of the United States, by the Constitution and the statutes of the United States, and as Commander in Chief of the armed services, it is hereby ordered as follows:

1. It is hereby declared to be the policy of the President that there shall be equality of treatment and opportunity for all persons in the armed services without regard to race, color, religion or national origin. This policy shall be put into effect as rapidly as

possible, having due regard to the time required to effectuate any necessary changes without impairing efficiency or morale.

2. There shall be created in the National Military Establishment an advisory committee to be known as the President's Committee on Equality of Treatment and Opportunity in the Armed Services, which shall be composed of seven members to be designated by the President.

3. The Committee is authorized on behalf of the President to examine into the rules, procedures and practices of the armed services in order to determine in what respect such rules, procedures and practices may be altered or improved with a view to carrying out the policy of this order. The Committee shall confer and advise with the Secretary of Defense, the Secretary of the Army, the Secretary of the Navy, and the Secretary of the Air Force, and shall make such recommendations to the President and to said Secretaries as in the judgment of the Committee will effectuate the policy thereof.

4. All executive departments and agencies of the Federal Government are authorized and directed to cooperate with the Committee in its work, and to furnish the Committee such information or the services of such persons as the Committee may require in the performance of its duties. . . .

—HARRY S TRUMAN, Executive Order 9981, 1948

10. Equal Opportunities for All: Truman's Civil Rights Program

Harry S. Truman

EDITORIAL NOTE: *In this notable message of February 2, 1948, President Truman called on Congress to implement the program recommended by his committee on civil rights. Although the message produced next to nothing in the way of legislation, it dramatized existing inequalities. Together with "To Secure These Rights," it helped prepare the way for public acceptance of the Supreme Court decision of 1954.*

TO THE CONGRESS OF THE UNITED STATES:

IN THE STATE of the Union message on January 7, 1948, I spoke of five great goals toward which we should strive in our constant effort to strengthen our democracy and improve the welfare of our people. The first of these is to secure fully our essential human rights. I am now presenting to the Congress my recommendations for legislation to carry us forward toward that goal.

This nation was founded by men and women who sought these shores that they might enjoy greater freedom and greater opportunity than they had known before. The founders of the United States proclaimed to the world the American belief that all men are created equal, and that governments are instituted to secure the inalienable rights with which all men are endowed. In the Declaration of Independence and the Constitution of the United

States they eloquently expressed the aspirations of all mankind for equality and freedom.

These ideals inspired the peoples of other lands, and their practical fulfillment made the United States the hope of the oppressed everywhere. Throughout our history men and women of all colors and creeds, of all races and religions, have come to this country to escape tyranny and discrimination. Millions strong, they have helped build this democratic Nation and have constantly reinforced our devotion to the great ideals of liberty and equality. With those who preceded them, they have helped to fashion and strengthen our American faith—a faith that can be simply stated:

We believe that all men are created equal and that they have the right to equal justice under law.

We believe that all men have the right to freedom of thought and of expression and the right to worship as they please.

We believe that all men are entitled to equal opportunities for jobs, for homes, for good health, and for education.

We believe that all men should have a voice in their government, and that government should protect, not usurp, the rights of the people.

These are the basic civil rights which are the source and the support of our democracy.

Today the American people enjoy more freedom and opportunity than ever before. Never in our history has there been better reason to hope for the complete realization of the ideals of liberty and equality.

We shall not, however, finally achieve the ideals for which this Nation was founded so long as any American suffers discrimination as a result of his race, or religion, or color, or the land of origin of his forefathers.

Unfortunately there still are examples—flagrant examples—of discrimination which are utterly contrary to our ideals. Not all groups of our population are free from the fear of violence. Not all groups are free to live and work where they please or to improve their conditions of life by their own efforts. Not all groups enjoy the full privileges of citizenship and participation in the Government under which they live.

We cannot be satisfied until all our people have equal opportunities for jobs, for homes, for education, for health, and for political expression, and until all our people have equal protection under the law. . . .

The protection of civil rights is the duty of every government which derives its powers from the consent of the people. This is equally true of local, State, and National Governments. There is much that the States can and should do at this time to extend their protection of civil rights. Wherever the law-enforcement measures of State and local governments are inadequate to discharge this primary function of government, these measures should be strengthened and improved.

The Federal Government has a clear duty to see that constitutional guarantees of individual liberties and of equal protection under the laws are not denied or abridged anywhere in our Union. That duty is shared by all three branches of the Government, but it can be fulfilled only if the Congress enacts modern, comprehensive civil-rights laws, adequate to the needs of the day, and demonstrating our continuing faith in the free way of life.

I recommend, therefore, that the Congress enact legislation at this session directed toward the following specific objectives:

1. Establishing a permanent Commission on Civil Rights, a Joint Congressional Committee on Civil Rights, and a Civil Rights Division in the Department of Justice.
2. Strengthening existing civil-rights statutes.
3. Providing Federal protection against lynching.
4. Protecting more adequately the right to vote.
5. Establishing a Fair Employment Practice Commission to prevent unfair discrimination in employment.
6. Prohibiting discrimination in interstate transportation facilities.
7. Providing home rule and suffrage in Presidential elections for the residents of the District of Columbia.
8. Providing statehood for Hawaii and Alaska and a greater measure of self-government for our island possessions.
9. Equalizing the opportunities for residents of the United States to become naturalized citizens.
10. Settling the evacuation claims of Japanese-Americans. . . .

The legislation I have recommended for enactment by the Congress at the present session is a minimum program if the Federal

Government is to fulfill its obligation of insuring the Constitutional guaranties of individual liberties and of equal protection under the law.

Under the authority of existing law the executive branch is taking every possible action to improve the enforcement of the civil-rights statutes and to eliminate discrimination in Federal employment, in providing Federal services and facilities, and in the armed forces.

I have already referred to the establishment of the Civil Rights Division of the Department of Justice. The Federal Bureau of Investigation will work closely with this new Division in the investigation of Federal civil-rights cases. Specialized training is being given to the Bureau's agents so that they may render more effective service in this difficult field of law enforcement.

It is the settled policy of the United States Government that there shall be no discrimination in Federal employment or in providing Federal services and facilities. Steady progress has been made toward this objective in recent years. I shall shortly issue an Executive order containing a comprehensive restatement of the Federal nondiscrimination policy, together with appropriate measures to ensure compliance.

During the recent war and in the years since its close we have made much progress toward equality of opportunity in our armed services without regard to race, color, religion, or national origin. I have instructed the Secretary of Defense to take steps to have the remaining instances of discrimination in the armed services eliminated as rapidly as possible. The personnel policies and practices of all the services in this regard will be made consistent.

I have instructed the Secretary of the Army to investigate the status of civil rights in the Panama Canal Zone with a view to eliminating such discrimination as may exist there. If legislation is necessary, I shall make appropriate recommendations to the Congress. . . .

The position of the United States in the world today makes it especially urgent that we adopt these measures to secure for all our people their essential rights.

The peoples of the world are faced with the choice of freedom or enslavement, a choice between a form of government which harnesses the state in the service of the individual and a form of government which chains the individual to the needs of the state.

We in the United States are working in company with other nations who share our desire for enduring world peace and who believe with us that, above all else, men must be free. We are striving to build a world family of nations—a world where men may live under governments of their own choosing and under laws of their own making.

As part of that endeavor, the Commission on Human Rights of the United Nations is now engaged in preparing an international bill of human rights by which the nations of the world may bind themselves by international covenant to give effect to basic human rights and fundamental freedoms. We have played a leading role in this undertaking designed to create a world order of law and justice fully protective of the rights and the dignity of the individual.

To be effective in these efforts, we must protect our civil rights so that by providing all our people with the maximum enjoyment of personal freedom and personal opportunity we shall be a stronger nation—stronger in our leadership, stronger in our moral position, stronger in the deeper satisfaction of a united citizenry.

We know that our democracy is not perfect. But we do know that it offers a fuller, freer, happier life to our people than any totalitarian nation has ever offered.

If we wish to inspire the peoples of the world whose freedom is in jeopardy, if we wish to restore hope to those who have already lost their civil liberties, if we wish to fulfill the promise that is ours, we must correct the remaining imperfections in our practice of democracy.

We know the ways. We need only the will.

—Harry S. Truman, Civil Rights Message, 1948

11. "Separate Educational Facilities are Inherently Unequal," 1954

Earl Warren

EDITORIAL NOTE: *The famous case of Brown* v. *Board of Education, one of the landmarks of American law, tested the validity of State laws providing for racial segregation in the public schools. In it the Court reversed the doctrine of Plessy* versus *Ferguson, that the Fourteenth Amendment does not outlaw segregation so long as equal facilities are provided for each race. The Court here ruled that "Separate educational facilities are inherently unequal." The Court followed this ruling with another on May 31, 1955, which established the principle that desegregation must proceed with "all deliberate speed" and assigned to the lower courts the responsibility for applying this principle. These rulings inaugurated a substantial revolution in the legal status of Negroes not only in the field of education but in other areas as well. We give here the first and historic opinion.*

WARREN, C. J.: THESE CASES COME to us from the State of Kansas, South Carolina, Virginia, and Delaware. They are premised on different facts and different local conditions, but a common legal question justifies their consideration together in this consolidated opinion.

In each of the cases, minors of the Negro race, through their legal representatives, seek the aid of the courts in obtaining admission to the public schools of their community on a nonsegregated basis. In each instance, they have been denied admission to schools attended by white children under laws requiring or permitting segregation according to race. This segregation was alleged to deprive the plaintiffs of the equal protection of the laws under the Fourteenth Amendment. In each of the cases other than the Delaware case, a three-judge federal district court denied relief to the plaintiffs on the so-called "separate but equal" doctrine announced by this Court in Plessy v. Ferguson. Under that doctrine, equality of treatment is accorded when the races are provided substantially equal facilities, even though these facilities be separate. In the Delaware case, the Supreme Court of Delaware adhered to that doctrine, but ordered that the plaintiffs be admitted to the white schools because of their superiority to the Negro schools.

The plaintiffs contend that segregated public schools are not "equal" and cannot be made "equal," and that hence they are deprived of the equal protection of the laws. Because of the obvious importance of the question presented, the Court took jurisdiction. Argument was heard in the 1952 term, and re-argument was heard this term on certain questions propounded by the Court.

Re-argument was largely devoted to the circumstances surrounding the adoption of the Fourteenth Amendment in 1868. It covered exhaustively consideration of the Amendment in Congress, ratification by the states, then existing practices in racial segregation, and the views of proponents and opponents of the Amendment. This discussion and our own investigation convince us that, although these sources cast some light, it is not enough to resolve the problem with which we are faced. At best, they are inconclusive. The most avid proponents of the post-War Amendments undoubtedly intended them to remove all legal distinctions among "all persons born or naturalized in the United States." Their opponents, just as certainly, were antagonistic to both the letter and the spirit of the Amendments and wished them to have the most limited effect. What others in Congress and the state legislatures had in mind cannot be determined with any degree of certainty.

An additional reason for the inconclusive nature of the Amendment's history, with respect to segregated schools, is the status of public education at that time. In the South, the movement toward free common schools, supported by general taxation, had not yet taken hold. Education of white children was largely in the hands of private groups. Education of Negroes was almost nonexistent, and practically all of the race were illiterate. In fact, any education of Negroes was forbidden by law in some states. Today, in contrast, many Negroes have achieved outstanding success in the arts and sciences as well as in the business and professional world. It is true that public education had already advanced further in the North, but the effect of the Amendment on Northern States was generally ignored in the congressional debates. Even in the North, the conditions of public education did not approximate those existing today. The curriculum was usually rudimentary; ungraded schools were common in rural areas; the school term was but three months a year in many states; and compulsory school attendance was virtually unknown. As a consequence, it is not surprising that there should be so little in the history of the Fourteenth Amendment relating to its intended effect on public education.

In the first cases in this Court construing the Fourteenth Amendment, decided shortly after its adoption, the Court interpreted it as proscribing all state-imposed discriminations against the Negro race. The doctrine of "separate but equal" did not make its appearance in this Court until 1896 in the case of Plessy v. Ferguson, supra, involving not education but transportation. American courts have since labored with the doctrine for over half a century. In this Court, there have been six cases involving the "separate but equal" doctrine in the field of public education. In Cumming v. Board of Education and Gong Lum v. Rice, the validity of the doctrine itself was not challenged. In more recent cases, all on the graduate school level, inequality was found in that specific benefits enjoyed by white students were denied to Negro students of the same educational qualifications. In none of these cases was it necessary to reexamine the doctrine to grant relief to the Negro plaintiff. And in Sweatt v. Painter, the Court expressly reserved decision on the question whether Plessy v. Ferguson should be held inapplicable to public education.

In the instant cases, that question is directly presented. Here unlike Sweatt v. Painter, there are findings below that the Negro and white schools involved have been equalized, or are being equalized, with respect to buildings, curricula, qualifications and salaries of teachers, and other "tangible" factors. Our decision, therefore, cannot turn on merely a comparison of these tangible factors in the Negro and white schools involved in each of the cases. We must look instead to the effect of segregation itself on public education.

In approaching this problem, we cannot turn the clock back to 1868 when the Amendment was adopted, or even to 1896 when Plessy v. Ferguson was written. We must consider public education in the light of its full development and its present place in American life throughout the Nation. Only in this way can it be determined if segregation in public schools deprives these plaintiffs of the equal protection of the laws.

Today, education is perhaps the most important function of state and local governments. Compulsory school attendance laws and the great expenditures for education both demonstrate our recognition of the importance of education to our democratic society. It is required in the performance of our most basic public responsibilities, even service in the armed forces. It is the very foundation of good citizenship. Today it is a principal instrument in awakening the child to cultural values, in preparing him for later professional training, and in helping him to adjust normally to his environment. In these days, it is doubtful that any child may reasonably be expected to succeed in life if he is denied the opportunity of an education. Such an opportunity, where the state has undertaken to provide it, is a right which must be made available to all on equal terms.

We come then to the question presented: Does segregation of children in public schools solely on the basis of race, even though the physical facilities and other "tangible" factors may be equal, deprive the children of the minority group of equal educational opportunities? We believe that it does.

In Sweatt v. Painter, in finding that a segregated law school for Negroes could not provide them equal educational opportunities, this Court relied in large part on "those qualities which are incapable of objective measurement but which make for greatness in a law school." In McLaurin v. Oklahoma State Regents, the Court, in requiring that a Negro admitted to a white graduate school be treated like all other students, again resorted to intangible considerations: ". . . his ability to study, to engage in discussions and exchange views with other students, and, in general, to learn his profession." Such considerations apply with added force to children in grade and high schools.

To separate them from others of similar age and qualifications solely because of their race generates a feeling of inferiority as to their status in the community that may affect their hearts and minds in a way unlikely ever to be undone. The effect of this separation on their educational opportunities was well stated by a finding in the Kansas case by a court which nevertheless felt compelled to rule against the Negro plaintiffs:

> Segregation of white and colored children in public schools has a detrimental effect upon the colored children. The impact is greater when it has the sanction of the law; for the policy of separating the races is usually interpreted as denoting the inferiority of the Negro group. A sense of inferiority affects the motivation of a child to learn. Segregation with the sanction of law, therefore, has a tendency to retard the educational and mental development of Negro children and to deprive them of some of the benefits they would receive in a racially integrated school system.

Whatever may have been the extent of psychological knowledge at the time of Plessy v. Ferguson, this finding is amply supported by modern authority. Any language in Plessy v. Ferguson contrary to this finding is rejected.

We conclude that in the field of public education the doctrine of "separate but equal" has no place. Separate educational facilities are inherently unequal. Therefore, we hold that the plantiffs and others similarly situated for whom the actions have been brought are, by reason of the segregation complained of, deprived of the equal protection of the laws guaranteed by the Fourteenth Amendment. This disposition makes unnecessary any discussion whether such segregation also violates the Due Process Clause of the Fourteenth Amendment.

Because these are class actions, because of the wide applicability of this decision, and because of the great variety of local conditions, the formulation of decrees in these cases presents problems of considerable complexity. On re-argument, the consideration of appropriate relief was necessarily subordinated to the primary question—the constitutionality of segregation in public education. We have now announced that such segregation is a denial of the equal protection of the laws. In order that we may have the full assistance of the parties in formulating decrees, the cases will be restored to the docket, and the parties are requested to present further argument. . . .

The Attorney General of the United States is again invited to participate. The Attorneys General of the states requiring or permitting segregation in public education will also be permitted to appear as *amici curiae* upon request to do so by September 15, 1954, and submission of briefs by October 1, 1954.

It is so ordered.

—Chief Justice Earl Warren, 1954

12. "Brown v. Topeka is a Naked Exercise of Judicial Power"

EDITORIAL NOTE: *Though the Supreme Court directed that integration proceed "with all deliberate speed," the deliberateness was far more conspicuous than the speed. There was at first some disposition to acquiesce in the judicial mandate, but opposition grew and hardened, and hastily organized White Citizens Councils conspired to frustrate the operation of the Brown Decision. On March 12, 1956, ninety-six Southern Congressmen—it was practically unanimous—issued a Declaration denouncing the Supreme Court decision as a violation of the Constitution, calling on their States to refuse obedience to it, and pledging themselves to resist it "by all lawful means."*

WE REGARD THE decision of the Supreme Court in the school cases as clear abuse of judicial power. It climaxes a trend in the Federal judiciary undertaking to legislate, in derogation of the authority of Congress, and to encroach upon the reserved rights of the states and the people.

The original Constitution does not mention education. Neither does the Fourteenth Amendment nor any other amendment. The debates preceding the submission of the Fourteenth Amendment clearly show that there was no intent that it should affect the systems of education maintained by the states.

The very Congress which proposed the amendment subsequently provided for segregated schools in the District of Columbia.

When the amendment was adopted in 1868, there were thirty-seven states in the Union. Every one of the twenty-six states that had any substantial racial differences among its people either approved the operation of segregated schools already in existence or subsequently established such schools by action of the same law-making body which considered the Fourteenth Amendment.

As admitted by the Supreme Court in the public school case (Brown v. Board of Education), the doctrine of separate but equal schools "apparently originated in Roberts v. City of Boston (1849), upholding school segregation against attack as being violative of a state constitutional guarantee of equality." This constitutional doctrine began in the North—not in the South—and it was followed not only in Massachusetts but in Connecticut, New York, Illinois, Indiana, Michigan, Minnesota, New Jersey, Ohio, Pennsylvania and other northern states until they, exercising their rights as states through the constitutional process of local self-government, changed their school systems.

In the case of Plessy v. Ferguson in 1896 the Supreme Court expressly declared that under the Fourteenth Amendment no person was denied any of his rights if the states provided separate but equal public facilities. This decision has been followed in many other cases. It is notable that the Supreme Court, speaking through Chief Justice Taft, a former President of the United States, unanimously declared in 1927 in Lum v. Rice that the "separate but equal" principle is ". . . within the discretion of the state in regulating its public schools and does not conflict with the Fourteenth Amendment."

This interpretation, restated time and again, became a part of the life of the people of many of the states and confirmed their habits, customs, traditions and way of life. It is founded on elemental humanity and common sense, for parents should not be deprived by Government of the right to direct the lives and education of their own children.

Though there has been no constitutional amendment or act of Congress changing this established legal principle almost a century old, the Supreme Court of the United States, with no legal basis for such action, undertook to exercise their naked judicial power and substituted their personal political and social ideas for the established law of the land.

This unwarranted exercise of power by the court, contrary to the Constitution, is creating chaos and confusion in the states principally affected. It is destroying the amicable relations between the white and Negro races that have been created through ninety years of patient effort by the good people of both races. It has planted hatred and suspicion where there has been heretofore friendship and understanding.

Without regard to the consent of the governed, outside agitators are threatening immediate and revolutionary changes in our public school systems. If done, this is certain to destroy the system of public education in some of the states.

With the gravest concern for the explosive and dangerous condition created by this decision and inflamed by outside meddlers:

We reaffirm our reliance on the Constitution as the fundamental law of the land.

We decry the Supreme Court's encroachments on rights reserved to the states and to the people, contrary to established law and to the Constitution.

We commend the motives of those states which have declared the intention to resist forced integration by any lawful means.

We appeal to the states and people who are not directly affected by these decisions to consider the constitutional principles involved against the time when they too, on issues vital to them, may be the victims of judicial encroachment.

Even though we constitute a minority in the present Congress, we have full faith that a majority of the American people believe in the dual system of government which has enabled us to achieve our greatness and will in time demand that the reserved rights of the states and of the people be made secure against judicial usurpation.

We pledge ourselves to use all lawful means to bring about a reversal of this decision which is contrary to the Constitution and to prevent the use of force in its implementation.

In this trying period, as we all seek to right this wrong, we appeal to our people not to be provoked by the agitators and troublemakers invading our states and to scrupulously refrain from disorder and lawless acts.

—"Southern Declaration on Integration," March 12, 1956

13. An Argument that the Negro is Inherently Inferior

Carleton Putnam

EDITORIAL NOTE: *The strongest and most elaborate argument against the desegregation decision came from Carleton Putnam, businessman, lawyer, and historian. Born in New York City and educated at Princeton and Columbia Universities, Putnam adopted, almost in toto, the traditional Southern view of the proper relations between the white and the Negro races. In 1959 he sent the following letter to Attorney-General William P. Rogers—with copies to the President and members of the Supreme Court. The following year he elaborated his argument in a book,* Race and Reason: A Yankee View, *which was received with immense enthusiasm throughout the South. Mr. Putnam's anthropolitical arguments, though generally rejected by scientists, received some support from the respected Professor Carleton Coon of the University of Pennsylvania.*

LETTER TO THE ATTORNEY-GENERAL OF THE UNITED STATES, MARCH 16, 1959

Following my correspondence with your Department in December, I have had a chance to review your briefs in the school desegregation cases and also to scan, as carefully as time permitted, the nine relevant volumes of the *Supreme Court's Records and Briefs.* I hesitate to impose further upon your kindness, but my survey has left one question in my mind upon which the record does not appear to touch, and which you may be able to answer.

I turn to you for the reason that, as a non-adversary party to these proceedings, I understand you to have represented the people of the United States. Since a majority of the population of the South are obviously against integration, and since the Gallup Poll for September 24, 1958, indicates that 58% of the white population of the North would not put their children in schools where more than half the enrollment is Negro, it becomes a close question whether the decision of the Supreme Court in these cases was not in fact contrary to the wishes of a national majority. While I recognize that this would in no way affect the validity of the decision, it would seem to have placed a peculiar responsibility upon you.

The matter which I find curious is the omission in your briefs of any challenge to the authorities cited by the Court in Footnote 11 to their opinion of May 17, 1954. I assume there must have been some indication, in argument or elsewhere, that these authorities were to be used. They appear, in large measure, to form the foundation of the decision. They reflect a point of view rooted in what I may call modern equalitarian anthropology—a school which holds that all races are currently equal in their capacity for culture, and that existing inequalities of status are due solely to inequalities of opportunity. While the briefs for the State of Virginia touch upon the qualifications of some of the individual psychologists who testified in the lower courts, they contain no examination of the underlying anthropological theory. It seems to me that such an examination should have been made. I have a science degree, I have read with some diligence in the field of anthropology and I have discussed the subject with competent anthropologists. It is my considered opinion that two generations of Americans have been victimized by a pseudo-scientific hoax in this field, that this hoax is part of an equalitarian propaganda typical of the left-wing overdrift of our times, and that it will not stand an informed judicial test. I do not believe that ever before has science been more warped by a self-serving few to the deception and injury of so many. On this subject there may be disagreement. But it is clear to me the Court should have been invited to examine the question.

Allow me to give my reasons for this opinion. The Court says in Footnote 11 "See generally Myrdal, *An American Dilemma,*" and I start with this book. I need hardly dwell upon the highly socialistic bias of its foreign author, and the startling remarks with which his text is peppered, such as his comment that the American Constitution "is in many respects impractical and ill-suited for modern conditions," that the Constitutional Convention of 1787 "was nearly a plot against the common people" and that in the conflict between liberty and equality in the United States "equality is slowly winning." A foreign socialist could not, perhaps, have realized that Jefferson's statement "all men are created equal" was a corruption from the Virginia Declaration of Rights, where the original wording read "all men are created equally free," nor that if equality (in any sense other than equality of opportunity and equality before the law) is defeating liberty in the United States, then everything America has stood for is in jeopardy, but certainly it was essential that these matters be called to the Court's attention in evaluating Myrdal's book.

I hasten, however, to the basic hypothesis underlying Myrdal's 1400 pages. On pages 90–91 he introduces the doctrines of Franz Boas, a foreign-born Columbia University professor who arrived in the United States in 1886, who was himself a member of a racial minority group, and who may be called the father of equalitarian anthropology in America. From these pages forward, Myrdal's *Dilemma* is founded upon the philosophy of Boas and his disciples. Thereafter, one constantly finds in Myrdal such sentences as these:

"The last two or three decades have seen a veritable revolution in scientific thought on the racial characteristics of the Negro. . . . By inventing and applying ingenious specialized research methods, the popular race dogma [that races are not by nature equal in their capacity for culture] is being victoriously pursued into every corner and effectively exposed as fallacious or at least unsubstantiated. . . . It is now becoming difficult for even popular writers to express other views than the ones of racial equalitarianism and still retain intellectual respect."

If you have not already read him, I invite you to a thorough and impartial study of Boas. I am confident you will find his views wholly unconvincing, his doctrines more "unsubstantiated" than those he attacks, and his approach so saturated with wishful thinking as to be pathetic. In even the most superficial analysis of the subject, Boas should have been challenged and his more obvious errors exposed. Boas, for example, may have been convinced that the average African's improvident indifference to "tomorrow" is just a healthy, "optimism", but I dare say the proverbial reasonable man on a jury would think of it less charitably.

If the deceptions of the Boas school were unconscious, they were nevertheless serious. People, for instance, were induced to believe that because early anthropologists put emphasis on brain pan size in their studies of race, and brain pan size later proved to be an invalid criterion, this automatically made all races equal. No one took the time to point out that not only is brain pan size not a final test of intelligence, but that, even if it were, equal brain size would not prove equal capacity for civilization. The character-intelligence index—the combination of intelligence with all of the qualities that go under the name of character, including especially the willingness to resist rather than to appease evil—forms the only possible index of the capacity for civilization as Western Europeans know it, and there is no test for this index save in observing the native culture in which it results. Such observation does not sustain the doctrine of equality.

Indeed, the entire foundation of the Boas theory rests on sand. It is based on the assumption that present day cultural differences between the Negro and other races are due, not to any natural limitations, but to isolation and historical accident. This theme has been taken up again and again by later anthropologists such as Kluckhohn of Harvard, and repeated as established scientific fact. I may illustrate the argument by comparing the condition of the white tribes of Northern Europe just before the fall of Rome with the Negro tribes in the Congo. Both were primitive and barbaric, both were isolated from civilization. With the conquest of Rome by the white barbarians, the northern tribes were brought in contact with the ancient Greco-Roman civilization and gradually absorbed its culture. The Negro, on the other hand, lacked such a contact and therefore remained in *statu quo.*

This was Boas' historical accident, and his explanation of the Negro's present level of civilization in Africa. Boas had various additional points and refinements of his thesis, such as the advantage the white barbarians enjoyed in contiguity of habitat and the more moderate differences in modes of manufacture in earlier times, which made it easier for backward peoples in those days to compete commercially with more advanced cultures than was the case in later centuries when our white civilization invaded Africa, but these arguments hang on the first point. In other words, had the Negroes shown the enterprise and initiative of the white barbarians, the Negroes themselves would have established a contiguity of habitat and had the advantage of more moderate differences in modes of manufacture.

As far as isolation is concerned, it hardly seems necessary to point out that the Alps did not keep the white barbarians out of Italy, and that the Nile Valley was open to the Negroes into Egypt. One observer, recently returned from an intensive tour of Africa and himself apparently a racial equalitarian, nevertheless feels compelled to include these sentences in his report:

"Why, when in China, India, Mesopotamia and on the Mediterranean coasts and islands, men isolated almost completely from one another, during some 5,000 years independently developed writing and metal tools, invented compasses, built temples and bridges, formulated philosophies, wrote books and poems—why, then, did similar progress not occur in Africa?

"I posed the question to many Africans. Their answer: the desert, the heat, disease, isolation—and always these words: 'For centuries our most vigorous young men were taken off as slaves.'

"The answer falls short. China has a desert; India's climate is as hot and as unhealthy; Mesopotamia indeed is hotter—and was surrounded by deserts. As for the slave trade, why were the Africans not making slaves of the Portuguese and the Arabs?"

This report, prepared by the assistant to the publisher of *Time* magazine, goes on to seek justification for the equalitarian viewpoint in the modern intelligence test and the modern performance of the exceptional Negro, answers which fall as far short as the others. The field of the intelligence test, like the field of Boas' anthropology, is filled with wishful thinking, with comparisons of the better Negroes and the poorer whites, with studies of mulattoes whose successes are largely proportionate to the admixture of white genes, and with similar avoidance of the essential point, namely, that in matters of race either the average of one must be compared with the average of the other, or the best of one must be compared with the best of the other.

If we are to compare averages, there is probably no better laboratory than the rural area around Chatham, Ontario, Canada. Chatham is a town at the northern end of the pre-Civil War "underground railroad" where a community of the descendants of escaped slaves has existed for 100 years. The social and economic situation of Negroes and whites in the rural area around Chatham is approximately equal. The schools have always been integrated, yet the tests of Negroes in these rural schools show them, after 100 years, to be as far below the whites in the same schools as the Negroes in the schools of the South are below the whites in the schools of the South. Dr. H. A. Tanser, now Superintendent of Schools at Chatham, published a study of this matter in 1939. The study is never mentioned by the modern school of equalitarian anthropology, but you will find it in the Library of Congress. Did your Department give it consideration?

In this connection, you are perhaps aware that Dr. Audrey M. Shuey, Chairman of the Department of Psychology at Randolph-Macon Woman's College, published a report in 1958 surveying and summarizing the results of 40 years of intelligence tests involving whites and Negroes. Dr. Shuey took her B.A. at the University of Illinois, her M.A. at Wellesley, and her Ph.D. at Columbia. Her book contains a foreword by Dr. Henry E. Garrett, former president of the American Psychological Association, the Eastern Psychological Association, the New York State Association of Applied Psychology and the Psychometric Society. In his foreword, Dr. Garrett says:

> Dr. Shuey finds that at several age levels and under a variety of conditions, Negroes regularly score below whites. There is, to be sure, an overlapping of scores, a number of Negroes scoring above the white medians. This overlap means that many individual Negroes achieve high scores on the tests. But the mean differences persist. Dr. Shuey concludes that the regularity and consistency of the results strongly implies a racial basis for these differences. I believe that the weight of evidence supports her conclusion.

Dr. Shuey states that "the remarkable consistency of test results . . . all point to the presence of some native differences between Negroes and whites determined by intelligence tests," and she adds the significant comment: "The tendency for the IQ's of colored children to become progressively lower with increase in age has been reported by a number of investigators who tested Negro children. . . . One is confronted with the probability of a continuance during adolescence of what seems to be a widening gap between the races." I recognize that Dr. Shuey's report was not extant at the time of the Brown decision, but a large part of her material was available, and in my opinion should have been submitted to the Court. I repeat that I do not consider the intelligence test decisive, as I believe character to be more important than intelligence, but in answer to those who use the intelligence test to support theories of racial equality, surely Tanser's and Shuey's material belonged in the record.

If, on the other hand, we compare the best with the best, the discrepancies are even clearer. I had occasion to ask Kluckhohn a question with respect to a statement in his *Mirror for Man* at page 126. This statement reads: "It is true that the total richness of Negro civilizations is *at least quantitatively* less impressive than that of Western or Chinese civilization." (Emphasis mine). I asked Kluckhohn if he would mind defining in what respects he found it *qualitatively* as impressive. I told him I was curious as to one poem equal to Milton's *Paradise Lost,* one history equal to Gibbon's *Decline and Fall,* one novel equal to Dickens' *David Copperfield,* one playwright equal to Shakespeare, one philosopher equal to Aristotle, one medical discovery equal to Salk's polio vaccine, one military leader equal to Napoleon, one inventor equal to Edison, one physicist equal to Einstein, one pioneer equal to Columbus, one statesman equal to Abraham Lincoln, one composer equal to Beethoven, one painter equal to Rembrandt. I have received no reply, but Kluckhohn's "at least quantitatively" seems to me typical of the deceptive words used by our modern equalitarian anthropology. The Court should not have been left in the dark on this tendency. Although they do not specifically cite Kluckhohn, he is one of the leaders of the modern school on which Myrdal rests his case.

I have found that a favorite method used by Boas and Kluckhohn for throwing dust in the eyes of the public is to create an impression that there is really no such thing as race. Although Kluckhohn begins the third paragraph of the fifth chapter of his *Mirror for Man* with the sentence "There are undoubtedly human races," he nevertheless entitles this chapter "Race: A Modern Myth." His thesis is that culture, not race, is what makes human beings what they are. Yet nowhere is the obvious fact examined that culture is absorbed, refined and advanced in proportion to racial capacity. There are, of course, certain modifying variables, among the chief of which are climate and economic conditions. The white culture of New England differs from the white culture of the Deep South, but not as much as the white culture of southern Florida differs from the black culture of Haiti, where the climate is approximately the same. That is to say, the effect of the variables is clearly less decisive than the fundamental difference in race.

Undoubtedly an individual or group, taken out of the cultural environment of their own race and brought up in that of another, will sometimes absorb some features of the culture of the new environment, but in such instances they become parasites upon the culture of the second race. They are carried up, or carried down, as the case may be, by the overwhelming impact of the environment of the second race. Their own capacity to contribute to, and to sustain, a culture can only be judged by the performance of their own race in its native habitat. And if that capacity is low, then too many of them, too freely integrated, must inevitably in the long run lower the culture of the second race.

There have, not unnaturally, been situations in which a race has captured the spark of culture in one habitat but not in another. In the case of the fall of the Roman Empire, the barbarians were, broadly speaking, members of the same race as the conquered. Here we find two branches of the white race, one of which had produced a culture while the other had not, and here the Boas theory of historical accident is tenable. Similarity of tinder permitted passage of the spark. It was still the white race that absorbed, and eventually carried forward, the Roman culture.

The essential question in this whole controversy is whether the Negro, given every conceivable help regardless of cost to the whites, is capable of full adaptation to our white civilization within a matter of a few generations, or whether the record indicates such adaptation cannot be expected save in terms of many hundreds, if not thousands, of years, and that complete integration of these races, especially in the heavy black belts of the South, can result only in a parasitic deterioration of white culture, with or without genocide. I am certain neither you nor the Court, nor any significant number of Northerners would knowingly shackle their racial brothers in the South against their will with a system which would produce either of the latter results. The sin of Cain would pale by comparison.

Yet to my mind it seems obvious that all the facts, and a preponderance of theory, are against Myrdal and his authorities. I would go so far as to say that in the last fifty years anthropology has been drafted to serve the demi-Goddess of Equalitarianism instead of the Goddess of Truth, and that the modern school in this field has a stern judgment to face, both at the bar of American public opinion and at the hands of two generations of youth whose thinking has been corrupted by it. One does not build a healthy society on error. One faces the truth, and deals with it as best one can.

I pass now from Myrdal, and the sources upon which his more general assumptions rest, to the remaining authorities cited in Footnote 11. All of these deal primarily with the adverse psychological effect of segregation upon Negroes and only secondarily with its alleged adverse effect upon white children. Nowhere is any study cited of a third question, namely, of the quite possible adverse effect of *integration* upon whites in schools with large percentages of Negroes. Was any such study made and presented to the Court?

The third question was well put by William Polk in his book *Southern Accent:* "If the Negro is entitled to lift himself up by enforced association with the white man, why should not the white man be entitled to prevent himself from being pulled down by enforced association with the Negro?" This question seems particularly important in view of the patent partiality of the authorities cited in favor of integration. The majority of these appear either to belong to Negro or other minority groups, or to have prepared their studies under the auspices of such groups. To expect these groups to present impartial reports on the subject of racial discrimination is like expecting a saloon keeper to prepare an impartial study on prohibition, or a meat packer to pass an unbiased judgment on the Humane Slaughter Bill. Their point of view is important and deserves consideration. Many of them are brilliant and consecrated men. But to permit them to provide the overwhelming preponderance of the evidence is manifestly not justice. If this is compounded by an absence of any consideration of the damaging effects of integration upon white children, it becomes doubly serious. While the brief for the State of Virginia touches upon the subject, it seems to me that the people of the United States, whom you represented, had a particular interest in seeing it more fully developed. I would appreciate your directing me to such a study, if one was made, and also your providing me with some explanation as to why the evidence on damage to the Negro was from such partisan sources.

Any American worthy of the name feels an obligation of kindness and justice toward his fellow man. He is willing to give every individual his chance, whatever his race, but in those circumstances where a race must be dealt with as a race, he realizes that the level of the average must be controlling, and that the relatively minor handicap upon the superior individual of the segregated race, if it be a handicap at all, must be accepted until the average has reached the point where desire for association is mutual.

This leads me to my final query. I will be frank to say that I was startled at the uncritical manner in which the Supreme Court was allowed to accept one phrase in the language of the lower court, to wit: "A sense of inferiority [produced by segregation] affects the motivation of a child to learn." Did neither you nor counsel for any of the appellees take occasion to point out that if a child is by nature inferior, enforced association with his superiors will increase his realization of his inferiority, while if he is by nature not inferior, any implication of inferiority in segregation, if such there be, will only serve as a spur to greater effort? Throughout history, challenges of this sort, acting upon individuals, groups and races of natural capacity, have proved a whip to achievement, times without number. The point was one of the legal hinges on which the case turned. In fact without it the decision falls apart, for there is no other even remotely arguable excuse why separate facilities cannot be made equal within any possible stretch of the meaning of the Fourteenth Amendment. Consequently, I would have thought it imperative that you raise it.

—Carleton Putnam, *Race and Reason. A Yankee View,* 1961

14. Southern Extremists Deplore "Black Monday," 1954

Judge Tom Brady

A. *The Press Charges the Court with Treason*

EDITORIAL NOTE: *Not all of the responses to the Supreme Court decision in Brown* v. *Topeka were as reasoned as that by Carleton Putnam. Much of the Southern press—and some Southern Congressmen—had recourse to unrestrained vituperation. Judge Tom Brady here brings together a few samples of these reactions.*

SUBSEQUENT TO THE decision, the outstanding editors in the South have candidly and fearlessly repudiated the action and warned the Court of the ultimate results. Major Frederick Sullens, editor of the Jackson Daily News, Jackson, Mississippi, on May 18th, the next day after Black Monday, came out with his candid editorial, "Bloodstains on White Marble Steps":

> . . . members of the Nation's highest tribunal may be learned in the law, but they were utterly lacking in common sense when they rendered Monday's decision, common sense of the kind that should have told them about the tragedy that will inevitably follow. When the courts toss common sense out the window and substitute specious reasoning, shallow subterfuge, silly sophistry and sordid politics, then our nation is in a deplorable plight! . . .
>
> Human blood may stain Southern soil in many places because of this

decision, but the dark red stains of that blood will be on the marble steps of the United States Supreme Court building.

This courageous editor has the benefit of almost half a century of association with and observation of the negro of the South. He has forgotten more about interracial problems than the Supreme Court will ever know. The poignant truth of the conditional potential which he stated is what is so terrifying.

Senator Richard Russell of Georgia, on the same day, sacrificed gladly any presidential possibilities he may have had in denouncing and bemoaning on the floor of the United States Senate the creation of this Frankenstein monster by the Supreme Court's decision.

On May 19th, 1954, Representative Williams in the House of Representatives boldly spoke out against the propriety and wisdom of the decision—branding May 17th as "Black Monday."

On May 27th Senator James O. Eastland delivered, on the floor of the United States Senate, the tersest, the clearest and most accurate analysis of the segregation problem yet propounded. This speech should go into the homes of every white and negro family in the South. It will do much to extinguish the widely scattered, smoldering fires of racial hate the decision has rekindled. It is fitting that a portion of that illustrious speech be quoted:

> The southern institution of racial segregation or racial separation was the correct, self-evident truth which arose from the chaos and confusion of the reconstruction period. Separation promotes racial harmony. It permits each race to follow its own pursuits, to develop its own culture, its own institutions, and its own civilization. Segregation is not discrimination. Segregation is not a badge of racial inferiority, and that it is not is recognized by both races in the Southern States. In fact, segregation is desired and supported by the vast majority of the members of both of the races in the South, who dwell side by side under harmonious conditions.
>
> The negro has made a great contribution to the South. We take pride in the constant advance he has made. It is where social questions are involved that Southern people draw the line. It is these social institutions with which Southern people, in my judgment, will not permit the Supreme Court to tamper.
>
> Let me make this clear, Mr. President: There is no racial hatred in the South. The negro race is not an oppressed race. A great Senator from the State of Idaho, Senator William E. Borah, a few years ago said on the

floor of the Senate: "Let us admit that the South is dealing with this question as best it can, admit that the men and women of the South are just as patriotic as we are, just as devoted to the principles of the Constitution as we are, just as willing to sacrifice for the success of their communities as we are. Let us give them credit as American citizens, and cooperate with them, sympathize with them, and help them in the solution of their problem, instead of condemning them. We are one people, one nation, and they are entitled to be treated upon this basis."

Mr. President, it is the law of nature, it is the law of God, that every race has both the right and the duty to perpetuate itself. All free men have the right to associate exclusively with members of their own race, free from governmental interference, if they so desire. Free men have the right to send their children to schools of their own choosing, free from governmental interference and to build up their own culture, free from governmental interference. These rights are inherent in the Constitution of the United States and in the American system of government, both state and national, to promote and protect this right.

Although these "lockings of the stable occurred subsequent to the stealing of the horse"—they should help deter future similar tyrannical acts. Communism disguised as "new democracy" is still communism, and tyranny masquerading as liberalism is still tyranny. The resistance of communism and tyranny, irrespective of whatever guise they may adopt, is not treason. It is the prerequisite of freedom, the very essence of liberty.

It is out of order to assume that the members of the new Sociological Supreme Court should have at least a working knowledge of anthropology, ethnology, biology, social evolution, and the science of society as well as the Constitution and decisions thereunder?

Is it expecting too much to anticipate that the United States Supreme Court, when deciding socio-legal questions, which profoundly affect the destiny of this nation, will take into consideration the great truths which these scientific studies have established, and what inestimable destruction the violation by it of these basic laws, which lie beyond its petty jurisdiction, will produce. Perhaps the United States Supreme Court is unconcerned with the ultimate destructive results of this tragic decision, since "there are none so blind as those who will not see."

—JUDGE TOM BRADY, "Black Monday," 1955

B. *Communist Masses Howled with Glee on "Black Monday"*

EDITORIAL NOTE: *Many Southerners persuaded themselves that the desegregation decision was no isolated event, but part of a conspiracy to socialize and Communize the United States. This was, indeed, almost the official view of the White Citizens Councils of America which exercised great influence in Alabama, Mississippi, and Louisiana. There is no better example of what Richard Hofstadter has called the "paranoiac style" in American politics than this argument by Judge Tom Brady that the whole thing was part of a Communist conspiracy. Judge Brady, at this time judge of the Fourteenth Judicial District, was a graduate of Yale University and, before he turned to law, taught sociology at the University of Mississippi.*

DO NOT ERRONEOUSLY suppose that the segregation ruling by the Supreme Court will satiate the inordinate hunger for power of these minority groups. Each one of their foresworn aims will be relentlessly prosecuted. . . .

It is unwise to prophesy, but socialized medicine, when such a case is prepared and comes for review upon appeal, will be ripe for legal validation by the present U. S. Supreme Court, under the "Open Sesame" interpretation of the Fourteenth Amendment. Such a decision would not be nearly as socialistic as the control and regulation of the schools of your State.

There will be more FHA's and more corruption, more TVA's, et ceteras. The Government will first control and then usurp the banking business, then it will manage and socialize transportation, agriculture and any other private enterprises where the totalitarian state will be advanced. We will all become socialized Federal workers, working for the glory of the State.

This is but a part of what lies ahead of "Black Monday." Sovereign States, do you know what lies behind it? The Communists of

America have been trying since 1936 to destroy the South. The bait which attracts them is the negro population. Hate campaigns against the Southern States were conducted in the North. Abuse and falsehoods were flagrantly utilized. Counsel and advice were given the negro leaders. A bloodless revolution was planned.

The negro was to be placed in office and in control, while the whites were to be driven out. A black empire was to be established in the Southern States of this nation, ruled by negroes. All public offices were to be held by negroes. The most fantastic and preposterous promises were made. The good will which had for eighty years existed between the races has been disturbed. Pilgrimages from the South to the North were encouraged where indoctrinization of the negroes took place. The new converts were returned to the South to disseminate their "new, glorious knowledge," and begin the creation of this fine socialistic Eden. Back of all this was but one motive, not the welfare of the negro, but the splitting away and controlling of a fine section of this nation, the segment which gave to democracy Thomas Jefferson, Washington, Madison, Monroe and Andrew Jackson. It was and is being done in behalf of Communist Russia. If the South, the stronghold of democracy, could be destroyed, then the nation could be destroyed.

This plan failed. The economic superiority of the white man or the innate loyalty of the Southern negro to this country, or both probably, caused the abandonment of the plan by the Communists. Then, too, it was prematurely conceived.

The plan to abolish segregation in the seventeen States, thirteen of which are Southern, was substituted. The medium through which this was to be accomplished was the National Association for the Advancement of Colored People, its affiliate organizations, together with the CIO.

Let us calmly and as impartially as possible review the facts.

In 1936, huge numbers of negroes migrated north to such cities as Chicago, Detroit, Akron, Pittsburgh, Philadelphia and New York. A little later, a migration went to California, the 1st District receiving a tremendous portion. In passing, James Roosevelt moved into this district and it was the block vote of these negroes which recently gave him the Democratic nomination to Congress.

Inflamed with their new power and fired by the promises of the

Roosevelt machine and the CIO, the negro vote switched with the CIO to the Democratic Party, making possible the election of Roosevelt to the presidency. The block vote of the negroes helped keep him there. It is partially responsible for the New Deal and all its socialism. Truman used the negro vote as a stirrup, and rewarded it with the Civil Rights agitation and the appointment of negroes to high offices. Satisfying their inordinate ambitions was one way of paying a political debt.

Catastrophes and epidemics such as the Great Fire of Chicago, the San Francisco earthquake, cholera and meningitis, the yellow fever and influenza epidemics, and the other pestilences which this country has undergone are disastrous and lamentable, but the most destructive force which we are subject to is mental (not insanity) and spiritual illness. This is the essence of communism and its corollary, socialism. They are the political and economic ills which destroy men's souls and decompose nations. The dubious have but to casually examine the economic and political conditions of the nations which have been thoroughly infected with the virus of communism. There is something mysterious about this dread governmental disease. The symptoms are so multiplex. It strikes where least expected with the speed and fury of a forest fire. It is a fanatical religion. It is an obsession. There is an abundance of satanic power embodied therein. It fascinates the quasi intelligent and it enthralls the ignorant. It appeals to rich and poor. To the indigent and maladjusted it is a panacea.

All the powers of darkness and evil are at its command. These are not idle words! Communism has always hitched to and ridden behind the four horsemen of the Apocalypse. Communism is the wine of Circe which transforms men into brutes. Though it is yet largely underground, it is rampant in our nation.

The Communist masses of Russia and Red China must have howled with glee on "Black Monday." They know the unanimous decision of the Supreme Court abolishing segregation in the four Districts and States involved was an illegal usurpation of the legislative prerogative of those State Legislatures and of Congress. The hoards of Russia and Red China know that another deadly blow has been dealt our Constitution, that outmoded, effete document which still precariously stands in the way of a new, brave communistic order in this country. They know that the South was struck below the belt, that the long governing principle of *stare decisis* is no longer operative in this country; that sociological criteria have supplanted laws in the deciding of cases in this country by our supreme judiciary.

Those muffled groans which were scarcely audible came from the graves of Chief Justices Marshall, Jay, Lamar, Taney, White, Hughes and Vinson.

The honor and glory, the courage and patriotism, the learning and wisdom of the highest judicial tribunal ever produced on this earth has been socialized and psychologized. Yes, the unanimous decision of the U. S. Supreme Court was to the constitutional rights of the sovereign states what the kiss of Iscariot in Gethsemane was to the Master.

—JUDGE TOM BRADY, *Black Monday,* 1955

15. The White Citizens Council Lets Loose the Winds of Fear

James Graham Cook

EDITORIAL NOTE: *During the depression years a group of ministers and social workers, deeply concerned about the position of the share-cropper of the South, set up a cooperative farm in the Delta country of Mississippi. It bore the auspicious name of Providence Farm and, with its medical clinic, school, credit union, and other social services, it enabled several hundred Negro farm families to achieve independence and social progress. Up until 1954 Providence Farm had been looked upon with indifference by the white community of the Delta region. After 1954 its desegregation policies aroused deep hostility. James Graham Cook describes how that hostility was organized by the White Citizens Council and how the Citizens Council managed to destroy Providence Farm and those connected with it.*

SITTING IN A BRIGHT Memphis restaurant one recent afternoon, a former Holmes County planter named Eugene Cox recalled the September 1955 day that Preacher Marsh Calloway had driven out to his place to warn him of a gathering that some Citizens Council members were planning to hold that night in the village of Tchula.

"Mr. Calloway, who was the Presbyterian minister over at Durant, had come hunting for me and my associate on the farm, Dr. David Minter. He said a mass meeting was being organized to hear a tape recording that concerned Dave and me. It wasn't officially called a

Citizens Council meeting, but I learned that J. P. Love, the head of the Council in Tchula, was going to preside."

The tape recording was of statements made to the county sheriff by four teen-age Negro boys, Cox was told. Some of the white citizens of Tchula seemed to figure that what the boys had said was proof that Cox and Minter favored racial integration.

Actually, Calloway's warning of the meeting did not come as a total surprise to Cox and Minter.

"For twenty years I had been talking to educators and business people in Mississippi, trying to get better schools for Negroes," said Cox. "Now that the 1954 decision had been handed down, we knew the extreme segregationists in the county were concerned about what might happen—that they were thinking: 'Who might cause us trouble?' "

Gene Cox looks like a Mississippi planter. He is a tall, strapping man in his fifties, with wavy gray hair and blue eyes. When he walks, he takes high, powerful strides, as if each step were carrying him over a cotton row. And when he sits reminiscing over a cup of coffee, he speaks in a soft drawl that is as soothingly slow as the Yazoo River.

But the plantation that he and Dr. David Minter operated near Tchula was an alien one to the delta. Even its name had an unfamiliar flavor: Providence Farm.

It was, in fact, a co-operative plantation, an outgrowth of an agricultural project sponsored back in the depression thirties by a group of ministers and professional do-gooders that included Reinhold Niebuhr, the theologian; Sherwood Eddy, the "Y" leader; and John Rust, the Memphis inventor of the Rust cotton picker. It was in part a religious missionary venture and in part an effort to help relocate some of the Arkansas sharecropper families who had been evicted during the attempt to organize the old Southern Tenant Farmers Union.

Cox had excellent qualifications for a job as one of the project's chief staff members. As a man "raised in the middle of a cotton patch in East Texas," he had some practical farming experience. Too, he and his wife had the kind of missionary inclinations that the project called for. Cox had studied for the ministry for a time before choosing to take a degree in sociology at Texas Christian

University. And his wife, who was born in Japan, was the daughter and granddaughter of Presbyterian missionaries.

The Delta Foundation project first located on a parcel of land in Bolivar County eighty miles or so northwest of Holmes. Jonathan Daniels, in *A Southerner Discovers the South,* described paying a 1937 visit there to Cox and the co-op's first manager, the Reverend Sam H. Franklin, and their helpers: "All the staff of the co-operative seemed to me like Robinson Crusoes washed up by good will on the delta of Mississippi where they were applying their city brains and missionary Christian enthusiasm energetically and ingeniously to the hard problems of the isolated land." And speaking of a donation that was being made to the project that year by some rich and philanthropic lady, Daniels remarked: "No better crop than such enthusiasm grows anywhere in the South and so long as such middle-aged Christians still bloom the members of the Delta can count on co-operative success. The boll weevil doesn't bite them."

In the beginning the co-op's participants were both white and Negro families. Then in the early 1940's the Foundation sold its land in Bolivar and moved the operation to a 2,600-acre farm in Holmes County. After that the great majority of the families served by the co-op were Negro.

The main pride of Providence Farm in Holmes County was its low-cost medical clinic, operated by Dr. Minter with the help of Cox's wife, who is a registered nurse. Minter, a former North Carolinian who is six years younger than Cox, had been with the project since 1938, except for a few years' tour of duty as an Air Corps medical officer during World War II. Like Cox, Minter had planned in his youth to become a minister; like Mrs. Cox, he came from a family of Presbyterian missionaries.

"In 1955 we had—in addition to the clinic—a small store and a credit union with about two hundred members, mostly Negroes," Cox recalled. "In years past we had had our own sawmill, dairy, and poultry unit, our own school, and a pretty extensive cotton-farming operation."

Then because of changes in the agricultural pattern of the delta—the replacement of tenant farming by large-scale mechanized cotton cultivation—Providence Farm by 1955 had greatly reduced the size of its cotton crop. And improvements in the state's program of schooling for Negroes had made some of the farm's educational activities unnecessary.

"But we were still active in organizing 'institutes' for farmers, planning summer camps for Negro children, and raising money for scholarships for some of the kids. We had a program of crafts and a nondenominational Bible school, and in the summers we would bring in Negro college students to staff the camps and coach the kids in sports."

Five white families were living on the farm in 1955—Cox and his wife and three teen-age daughters, the Minters and their three children, and the families of the staff carpenter, tractor driver, and sawmiller.

These were the last of the "Robinson Crusoes" still dwelling on Providence Farm when the Reverend Marsh Calloway drove out to warn them that something more serious than the boll weevil might be just about to bite.

After hearing the minister out, Cox decided to telephone the Tchula Citizens Council leader, J. P. Love, who only recently had been elected as Holmes County's next representative in the Mississippi Legislature.

"Love said he was sorry Dave and I hadn't been notified about the meeting earlier. I told him we wanted to go to it ourselves, that we'd rather do that than have somebody coming out to the farm at one o'clock in the morning to tell us what it was all about. I assumed then that it was something designed to discredit us."

Not until Cox and Minter arrived at the meeting did they come to realize that its design was a far more remarkable one: the purpose of the meeting was to excommunicate them from Holmes County.

The prelude to the extraordinary meeting that was being organized that September day of 1955 had begun one Saturday night away back in July 1954 which—coincidentally—was the very month that the first Citizens Council was formed in Holmes County.

On that Saturday night a Negro named Henry Randale was brought to Dr. Minter at the Providence Farm clinic with a bullet wound in the back of his thigh. He had been shot, he said, by the county sheriff, Richard Byrd.

Randale and several other Negroes had been standing beside a railroad crossing in Tchula, laughing and engaging in Saturday-night talk of this and that, when Sheriff Byrd drove up. The sheriff, a hefty fellow who had a reputation as a lawman who was "hard on niggers," ordered them to cut out their "whooping" and move on. Seizing on Randale, Byrd demanded to know what all the whooping was about.

Randale replied, " 'Twarn't none of me that whooped."

The sheriff, apparently considering this a not adequately respectful answer, beat him on the head, then, as Randale tried to run from him, fired a bullet into the back of his leg, and drove off. Randale's friends picked him up and carried him out to Dr. Minter at Providence Farm.

Many small-town Southern newspapers might have overlooked such an event as merely another routine incident in "The Law's" Saturday-night process of policing the Negroes. But the owner of two Holmes County newspapers, Mrs. Hazel Brannon Smith of Lexington, was a publisher with an outspokenness rare in rural Southern journalism.

An energetic, plumply attractive woman who was born and reared in Alabama, she had come to the delta in 1936 to publish the Durant *News.* She soon acquired a second paper, the Lexington *Advertiser,* and developed one of the more prosperous weekly publishing operations in Mississippi. Her success came largely because she was a skillful writer who seemed not to mind stepping on the toes of advertisers or elected officials when she felt it was in the public interest. She was especially noted for her editorial campaigns against the local bootlegging industry. This editorial straightforwardness—plus, perhaps, the fact that her husband was a Yankee, born in Philadelphia—naturally had won her a number of enemies in her circulation area.

In the editions of her Lexington *Advertiser* and Durant *News* immediately following the shooting of Henry Randale, Hazel Smith made it plain that she felt the incident proved Richard Byrd was not a fit man for the office of sheriff.

> The laws in America are for everyone—rich and poor, strong and weak, white and black. . . . Laws were made to protect the weak from

> the strong. . . . This man was shot in the back. He was running only because he had been told to "get goin'" by the Sheriff. He had not violated any law. . . . He just made the one mistake of being around when the Sheriff drove up.

Sheriff Byrd promptly filed a $57,500 libel suit against Mrs. Smith.

Dr. Minter, who had treated Randale's wound and had heard his account of the shooting, was the main witness for the defense. The physician later remarked on the atmosphere that existed as he prepared to testify: "As part of the pre-trial campaign to discredit Mrs. Smith and also to discredit me as a witness there were many rumors spread all over the county that I was a Communist, that I was heading a spy ring and holding secret meetings, that I was distributing communist literature."

Cox said that he understood that Sheriff Byrd's attorney asked Minter just one cross-examination question: "Do you live in a community called Providence?"

It was felt by some spectators that the most valuable witness in Byrd's behalf was one who testified that Hazel Smith once had a Negro woman to dinner in her home. Mrs. Smith denied this.

Nevertheless, the jury brought in a verdict against her, awarding Sheriff Byrd $10,000 in damages.

Although no actual money payment was made pending Mrs. Smith's appeal of the case to the State Supreme Court, the verdict obviously renewed Sheriff Byrd's self-confidence as a guardian of the Southern Way of Life. With the belief that Hazel Smith had been permanently squelched, Byrd and other dedicated segregationists of the county focused their attention on Dr. Minter and his friend Cox.

Their chance finally came in September 1955, when Byrd arrested four Negro boys.

Byrd accused them of whistling at a white girl—a serious charge to be leveled at a Mississippi Negro at any time, and particularly grave just at that time; the Emmett Till slaying had occurred in an adjoining delta county only the previous month.

When it was learned that the four boys lived near Providence Farm and their families had taken part in some of the co-op's activities, the questioning of them was intensified. After interrogating the terrified youths through a weekend, a two-hour recording of their answers to questions was taped on Monday. It was later in that day that Preacher Calloway heard that the mass meeting was being organized.

When Cox and Minter, along with Calloway, drove in to Tchula that night, they found that a crowd of 700 white men from all over the county had gathered at the high-school auditorium.

"As I say, they didn't officially call it a Citizens Council meeting," Cox recollected. "But J. P. Love was presiding. And there to play the tape recorder was William Moses, who was chairman of the Holmes County Citizens Council."

Moses worked for the same auto sales firm in Lexington that had employed Richard Byrd before his election as sheriff.

Byrd was there, of course, and—according to a later United Press report—so was Holmes County Attorney Pat Barrett, head of the Lexington chapter of the Citizens Council.

(Whether the gathering was really a "Citizens' Council meeting" is debatable, but not very pertinent, for by September 1955 the Council membership was so interwoven with the white community in general that it was practically impossible to distinguish the one from the other. As a Council leader later remarked, even as he was denying that Love's chairmanship of the Tchula gathering made it a CC meeting per se: "How could you have a meeting in this county without one of our members in the chair?")

Soon after Love called the meeting to order, said Cox, Moses switched on the tape recorder.

"The tape was two hours long," Cox remembers. "The boys who had been questioned lived on a place adjoining Providence Farm. Their families had come to the clinic, were members of our credit union, and had attended some of the institutes we'd held. The tape was full of loaded and leading questions. The answers the boys gave to them built up the image that Negroes and whites swam together in our pool at the farm, and that Dave Minter and I advocated school integration."

In a gesture of fair play Love invited Minter and Cox up to the auditorium stage to make their answers to the implications of the recording.

"So we went right up in front of the footlights," said Cox. "Dave told the crowd that to his knowledge there had been no interracial swimming at the farm. But a planter out in the audience stood up and said he had personally seen it taking place. I said they both might be right. I explained that my wife had hired a Negro girl as a maid to watch over our three daughters whenever they went into the pool, and she'd given the maid a swim suit to wear when she went with them. That fellow probably had seen the Negro maid with my children; that was probably it."

Both Cox and Minter denied that they had promoted any kind of social integration at Providence Farm.

"Since there's a Mississippi state law that says there must be no activities between Negroes and whites that might lead to intermarriage, the trustees and staff of the project had decided long ago not to have any interracial activities on the farm at the social level."

After Cox and Minter had presented their "defense," there was a pause. Then one of the planters in the audience got up and made the motion for excommunication. The motion was that Cox and Minter be asked to move away "in the best interest of the county."

The Reverend Marsh Calloway rose to protest the motion. The whole evening's ceremony in the auditorium, he declared, was "un-American and un-Christian."

But when the vote was taken, all but two members of the audience stood up and were counted for excommunication and the Southern Way of Life.

"One of the two that voted for us was Marsh Calloway," Cox remembered. "The other was a fellow—a welder or machinist, I believe he was—who'd told the crowd, 'Gentlemen, I think we ought to pray about this.' "

Cox and Minter felt determined not to accept their neighbors' decision that they must leave the county. They vowed to stick it out.

But there were discouragements.

For one thing, the elders of Marsh Calloway's church in Durant met soon after the meeting and voted in favor of a resolution asking him to resign his pulpit. A spokesman for the elders said Calloway's remarks had caused many of his church's members to "lose faith" in him. "His usefulness is at an end here," the elder spokesman said.

Cox said that the last he heard Calloway had been living in Louisiana, but he understood the minister had moved on from there since then.

Too, there were discomforts and inconveniences.

"We got a lot of anonymous telephone calls threatening us, and then they cut our telephone line," Cox remembered. "We heard rumors we were going to be burned out; the sheriff set up a road block for about a week and kept the deputies around the place. People were afraid to come to the clinic, and soon Dave's practice fell off to practically nothing.

"Another thing: Dave's insurance was canceled. The company said it was because he was considered an 'unusual risk.' Dave had to scout around a long time for a company that would sell him insurance. He finally found that Lloyd's of London was the only one that would insure him."

Ten months after the excommunication ceremony at the Tchula auditorium Dr. Minter packed up his family and moved to Tucson, Arizona. The move was made partly to benefit the health of one of his children. But the main reason, obviously, was that without a medical practice his usefulness in Holmes County—like Marsh Calloway's "usefulness" to his congregation—had come to an end.

Dave Minter commented later:

> Most planters [had] stopped sending patients to me. There were a few exceptions, but there was evidently a concerted effort on the part of council members to boycott me. . . . One former patient [a white man] confided to me while drinking that he would have been to see me but that the council had told [people] to stay away. . . . There is very little which can be definitely blamed on the councils or rather the organized efforts of the councils. . . . It is hard to say if the council would have bothered about us if the Sheriff had not laid the groundwork, although eventually there would have been something done because of our opposition to them (not open but just the fact that we did not join). . . . Although no one admitted that the CC planned the [Tchula] meeting, it was certainly through their organization that word spread; also, at the meeting that night one prominent man from Goodman [another

Holmes County town] recommended that a committee be appointed to investigate and report to the councils!

The Council organization clamped no "real boycott" on him and Cox, said Minter. They could still buy gasoline and groceries for the farm as usual.

The thing that the council did was to let loose "the winds of fear." . . .

A month after the Minter family's departure Cox and his wife and three daughters left. By then all the other white families had gone, too.

After twenty years the Providence Farm project was no more.

—James Graham Cook, *The Segregationists,* 1962

16. Crisis in Little Rock

A. *The Eisenhower Address on Little Rock, September 24, 1957*

Dwight D. Eisenhower

EDITORIAL NOTE: *With the passing of time, Southern resistance to desegregation grew and became "massive." Within a few months, in 1956, five Southern States adopted forty-two segregation measures. Georgia made it a felony for any school official to spend tax money for public schools in which the races were mixed; Mississippi made it a crime for any organization to institute desegregation proceedings in the State courts; Virginia went to the extreme of closing some of her public schools altogether. State resistance came to a head in Arkansas. In the late summer of 1957, Governor Orville Faubus called out the State National Guard under orders, not to protect Negro children in their right to attend school, but to prevent them from exercising that right. When these troops were withdrawn on order of the Federal district judge, mobs aided by the local authorities prevented Negroes from entering the local high school. On September 24, President Eisenhower ordered Federal troops to Little Rock to preserve order; at the same time he addressed the nation on the subject. The people of Arkansas responded by re-electing Faubus to the governorship, and Faubus persisted in his tactics of obstruction until the following year. Eventually order was restored, the troops withdrawn, and token desegregation took place.*

MY FELLOW CITIZENS . . . I must speak to you about the serious situation that has arisen in Little Rock. . . . In that city, under the leadership of demagogic extremists, disorderly mobs have deliberately prevented the carrying out of proper orders from a federal court. Local authorities have not eliminated that violent opposition and, under the law, I yesterday issued a proclamation calling upon the mob to disperse.

This morning the mob again gathered in front of the Central High School of Little Rock, obviously for the purpose of again preventing the carrying out of the court's order relating to the admission of Negro children to that school.

Whenever normal agencies prove inadequate to the task and it becomes necessary for the executive branch of the federal government to use its powers and authority to uphold federal courts, the President's responsibility is inescapable.

In accordance with that responsibility, I have today issued an Executive Order directing the use of troops under federal authority to aid in the execution of federal law at Little Rock, Arkansas. This became necessary when my Proclamation of yesterday was not observed, and the obstruction of justice still continues.

It is important that the reasons for my action be understood by all our citizens.

As you know, the Supreme Court of the United States has decided that separate public educational facilities for the races are inherently unequal and therefore compulsory school segregation laws are unconstitutional. . . .

During the past several years, many communities in our southern states have instituted public school plans for gradual progress in the enrollment and attendance of school children of all races in order to bring themselves into compliance with the law of the land.

They thus demonstrated to the world that we are a nation in which laws, not men, are supreme.

I regret to say that this truth—the cornerstone of our liberties—was not observed in this instance. . . .

Here is the sequence of events in the development of the Little Rock school case.

In May of 1955, the Little Rock School Board approved a moderate plan for the gradual desegregation of the public schools in that city. It provided that a start toward integration would be made at the present term in the high school, and that the plan would be in full operation by 1963. . . . Now this Little Rock plan was challenged in the courts by some who believed that the period of time as proposed in the plan was too long.

The United States Court at Little Rock, which has supervisory responsibility under the law for the plan of desegregation in the public schools, dismissed the challenge, thus approving a gradual rather than an abrupt change from the existing system. The court found that the school board had acted in good faith in planning for a public school system free from racial discrimination.

Since that time, the court has on three separate occasions issued orders directing that the plan be carried out. All persons were instructed to refrain from interfering with the efforts of the school board to comply with the law.

Proper and sensible observance of the law then demanded the respectful obedience which the nation has a right to expect from all its people. This, unfortunately, has not been the case at Little Rock. Certain misguided persons, many of them imported into Little Rock by agitators, have insisted upon defying the law and have sought to bring it into disrepute. The orders of the court have thus been frustrated.

The very basis of our individual rights and freedoms rests upon the certainty that the President and the Executive Branch of Government will support and insure the carrying out of the decisions of the federal courts, even, when necessary with all the means at the President's command. . . .

Mob rule cannot be allowed to override the decisions of our courts.

Now, let me make it very clear that federal troops are not being used to relieve local and state authorities of their primary duty to preserve the peace and order of the community. . . .

The proper use of the powers of the Executive Branch to enforce the orders of a federal court is limited to extraordinary and compelling circumstances. Manifestly, such an extreme situation has been created in Little Rock. This challenge must be met and with such measures as will preserve to the people as a whole their lawfully protected rights in a climate permitting their free and fair exercise.

The overwhelming majority of our people in every section of the country are united in their respect for observance of the law—even in those cases where they may disagree with that law. . . .

A foundation of our American way of life is our national respect for law.

In the South, as elsewhere, citizens are keenly aware of the tremendous disservice that has been done to the people of Arkansas in the eyes of the nation, and that has been done to the nation in the eyes of the world.

At a time when we face grave situations abroad because of the hatred that communism bears toward a system of government based on human rights, it would be difficult to exaggerate the harm that is being done to the prestige and influence, and indeed to the safety, of our nation and the world.

Our enemies are gloating over this incident and using it everywhere to misrepresent our whole nation. We are portrayed as a violator of those standards of conduct which the peoples of the world united to proclaim in the Charter of the United Nations. There they affirmed "faith in fundamental human rights" and "in the dignity and worth of the human person" and they did so "without distinction as to race, sex, language or religion."

And so, with deep confidence, I call upon the citizens of the State of Arkansas to assist in bringing to an immediate end all interference with the law and its processes. If resistance to the federal court orders ceases at once, the further presence of federal troops will be unnecessary and the City of Little Rock will return to its normal habits of peace and order and a blot upon the fair name and high honor of our nation in the world will be removed.

Thus will be restored the image of America and of all its parts as one nation, indivisible, with liberty and justice for all.

—Eisenhower's Address on Little Rock, 1957

B. *Cooper v. Aaron, 1958*

EDITORIAL NOTE: *Arkansas undertook to nullify the decision of the Supreme Court as Georgia had nullified the decision of the Court in*

1832. In this opinion, notable because in it each judge concurred by name, the Court resoundingly rejected a doctrine which, if permitted to stand, would have made the Constitution, in the words of Marshall, "a magnificent structure to look at but totally unfit for use."

OPINION OF THE COURT BY THE CHIEF JUSTICE MR. JUSTICE BLACK, MR. JUSTICE FRANKFURTER, MR. JUSTICE DOUGLAS, MR. JUSTICE BURTON, MR. JUSTICE CLARK, MR. JUSTICE HARLAN, MR. JUSTICE BRENNAN, AND MR. JUSTICE WHITTAKER.

As THIS CASE reaches us it raises questions of the highest importance to the maintenance of our federal system of government. It necessarily involves a claim by the governor and legislature of a state that there is no duty on state officials to obey federal court orders resting on this Court's considered interpretation of the United States Constitution. Specifically it involves actions by the governor and legislature of Arkansas upon the premise that they are not bound by our holding in Brown v. Board of Education. . . .

On May 17, 1954, this Court decided that enforced racial segregation in the public schools of a state is a denial of the equal protection of the laws enjoined by the Fourteenth Amendment. Brown v. Board of Education.

The Court postponed, pending further argument, formulations of a decree to effectuate this decision. That decree was rendered May 31, 1955. Brown v. Board of Education, . . . [under which] the district courts were directed to require "a prompt and reasonable start toward full compliance," and to take such action as was necessary to bring about the end of racial segregation in the schools "with all deliberate speed." . . .

On May 20, 1954, three days after the first Brown opinion, the Little Rock District School Board adopted, and on May 23, 1954, made public, a statement of policy entitled "Supreme Court Decision —Segregation in the Public Schools." In this statement the Board recognized that "It is our responsibility to comply with Federal Constitutional Requirements and we intend to do so when the Supreme Court of the United States outlines the method to be followed."

Thereafter the Board undertook studies of the administrative problems confronting the transition to a desegregated public school system in Little Rock. It instructed the Superintendent of Schools to prepare a plan . . . The plan provided for desegregation at the senior high school level (grades 10 through 12) as the first stage. Desegregation at the junior high and elementary levels was to follow. It was contemplated that desegregation at the high school level would commence in the fall of 1957, and the expectation was that complete desegregation of the school system would be accomplished by 1963. . . .

While the School Board was thus going forward with its preparation for desegregating the Little Rock school system, other state authorities, in contrast, were actively pursuing a program designed to perpetuate in Arkansas, the system of racial segregation which this Court had held violated the Fourteenth Amendment. First came, in November 1956, an amendment to the State Constitution flatly commanding the Arkansas General Assembly to oppose "in every Constitutional manner the Un-Constitutional desegregation decisions of May 17, 1954 and May 31, 1955 of the United States Supreme Court," Ark. Const. Amend. 44, and, through the initiative, a pupil assignment law. Pursuant to this state constitutional command, a law relieving school children from compulsory attendance at racially mixed schools, was enacted by the General Assembly in February, 1957. . . .

On September 2, 1957, the day before these Negro students were to enter Central High, the school authorities were met with drastic opposing action on the part of the Governor of Arkansas who dispatched units of the Arkansas National Guard to the Central High School grounds, and placed the school "off limits" to colored students.

The next school day was Monday, September 23, 1957. The Negro children entered the high school . . . under the protection of the Little Rock Police Department and members of the Arkansas State Police. But the officers caused the children to be removed from the school during the morning because they had difficulty controlling a large and demonstrating crowd which had gathered at the high school. On September 25, however, the President of the United States dispatched federal troops to Central High School and admission of the Negro students to the school was thereby effected. Regular army troops continued at the high school until November 27, 1957.

They were then replaced by federalized National Guardsmen who remained throughout the balance of the school year. Eight of the Negro students remained in attendance at the school throughout the school year.

We come now to the aspect of the proceedings presently before us. On February 20, 1958, the School Board and the Superintendent of Schools filed a petition in the District Court seeking a postponement of their program of desegregation. Their position in essence was that because of extreme hostility, which they stated had been engendered largely by the official attitudes and actions of the Governor and Legislature, the maintenance of a sound educational program at Central High School, with the Negro students in attendance, would be impossible. The Board therefore proposed that the Negro students already admitted to the school be withdrawn and sent to segregated schools, and that all further steps to carry out the Board's desegregation program be postponed for a period later suggested by the Board to be two and one-half years. . . .

One may well sympathize with the position of the Board in the face of the frustrating conditions which have confronted it, but regardless of the Board's good faith, the actions of the other state agencies responsible for those conditions compel us to reject the Board's legal position. . . .

The constitutional rights of respondents are not to be sacrificed or yielded to the violence and disorder which have followed upon the actions of the Governor and Legislature. . . .

. . . the constitutional rights of children not to be discriminated against in school admission on grounds of race or color declared by this Court in the Brown case can neither be nullified openly and directly by state legislators or state executive or judicial officers, nor nullified indirectly by them through evasive schemes for segregation whether attempted "ingeniously or ingenuously." . . .

What has been said, in the light of the facts developed, is enough to dispose of the case. However, we should answer the premise of the actions of the Governor and Legislature that they are not bound by our holding in the Brown case. It is necessary only to recall some basic constitutional propositions which are settled doctrine.

Article VI of the Constitution makes the Constitution the "supreme Law of the Land." In 1803, Chief Justice Marshall, speaking for a unanimous Court, referring to the Constitution as "the fundamental and paramount law of the nation," declared in the notable case of Marbury v. Madison that "It is emphatically the province and duty of the judicial department to say what the law is." This decision declared the basic principle that the federal judiciary is supreme in the exposition of the law of the Constitution, and that principle has ever since been respected by this Court and the country as a permanent and indispensable feature of our constitutional system. It follows that the interpretation of the Fourteenth Amendment enunciated by this Court in the Brown case is the supreme law of the land . . .

No state legislator or executive or judicial officer can war against the Constitution without violating his undertaking to support it . . .

It is, of course, quite true that the responsibility for public education is primarily the concern of the states, but it is equally true that such responsibilities, like all other state activity, must be exercised consistently with federal constitutional requirements as they apply to state action. The Constitution created a government dedicated to equal justice under law. The Fourteenth Amendment embodied and emphasized that ideal. State support of segregated schools through any arrangement, management, funds, or property cannot be squared with the Amendment's command that no state shall deny to any person within its jurisdiction the equal protection of the laws. The right of a student not to be segregated on racial grounds in schools so maintained is indeed so fundamental and pervasive that it is embraced in the concept of due process of law. . . . The basic decision in Brown was unanimously reached by this Court only after the case had been briefed and twice argued and the issue had been given the most serious consideration. Since the first Brown opinion three new Justices have come to the Court. They are at one with the Justices still on the Court who participated in that basic decision as to its correctness, and that decision is now unanimously reaffirmed. The principles announced in that decision and the obedience of the states to them, according to the command of the Constitution, are indispensable for the protection of the freedoms guaranteed by our fundamental charter for all of us. Our constitutional idea of equal justice under law is thus made a living truth.

—Cooper *v.* Aaron, 1958

17. The Court Vindicates the NAACP, 1958

John Marshall Harlan

EDITORIAL NOTE: *The NAACP had long spearheaded the struggle for Negro rights in the South. One method whereby Southern whites fought back, against the Brown and other decisions and the new program for civil rights, was a rash of laws harassing the NAACP. On the surface, these laws merely required of the NAACP—and of other organizations—full disclosure: membership lists, records, finances, and so forth. Clearly membership lists gave State and local authorities an opportunity to bring social or economic pressure on members of unpopular organizations. Though the task of weighing the interest of society in full disclosure and the interest of society in voluntary association was a difficult one, the court rightly held that the legislation was a violation of the freedom of association and therefore void.*

HARLAN, J.: WE REVIEW FROM the standpoint of its validity under the Federal Constitution a judgment of civil contempt entered against the National Association for the Advancement of Colored People, in the courts of Alabama. The question presented is whether Alabama, consistently with the Due Process Clause of the Fourteenth Amendment, can compel petitioner to reveal to the State's Attorney General the names and addresses of all its Alabama members and agents, without regard to their positions or functions in the Association. The judgment of contempt was based upon petitioner's refusal to comply fully with a court order requiring in part the production of membership lists. Petitioner's claim is that the order, in the circumstances shown by this record, violated rights assured to petitioner and its members under the Constitution. . . .

Petitioner produced substantially all the data called for . . . except its membership lists, as to which it contended that Alabama could not constitutionally compel disclosure. . . .

The Association both urges that it is constitutionally entitled to resist official inquiry into its membership lists, and that it may assert, on behalf of its members, a right personal to them to be protected from compelled disclosure by the State of their affiliation with the Association as revealed by the membership lists. We think that petitioner argues more appropriately the rights of its members, and that its nexus with them is sufficient to permit that it act as their representative before this Court. In so concluding, we reject respondent's argument that the Association lacks standing to assert here constitutional rights pertaining to the members, who are not of course parties to the litigation. . . .

If petitioner's rank-and-file members are constitutionally entitled to withhold their connection with the Association despite the production order, it is manifest that this right is properly assertable by the Association. To require that it be claimed by the members themselves would result in nullification of the right at the very moment of its assertion. . . .

We thus reach petitioner's claim that the production order in the state litigation trespasses upon fundamental freedoms protected by the Due Process Clause of the Fourteenth Amendment. Petitioner argues that in view of the facts and circumstances shown in the record, the effect of compelled disclosure of the membership lists will be to abridge the rights of its rank-and-file members to engage in lawful association in support of their common beliefs. It contends that governmental action which, although not directly suppressing association, nevertheless carries this consequence, can be justified only upon some overriding valid interest of the State.

Effective advocacy of both public and private points of view, particularly controversial ones, is undeniably enhanced by group association, as this Court has more than once recognized by remarking upon the close nexus between the freedoms of speech and assembly.

It is beyond debate that freedom to engage in association for the advancement of beliefs and ideas is an inseparable aspect of the "liberty" assured by the Due Process Clause of the Fourteenth Amendment, which embraces freedom of speech. [Cites cases] Of course, it is immaterial whether the beliefs sought to be advanced by association pertain to political, economic, religious or cultural matters, and state action which may have the effect of curtailing the freedom to associate is subject to the closest scrutiny.

The fact that Alabama, so far as is relevant to the validity of the contempt judgment presently under review, has taken no direct action to restrict the right of petitioner's members to associate freely, does not end inquiry into the effect of the production order. In the domain of these indispensable liberties, whether of speech, press, or association, the decisions of this Court recognize that abridgement of such rights, even though unintended, may inevitably follow from varied forms of governmental action. . . .

It is hardly a novel perception that compelled disclosure of affiliation with groups engaged in advocacy may constitute as effective a restraint on freedom of association as the forms of governmental action in the cases above were thought likely to produce upon the particular constitutional rights there involved. This Court has recognized the vital relationship between freedom to associate and privacy in one's associations. When referring to the varied forms of governmental action which might interfere with freedom of assembly, it said in American Communications Ass'n v. Douds, "A requirement that adherents of particular religious faiths or political parties wear identifying arm-bands, for example, is obviously of this nature." Compelled disclosure of membership in an organization engaged in advocacy of particular beliefs is of the same order. Inviolability of privacy in group association may in many circumstances be indispensable to preservation of freedom of association, particularly where a group espouses dissident beliefs.

We think that the production order, in the respects here drawn in question, must be regarded as entailing the likelihood of a substantial restraint upon the exercise by petitioner's members of their right to freedom of association. Petitioner has made an uncontroverted showing that on past occasions revelation of the identity of its rank-and-file members has exposed these members to economic reprisals, loss of employment, threat of physical coercion, and other manifestations of public hostility. . . .

It is not sufficient to answer, as the State does here, that whatever repressive effect compulsory disclosure of names of petitioner's members may have upon participation by Alabama citizens in petitioner's activities follows not from *state* action but from *private* community pressures. The crucial factor is the interplay of governmental and private action, for it is only after the initial exertion of state power represented by the production order that private action takes hold. . . .

—JUSTICE JOHN MARSHALL HARLAN,
Opinion in NAACP *v.* Alabama, 1958

18. Crisis in Montgomery

Martin Luther King, Jr.

EDITORIAL NOTE: *During the decade of the fifties a new, more vigorous, and more resourceful group of young Negroes seized the leadership of the movement for Negro rights. Chief among these was the Reverend Dr. Martin Luther King, Jr., a graduate of Morehouse College, Crozer Theological Seminary, with a doctor's degree from Boston University. The Reverend Dr. King early came under the influence of the great Indian leader Mahatma Gandhi, and saw the possibilities of combining Gandhi's program of civil disobedience with the Christian doctrines of nonviolence. The first major test of his philosophy and of this new leadership came in Montgomery, Alabama, in the mid-1950's. The new philosophy proved effective, and, as the Reverend Dr. King tells us, "integrated buses now roll daily through the city . . . a meaning-crowded symbolism."*

THE LAST HALF century has seen crucial changes in the life of the American Negro. The social upheavals of the two world wars, the great depression, and the spread of the automobile have made it both possible and necessary for the Negro to move away from his former isolation on the rural plantation. The decline of agriculture and the parallel growth of industry have drawn large numbers of Negroes to urban centers and brought about a gradual improvement in their economic status. New contacts have led to a broadened outlook and new possibilities for educational advance. All of these factors have conjoined to cause the Negro to take a fresh look at himself. His expanding life experiences have created within him a consciousness that he is an equal element in a larger social compound and accordingly should be given rights and privileges commensurate with his new responsibilities. Once plagued with a tragic sense of inferiority resulting from the crippling effects of slavery and segregation, the Negro has now been driven to re-evaluate himself. He has come to feel that he is somebody. His religion reveals to him that God loves all His children and the the important thing about a man is not "his specificity but his fundamentum"—not the texture of his hair or the color of his skin but his eternal worth to God. . . .

Along with the Negro's changing image of himself has come an awakening moral consciousness on the part of millions of white Americans concerning segregation. Ever since the signing of the Declaration of Independence, America has manifested a schizophrenic personality on the question of race. She has been torn between selves —a self in which she proudly professed democracy and a self in which she has sadly practiced the antithesis of democracy. The reality of segregation, like slavery, has always had to confront the ideals of democracy and Christianity. Indeed, segregation and discrimination are strange paradoxes in a nation founded on the principle that all men are created equal. This contradiction has disturbed the consciences of whites both North and South, and has caused many of them to see that segregation is basically evil.

Climaxing this process was the Supreme Court's decision outlawing segregation in the public schools. For all men of good will May 17, 1954, marked a joyous end to the long night of enforced segregation. In unequivocal language the Court affirmed that "separate but equal" facilities are inherently unequal, and that to segregate a child on the basis of his race is to deny that child equal protection of the law. This decision brought hope to millions of disinherited Negroes who had formerly dared only to dream of freedom. It further enhanced the Negro's sense of dignity and gave him even greater determination to achieve justice.

This determination of Negro Americans to win freedom from all forms of oppression springs from the same deep longing that motivates oppressed peoples all over the world. The rumblings of discontent in Asia and Africa are expressions of a quest for freedom and human dignity by people who have long been the victims of colonialism and imperialism. So in a real sense the racial crisis in America is a part of the larger world crisis.

But the numerous changes which have culminated in a new sense of dignity on the part of the Negro are not of themselves responsible for the present crisis. If all men accepted these historical changes in good faith there would be no crisis. The crisis developed when the collective pressures to achieve fair goals for the Negro met with tenacious and determined resistance. Then the emerging new order, based on the principle of democratic equalitarianism, came face to face with the older order, based on the principles of paternalism and subordination. The crisis was not produced by outside agitators, NAACP'ers, Montgomery Protesters, or even the Supreme Court. The crisis developed, paradoxically, when the most sublime principles of American democracy—imperfectly realized for almost two centuries—began fulfilling themselves and met with the brutal resistance of forces seeking to contract and repress freedom's growth.

The resistance has risen at times to ominous proportions. Many states have reacted in open defiance. The legislative halls of the South still ring loud with such words as "interposition" and "nullification." Many public officials are using the power of their offices to defy the law of the land. Through their irresponsible actions, their inflammatory statements, and their dissemination of distortions and half-truths, they have succeeded in arousing abnormal fears and morbid antipathies within the minds of underprivileged and uneducated whites, leaving them in such a state of excitement and confusion that they are led to acts of meanness and violence that no normal person would commit.

This resistance to the emergence of the new order expresses itself in the resurgence of the Ku Klux Klan. Determined to preserve segregation at any cost, this organization employs methods that are crude and primitive. It draws its members from underprivileged groups who see in the Negro's rising status a political and economic threat. Although the Klan is impotent politically and openly denounced from all sides, it remains a dangerous force which thrives on racial and religious bigotry. Because of its past history, whenever the Klan moves there is fear of violence.

Then there are the White Citizens Councils. Since they occasionally recruit members from a higher social and economic level than the Klan, a halo of partial respectability hovers over them. But like the Klan they are determined to preserve segregation despite the law. Their weapons of threat, intimidation, and boycott are directed both against Negroes and against any whites who stand for justice. They demand absolute conformity from whites and abject submission from Negroes. The Citizens Councils often argue piously that they abhor violence, but their defiance of the law, their unethical methods, and their vitriolic public pronouncements inevitably create the atmosphere in which violence thrives. . . .

As in other social crises the defenders of the status quo in the South argue that they were gradually solving their own problems until external pressure was brought to bear upon them. The familiar complaint in the South today is that the Supreme Court's decision on education has set us back a generation in race relations, that people of different races who had long lived at peace have now been turned against one another. But this is a misinterpretation of what is taking place. When a subject people moves toward freedom, they are not creating a cleavage, but are revealing the cleavage which apologists of the old order have sought to conceal. It is not the movement for integration which is creating a cleavage in the United States today. The depth of the cleavage that existed, the true nature of which the moderates failed to see and make clear, is being revealed by the resistance to integration.

During a crisis period, a desperate attempt is made by the extremists to influence the minds of the liberal forces in the ruling majority. So, for example, in the present transition white Southerners attempt to convince Northern whites that the Negroes are inherently criminal. They seek instances of Negro crime and juvenile delinquency in Northern communities and then say: "You see, the Negroes are problems to you. They create problems wherever they go." The accusation is made without reference to the true nature of the situation. Environmental problems of delinquency are interpreted as evidence of racial criminality. Crises arising in Northern schools are interpreted as proofs that Negroes are inherently delinquent. The extremists do not recognize that these school problems are symptoms of urban dislocation, rather than expressions of racial deficiency.

Criminality and delinquency are not racial; poverty and ignorance breed crime whatever the racial group may be.

In the attempt to influence the minds of Northern and Southern liberals, the segregationists are often subtle and skillful. Those who are too smart to argue for the validity of segregation and racial inferiority on the basis of the Bible set forth their arguments on cultural and sociological grounds. The Negro is not ready for integration, they say; because of academic and cultural lags on the part of the Negro, the integration of schools will pull the white race down. They are never honest enough to admit that the academic and cultural lags in the Negro community are themselves the result of segregation and discrimination. The best way to solve any problem is to remove its cause. It is both rationally unsound and sociologically untenable to use the tragic effects of segregation as an argument for its continuation.

All of these calculated patterns—the defiance of Southern legislative bodies, the activities of White Supremacy organizations, and the distortions and rationalizations of the segregationists—have mounted up to massive resistance. This resistance grows out of the desperate attempt of the white South to perpetuate a system of human values that came into being under a feudalistic plantation system and which cannot survive in a day of growing urbanization and industrial expansion. These are the rock-bottom elements of the present crisis. . . .

History has thrust upon our generation an indescribably important destiny—to complete a process of democratization which our nation has too long developed too slowly, but which is our most powerful weapon for world respect and emulation. How we deal with this crucial situation will determine our moral health as individuals, our cultural health as a region, our political health as a nation, and our prestige as a leader of the free world. The future of America is bound up with the solution of the present crisis. The shape of the world today does not permit us the luxury of a faltering democracy. The United States cannot hope to attain the respect of the vital and growing colored nations of the world unless it remedies its racial problems at home. If America is to remain a first-class nation, it cannot have a second-class citizenship.

The Negro himself has a decisive role to play if integration is to become a reality. Indeed, if first-class citizenship is to become a reality for the Negro he must assume the primary responsibility for making it so. Integration is not some lavish dish that the federal government or the white liberal will pass out on a silver platter while the Negro merely furnishes the appetite. One of the most damaging effects of past segregation on the personality of the Negro may well be that he has been victimized with the delusion that others should be more concerned than himself about his citizenship rights. . . .

Oppressed people deal with their oppression in three characteristic ways. One way is acquiescence: the oppressed resign themselves to their doom. They tacitly adjust themselves to oppression, and thereby become conditioned to it. In every movement toward freedom some of the oppressed prefer to remain oppressed. . . .

A second way that oppressed people sometimes deal with oppression is to resort to physical violence and corroding hatred. Violence often brings about momentary results. Nations have frequently won their independence in battle. But in spite of temporary victories, violence never brings permanent peace. It solves no social problem; it merely creates new and more complicated ones. . . .

If the American Negro and other victims of oppression succumb to the temptation of using violence in the struggle for freedom, future generations will be the recipients of a desolate night of bitterness, and our chief legacy to them will be an endless reign of meaningless chaos. Violence is not the way.

The third way open to oppressed people in their quest for freedom is the way of nonviolent resistance. Like the synthesis in Hegelian philosophy, the principle of nonviolent resistance seeks to reconcile the truths of two opposites—acquiescence and violence—while avoiding the extremes and immoralities of both. The nonviolent resister agrees with the person who acquiesces that one should not be physically aggressive toward his opponent; but he balances the equation by agreeing with the person of violence that evil must be resisted. He avoids the nonresistance of the former and the violent resistance of the latter. With nonviolent resistance, no individual or group need submit to any wrong, nor need anyone resort to violence in order to right a wrong.

It seems to me that this is the method that must guide the actions of the Negro in the present crisis in race relations. Through nonviolent resistance the Negro will be able to rise to the noble height of opposing the unjust system while loving the perpetrators of the system. The Negro must work passionately and unrelentingly for full stature as a citizen, but he must not use inferior methods to gain it. He must never come to terms with falsehood, malice, hate, or destruction.

Nonviolent resistance makes it possible for the Negro to remain in the South and struggle for his rights. The Negro's problem will not be solved by running away. He cannot listen to the glib suggestion of those who would urge him to migrate en masse to other sections of the country. By grasping his great opportunity in the South he can make a lasting contribution to the moral strength of the nation and set a sublime example of courage for generations yet unborn.

By nonviolent resistance, the Negro can also enlist all men of good will in his struggle for equality. The problem is not a purely racial one, with Negroes set against whites. In the end, it is not a struggle between people at all, but a tension between justice and injustice. Nonviolent resistance is not aimed against oppressors but against oppression. Under its banner consciences, not racial groups, are enlisted.

If the Negro is to achieve the goal of integration, he must organize himself into a militant and nonviolent mass movement. All three elements are indispensable. The movement for equality and justice can only be a success if it has both a mass and militant character; the barriers to be overcome require both. Nonviolence is an imperative in order to bring about ultimate community. . . .

Nonviolence can touch men where the law cannot reach them. When the law regulates behavior it plays an indirect part in molding public sentiment. The enforcement of the law is itself a form of peaceful persuasion. But the law needs help. The courts can order desegregation of the public schools. But what can be done to mitigate the fears, to disperse the hatred, violence and irrationality gathered around school integration, to take the initiative out of the hands of racial demagogues, to release respect for the law? In the end, for laws to be obeyed, men must believe they are right.

Here nonviolence comes in as the ultimate form of persuasion. It is the method which seeks to implement the just law by appealing to the conscience of the great decent majority who through blindness, fear, pride, or irrationality have allowed their consciences to sleep.

The nonviolent resisters can summarize their message in the following simple terms: We will take direct action against injustice without waiting for other agencies to act. We will not obey unjust laws or submit to unjust practices. We will do this peacefully, openly, cheerfully because our aim is to persuade. We adopt the means of nonviolence because our end is a community at peace with itself. We will try to persuade with our words, but if our words fail, we will try to persuade with our acts. We will always be willing to talk and seek fair compromise, but we are ready to suffer when necessary and even to risk our lives to become witnesses to the truth as we see it.

—MARTIN LUTHER KING, JR., "Where Do We Go from Here?" 1958

19. Justice Douglas Vindicates the Negro Sit-Ins, 1961

William O. Douglas

EDITORIAL NOTE: *Most of the pressure for vindicating the rights of Negroes had traditionally come from the North, and from the white community, though always with the inspiration and guidance of far-sighted Negro leaders like Frederick Douglass, Booker T. Washington, W. E. B. Du Bois, and Thurgood Marshall. In the 1950's Southern Negroes began to take matters into their own hands. In a number of Southern cities they staged successful demonstrations against segregation in streetcars and buses. In the spring of 1960, Negro students, inspired by Gandhi's passive resistance movement, began to "sit in" at lunch counters in drugstores and at shopping centers, and within a short time this "sit-in" movement had swept across the whole South. Southern authorities responded with wholesale arrests. Garner* versus *Lousiana, the first of these cases to reach the Supreme Court, upheld the "sit-ins" on somewhat narrow grounds, but Justice Douglas' concurring opinion, which we give here, took much broader ground. In subsequent decisions the Court tended to adopt the Douglas position on the rights of access to public facilities of all kinds.*

DOUGLAS, J., concurring: IF THESE CASES had arisen in the Pacific northwest—the area I know best—I could agree with the opinion of the Court. For while many communities north and south, east and west, at times have racial problems, those areas which have never known segregation would not be inflamed or aroused by the presence of a member of a minority race in a restaurant. But in Louisiana racial problems have agitated the people since the days of slavery. The landmark case of Plessy v. Ferguson—the decision that announced in 1896 the now-repudiated doctrine of "separate but equal" facilities for whites and blacks—came from Louisiana which had enacted in 1890 a statute requiring segregation of the races on railroad trains. In the environment of a segregated community I can understand how the mere presence of a Negro at a white lunch counter might inflame some people as much as fisticuffs would in other places. For the reasons stated by Mr. Justice Harlan in these cases, I read the Louisiana opinions as meaning that this law includes "peaceful conduct of a kind that foreseeably may lead to public disturbance"—a kind of "generally known condition" that may be "judicially noticed" even in a criminal case.

It is my view that a state may not constitutionally enforce a policy of segregation in restaurant facilities. Some of the arguments assumed that restaurants are "private" property in the sense that one's home is "private" property. They are, of course, "private" property for many purposes of the Constitution. Yet so are street railways, power plants, warehouses, and other types of enterprises which have long been held to be affected with a public interest. Where constitutional rights are involved, the proprietary interests of individuals must give way. Towns, though wholly owned by private interests, perform municipal functions and are held to the same constitutional requirements as ordinary municipalities. Marsh v. State of Alabama. State regulation of private enterprise falls when it discriminates against interstate commerce. Port Richmond Ferry v. Board of Chosen Freeholders of Hudson County. State regulation of private enterprise that results in impairment of other constitutional rights should stand on no firmer footing, at least in the area where facilities of a public nature are involved.

Long before Chief Justice Waite wrote the opinion in Munn v. State of Illinois, holding that the prices charged by grain warehouses could be regulated by the state, a long list of businesses had been held to be "affected with a public interest." Among these were ferries, common carriers, hackmen, bakers, millers, wharfingers, and innkeepers. The test used in Munn v. State of Illinois was stated as follows: "Property does become clothed with a public interest when used in a manner to make it of public consequence, and affect the community at large." In reply to the charge that price regulation deprived the warehouses of property. Chief Justice Waite stated, "There is no attempt to compel these owners to grant the public an interest in their property, but to declare their obligations, if they use it in this particular manner."

There was a long span between Munn v. Illinois and Nebbia v. People of State of New York, which upheld the power of a state to fix the price of milk. A business may have a "public interest" even though it is not a "public utility" in the accepted sense, even though it enjoys no franchise from the state, and even though it enjoys no monopoly. The examples cover a wide range from price control to prohibition of certain types of business. Various systems or devices designed by states or municipalities to protect the wholesomeness of food in the interests of health are deep-seated as any exercise of the police power. Adams v. City of Milwaukee. . . .

Under Louisiana law, restaurants are a form of private property affected with a public interest. Local Boards of Health are given broad powers. The city of Baton Rouge in its City Code requires all restaurants to have a permit. The Director of Public Health is given broad powers of inspection and permits issued can be suspended. Permits are not transferable. One who operates without a permit commits a separate offense each day a violation occurs. Moreover, detailed provisions are made concerning the equipment that restaurants must have, the protection of ready-to-eat foods and drink, and the storage of food.

Restaurants, though a species of private property, are in the public domain. Or to paraphrase the opinion in Nebbia v. New York, restaurants in Louisiana have a "public consequence" and "affect the community at large."

While the concept of a business "affected with a public interest" normally is used as a measure of a state's police power over it, it also has other consequences. A state may not require segregation of the races on conventional public utilities any more than it can segregate them in ordinary public facilities. . . . It was this idea that the first Mr. Justice Harlan, dissenting in Plessy v. Ferguson, advanced. Though a common carrier is private enterprise, "its work" he maintained is public. And there can be no difference, in my view, between one kind of business that is regulated in the public interest and another kind so far as the problem of racial segregation is concerned. I do not believe that a state that licenses a business can license it to serve only whites or only blacks or only yellows or only browns. Race is an impermissible classification when it comes to parks or other municipal facilities by reason of the Equal Protection Clause of the Fourteenth Amendment. By the same token, I do not see how a state can constitutionally exercise its licensing power over business either in terms or in effect to segregate the races in the licensed premises. The authority to license a business for public use is derived from the public. Negroes are as much a part of that public as are whites. A municipality granting a license to operate a business for the public represents Negroes as well as other races who live there. A license to establish a restaurant is a license to establish a public facility and necessarily imports, in law, equality of use for all members of the public. I see no way whereby licenses issued by a state to serve the public can be distinguished from leases of public facilities for that end.

One can close the doors of his home to anyone he desires. But one who operates an enterprise under a license from the government enjoys a privilege that derives from the people. Whether retail stores, not licensed by the municipality, stand on a different footing is not presented here. But the necessity of a license shows that the public has rights in respect to those premises. The business is not a matter of mere private concern. Those who license enterprises for public use should not have under our Constitution the power to license it for the use of only one race. For there is the overriding constitutional requirement that all state power be exercised so as not to deny equal protection to any group. As the first Mr. Justice Harlan stated in dissent in Plessy v. Ferguson, "in view of the constitution, in the eyes of the law, there is in this country no superior, dominant, ruling class of citizens. There is no caste here. Our constitution is colorblind. . . ."

—JUSTICE WILLIAM DOUGLAS, Opinion in Garner *v.* Louisiana, 1961

20. Policy and Reality in Negro Employment

William Peters

EDITORIAL NOTE: *Back in the 1880's Frederick Douglass had made clear that without economic security the Negro would be helpless. Without economic security, Booker T. Washington added, the Negro could not hope to win political rights. Increasingly even the sharpest critics of the Douglass-Washington school of thought came to see the validity of this position. For notwithstanding the most persistent efforts by state and federal governments to insure fair treatment in employment practices, the Negro was still almost everywhere fobbed off with the lowest paid jobs; he was the last to be hired and the first to be fired. William Peters, a Northern journalist, here describes for us how even the Federal Government lent itself to this conspiracy.*

TO SEE THE situation in detail, let us look first at the question of federal government employment. In principle at least, equal opportunity for federal employment has existed since the Civil Service Act of 1883, which provided for open competitive examinations, with vacancies to be filled from the three highest scorers, "with sole reference to merit and fitness." It was not, however, until 1940 that the use of photographs in applications was discontinued and the word "race" added to a general prohibition of discrimination for "political or religious opinions."

In 1941, when President Roosevelt set up his Committee on Fair Employment Practice, its duties were primarily to halt discrimination in work on defense contracts, though it also received reports from the Civil Service Commission on all complaints of discrimination in federal employment. The effectiveness of the Commission's anti-discrimination program under this arrangement can be surmised from its 1946 report to President Truman that with more than eight million placements, not to mention thousands of other personnel actions in the federal service since 1941, only 1,871 complaints of discrimination had been received. Of these a finding of discrimination had been made in exactly fifty-eight cases, an average of less than twelve per year.

In 1948, President Truman, re-emphasizing the government's policy, created a Fair Employment Practice Board within the Civil Service Commission. In 1955, President Eisenhower replaced it with his Committee on Government Employment Policy. A significant difference between the two groups is that the Truman Board, while it had, like the Eisenhower Committee, power only to recommend action to the heads of departments, was specifically ordered to report to the President any instance in which its recommendation was not "promptly and fully carried out." The present Committee is under no such stricture.

There appears to be no question today of what the government's policy is. In his order creating the Committee on Government Employment Policy, President Eisenhower stated in unmistakable language that "it is the policy of the United States Government that equal opportunity be afforded all qualified persons, consistent with law, for employment in the Federal Government," and that "this policy necessarily excludes and prohibits discrimination against any employee or applicant for employment in the Federal Government because of race, color, religion, or national origin."

Under such a policy, rigidly adhered to, it would be reasonable to expect that Negroes, widely excluded from skilled, semi-skilled, clerical, and supervisory jobs in private business and industry in the South, would turn in large numbers to the federal government, where "merit and fitness" are the only tests. This is particularly true when the wide discrepancy between white and Negro incomes in the South is considered—a discrepancy which widens sharply as educational level increases. It stands to reason that well-educated Negroes with equal access to federal government jobs in the South would be found perhaps even in disproportionately large numbers among the upper echelons of Southern federal employees.

To determine the actual situation, a number of independent studies of federal agencies in several Southern cities were made during 1958 at the instance of this writer. The results indicate with remarkable consistency that, with rare exceptions, Negroes are not employed above the level of janitorial and labor services by federal agencies in the South.

Consider, for example, Greensboro, North Carolina, a city which houses more than twenty federal agencies. Of them only two currently employ Negroes in other than menial jobs. Here, as in most places in the South, the Post Office Department is the outstanding exception. Greensboro's post office employs approximately twenty-five Negro clerks and carriers, while the Postal Transportation Service hires about a hundred Negroes as mail handlers and even has two in supervisory capacities, both as foremen on the highway post offices. The other exception is the Internal Revenue Service, where six of the approximately four hundred employees are Negroes: three working as clerks, three more as tax agents or examiners.

But the other federal agencies in Greensboro, including the Departments of Agriculture, the Air Force, the Army, Commerce, the Interior, Labor, the Navy, State, and the Treasury, as well as the offices of the U. S. Attorney, District Court, FBI, Marine Corps, U. S. Marshal, Bureau of Narcotics, Probation Office, Selective Service and Social Security Boards, Veterans Employment Service, and Weather Bureau have among them *not a single Negro employee* above the level of janitor or laborer.

In Charleston, South Carolina, where the U. S. Naval Yard provides employment for about seven thousand people and the activities and spending of the Navy Department and naval personnel constitute a major factor in the economy, the picture is not much better. For while it is true that about 40 per cent of the Naval Yard employees are Negroes, only a half dozen at most hold supervisory jobs, and some of these are supervisors in name only, since they have few, if any, employees working under them. In the entire clerical department of the Naval Yard there are exactly three Negro women typists; the civilian police department guarding this vast establishment includes a single Negro, with the rank of private.

With this kind of record, it is ironic that Charleston's Naval Yard has sometimes been cited as an example of successful integration, though it is true that some years ago eating and toilet facilities at the installation were desegregated. Yet Eli Ginzberg, in his recent book, *The Negro Potential*, records as fact the testimony of a senior naval officer in the spring of 1954. "At a regional conference on the problem of skill called by the National Manpower Council," he writes, "he reported that at the Charleston Naval Shipyard there was no longer any discrimination whatever against the Negro." The recent appraisal of an informant in a position to know is probably nearer the mark: that a token representation of Negroes in jobs other than menial ones is all that the local administrators of the Naval Yard are granting or are willing to grant.

Elsewhere in Charleston the picture is even bleaker. At Headquarters, Sixth Naval District, there is one Negro mimeograph operator and a Negro janitor. In the U. S. Customs House there are no Negroes. Above the level of janitorial and labor services there are no Negroes in Charleston's Internal Revenue Service, none in the Justice Department, none in the federal court, and none in any of the other branches of the federal judiciary. Here again the Post Office is the outstanding exception, with three or four Negro clerks, a majority of Negro carriers, but no Negroes in supervisory jobs.

The Post Office is also a major exception to the general picture in Birmingham, Alabama, with fifty-six Negro mail handlers, forty Negro clerks, and eighty-five Negro carriers. Once again, though, while intelligent, well-trained, experienced, and well-educated Negroes have frequently taken examinations for promotions above the clerk and carrier level, these promotions in Birmingham have gone only to whites. Early in 1958 a Negro clerk was assigned to the post office at Ensley, a suburb of Birmingham. When objections were raised, Post Office officials capitulated, and the man was transferred. He resigned in disgust and moved to California.

In connection with Veterans Hospitals, it should be noted that several years ago, under orders from Washington, patients in all V. A. Hospitals were integrated. The results, as in the case of the armed forces, were a vivid illustration of what could be done where there was a firm determination to apply non-discrimination policies. Overnight, for example, in the V. A. Hospital at Jackson, Mississippi, patients were moved into newly painted wards on a completely integrated basis. Within the hospital there was no difficulty. And when a bill was introduced in the 1957 special session of the Mississippi State Legislature to cancel the state's authority to donate land for a new eleven-million-dollar V. A. Hospital in Jackson, Governor J. P. Coleman warned the legislators, "There's a great movement now to build a new V. A. Hospital in Memphis, and it would be an easy thing for them to switch this hospital to Memphis if we made what they considered unreasonable restrictions." The threat of loss to the state of eleven million dollars of federal money was sufficient to stem the tide, and the Veterans Hospital in which Negroes and whites will share wards equally will remain in Jackson.

In Knoxville, Tennessee, the Departments of Agriculture, Commerce, Health, Education and Welfare, Labor and the Treasury, as well as the FBI, Federal Housing Authority, Geological Survey, Small Business Administration, Referee in Bankruptcy, and Veterans Administration have no Negroes employed *in any capacity,* while the federal judiciary has only a single Negro court crier. Here the exceptions are the Post Office, with twenty-four Negro carriers, clerks, and custodial employees out of a work force of more than five hundred, and the Tennessee Valley Authority, with some twenty Negroes, including an assistant to the general manager, an electrical engineer, an economic statistician, and clerks, a typist, a receptionist, and a guard in addition to some forty Negroes employed as janitors, laborers, and tradesmen. Total employment with the TVA is more than fourteen hundred. With a federal payroll of more than twenty-two hundred in Knoxville, fewer than a hundred jobs are held by Negroes, even if janitorial and labor services are included.

But of all the Southern cities in which information was gathered, the most shocking results came from Atlanta, the South's largest city. They were the more shocking in view of Atlanta's record of good race relations and the fact that, where desegregation of public facilities has been accomplished—as in Atlanta's golf courses—there has been no difficulty. It is also worth noting that under Mayor William B. Hartsfield's enlightened guidance Atlanta has hired Negro policemen, two of whom were promoted to the rank of detective in 1955. In 1956, Atlanta's railroad station waiting rooms for interstate passengers were desegregated, and a year earlier the first Atlanta

Arts Festival open to Negro exhibitors and spectators was held in Piedmont Park marking the park's first use for an integrated event.

Atlanta is one of the Southern cities which has elected a Negro to its school board and in which a Negro has served on the policy board of the Community Chest. Here, too, the traditional excuse that Negroes are unqualified for semi-skilled, skilled, and white collar jobs is belied by the presence of six Negro colleges which in 1958 alone handed out 573 graduate and undergraduate degrees. Here, then, is one Southern city in which the city adminstration and business and civic leaders have demonstrated the possibilities for progress and in which trained and educated Negroes are readily available.

Yet of more than thirty major federal agencies in Atlanta, many with numerous important subdivisions, only five have permanent Negro employees above the level of janitorial and labor services. Of these three qualify only as technical exceptions: one—the Army—has a single Negro clerical worker, another—the housing agencies—has Negro race relations advisers and their secretaries (where, by definition, the jobs must be filled by Negroes), and a third—the U. S. Penitentiary—has a Negro chaplain, and Negro guards and parole officers all for work primarily with Negroes. In all Atlanta there are only two federal agencies in which Negroes can honestly be said to have been hired or promoted above menial employment on an unsegregated basis. One is the Health Education and Welfare Department's Communicable Disease Center, where two Negro technicians and two or three Negro biologic aides are employed. The other, not surprisingly, is the Post Office, where Negroes are working as carriers, clerks, truck drivers, and mail handlers. In addition two Negroes supervise segregated departments, and two Negro substation superintendents serve in segregated sub-stations.

The list of federal agencies in Atlanta in which no Negroes are employed in clerical, administrative, or supervisory capacities—or, indeed, in any capacity other than janitorial and labor services—is too long to include here. . . .

This, then, is the true state of federal government employment in the South today: non-discriminatory policies are flagrantly violated and Negroes, even in the Post Office Department, are systematically excluded from higher paying, more responsible jobs for which many are qualified. How is it done? To answer that question, it is necessary to look briefly into the system of federal hiring and the complaint procedures of the President's Committee on Government Employment Policy. . . .

These failures of the federal government to give more than lip service to its own policies with regard to discrimination in employment unfortunately fit snugly into the basic strategy of Southern segregationists, making the federal executive the unwitting accomplice of the general plot on the part of segregationists to deny jobs to Southern Negroes. With this as their announced policy, Southern segregationists can hardly fail to appreciate the federal government's obvious reluctance to make its employment policies work. And if there were any doubt in the South about where the federal government stood, it would most surely be dispelled by the knowledge that segregation itself is being perpetuated by agencies of the federal government.

Throughout the South, for example, the U. S. Department of Agriculture has employed Negro county agents to advise Negro farmers on better farming practices. Not only is this county agent program segregated in the sense that Negro agents work only with Negro farmers, but with perhaps fifty exceptions, the nine hundred Negro county agents in the South have segregated offices in other parts of town from their white counterparts. Even the lines of supervision of Negro and white county agents have traditionally been separate, and where this pattern has recently begun to change, the Negro agent has invariably become the assistant to the white agent, thus effectively holding his income below that of his white colleague.

Much the same situation prevails in the case of the Agriculture Department's home demonstration agents in the South, and when one turns to soil conservation technicians the picture is even worse. Of the nearly three thousand government soil conservation technicians in the U. S., fewer than thirty are Negroes, and the proof that these few jobs are allocated on a segregated basis lies in the fact that in all the Northern states not a single Negro is employed in such a job. The same is true of the farmers' home supervisors, who in each agricultural county supervise farm loans. Of the nearly five thousand such individuals employed by the Department of Agriculture, either as supervisors or assistants, and with a case load of nearly sixty thousand Negro farmers, there are few Negroes in these jobs—one or two in each of several Southern states at most. It is a sad corollary that most of the farm loans made to Negroes in the South are made in those few counties where there is a Negro supervisor or assistant.

This means, in plain language, that white employees of the federal government are using their offices to discriminate against Negroes in such things as the granting of government loans. And there are clear indications throughout the South today that this kind of discrimination is increasingly being aimed at Negroes outspoken in their insistence on public school desegregation, the right to vote, and other causes unpopular with the segregationists.

—William Peters, *The Southern Temper*, 1959

21. A Southern Student is Loyal to the Traditions of the Old South

Margaret Long

EDITORIAL NOTE: *The code of the ante-bellum Southern planter was a simple thing and, to those who formulated it and subscribed to it, wholly admirable. It asserted that slavery was a blessing alike to Negro and to white, that the "peculiar institution" itself was, with a few tragic exceptions, benevolent; that slaves loved their masters and masters cared tenderly for their slaves; and that only the Southern planter really understood the Negro. Neither the destruction of slavery nor Reconstruction dimmed this bright image or changed these convictions. Quite the contrary: the War and Reconstruction threw a romantic aura over the "peculiar institution." During the century after the War the heirs of the planter tradition—joined now by those who were not but wanted to be—added to this religion a further article of faith: that if only the rest of the world would leave the South alone, whites and Negroes would, between them, work out a happy and productive relationship. It is not surprising then that the Negro unrest of the fifties and sixties was blamed almost entirely on "outside agitators"—Northerners, or worse, who did not and indeed could not understand the virtues of the traditional South. Margaret Long, a novelist and the editor of the courageous magazine,* New Youth, *gives us here a fascinating interview with a young man at the University of Mississippi which helps us understand how it was possible for even the post-war generation—this was in 1963—to subscribe uncritically to the code of the Old South.*

OXFORD, MISS. THE HARSH AND hating faces of young Southerners photographed in troubled scenes of the desegregating Deep South have shocked and baffled most other Americans, among them, indeed, many rational and peaceable people in Dixie. To investigate the ideas and feelings that fire many of these boys and girls I made a mission to Mississippi, the state where segregationist sentiment is most intense. Here I found many attractive and voluble youngsters eager to proclaim white superiority, Southern culture and Negro contentment. These high-school and college boys and girls exhibited a common innocence of the Negro movement, which they believe is fomented by outsiders and Communists. (The N.A.A.C.P., the only civil-rights organization most of them know, seems to them a blend of both.) They also showed intense emotions of both affection and revulsion toward Negroes.

The sweetly mannered young people I talked to seemed most of all gripped by a poignant loyalty to the precarious present and the easy past of the white South, a fealty uncorrupted by alien facts and ideas from beyond the tight and turbulent little world of Mississippi.

From here, the common ground fell away into varying attitudes, ranging from the valiant "Never!" of one Delta boy who would "die for" segregation, to the "It's coming" of several others and the pained confusion of a 17-year-old girl who thought, "It's *awful* Nigras can't come to our *churches*."

The Confederate dedication of one 18-year-old probably best expressed the adamant segregationist mood typical of many young people of the Deep South. He was Don Barrett, a Phi Delta Theta pledge at the University of Mississippi at Oxford, who answered questions at word-tumbling length, his replies replete with nice, old-fashioned "Yes'ms" and "No'ms." His forebears came to Mississippi from Virginia and South Carolina, and his great-grandmother, he said, gave $80,000 that she had hidden away to the Confederate Army after her plantation, Newstead, was used by Grant as headquarters during the Vicksburg campaign and then was sacked and ruined.

"She turned it over, lock, stock and barrel," he said, his round, rosy face glowing and his eyes dark with love. "That's the kind of heritage I come from—and I'm proud of it."

Young Barrett's more immediate heritage includes a pleasant childhood of play in backyard pecan treehouses, fishing and hunting, adoration of a beautiful mother (she was beauty queen in high school, at Millsaps College in Jackson, and at Ole Miss) and a trusting attachment to his energetic and commanding father. ("He's got more sense in a minute than I've got in three weeks. He's the wisdom I draw on.") He also exhibits the usual masculine pleasure in two little sisters and pride tinged perhaps with rivalry, in an older brother, Pat Jr., who is taking psychology at Millsaps and planning to study law at Ole Miss.

"Yes, of course, I used to play with Negro children," he said. "We quit, well, we quit when . . . when we both realized the difference, and they went their way and I went mine. You may be surprised that our next-door neighbors were Nigras. They lived catty-corner across the street from us . . . the nearest neighbors."

Mr. Barrett spoke ardently of the good Negroes and his affection for them and their profound loyalty to him and his. He smiled quickly and radiantly at the memory of these ancient felicities. Dora, who cooks and cleans up, is "a young 43"—like his mother. They were born on the same day and exchange birthday presents. Allie Mae, a registered nurse by correspondence course, "respected by the white community and venerated by the Negro community," nursed Don when he was born and promised his grandmother "she'd always take care of Sara," his mother. Allie May visits frequently in Miss Sara's bedroom and on the phone. Amelia, older, cooks on Sunday, and Pecolia, he confided with a flash of delight, "is making me a quilt." There are several Negro hands on his father's cattle farms who are also life-long familiars at the Barrett house in Lexington.

Lexington is the seat of Holmes County, seven miles in the hills at the edge of the Delta, "the heart of Mississippi and the citadel of Southern rights," with "stark nekkid bluffs looking out to the Mississippi River." It is to him the most beautiful place in the world, a rich center of farming which produces the best crops and "the best people, too." The citadel of Holmes County has 19,600 Negro citizens and 7,000 whites.

"I feel, as do most of the white population of the South, that the Negro is inherently unequal," Barrett said. "Now they say it's lack of opportunity, cause and result, the reason men first took the fire and light of learning, that the Nigras never had the need in

Africa because they could just pluck the fruit of the woods and all, and sustain life on that. But you can't say they didn't get learning and civilization because of the easy climate, because they've got a range of all climates and mountains and jungles. They came into contact with the Saracens in North Africa. And Alexander the Great and they never did catch the light of learning, nobody in the region. If they hadn't been taken over by the white man . . .

"Well, where they're not, they're still eating each other," he said, his voice vibrant with triumph and disgust.

"But the white South has taken the Neegra, fed, clothed, taught them how to speak and wear clothes and taught him Christianity. Still, look at 'em, their illegitimacy rate!"

Mr. Barrett was at such polite pains to say the respectful Southern "Nigra" and never to lapse into the easy and offensive "nigger," and I was so vigilant with my proper and hard-learned "Negro," that we quite rattled one another. Once, in the heat of exchange, he said "Neegra" and, again, "Neeger," and I once wildly pronounced it "Nigroo," to our mutual dismay. But we both behaved well upon these lapses, quite as if they had not occurred, and proceeded as nice as you please.

"In my opinion," he said, "the South made its biggest mistake—because they hated to do it out of our love and affection for the Nigras—but our mistake is in talking states' rights instead of anthropology.

"The moderates [and here Barrett used the term as it is widely understood in Mississippi, as equivalent to Communists or other enemies of order and freedom], prophets of gloom and doom, say it's coming—we gotta accept it. I think if the Nigra is able to live on an equal footing after the troops leave, then we are wrong—wrong when we say the Nigra is not capable.

"Yes'm, I expect there'll have to be an occupation before there'll be integration in Mississippi, and the Kennedy twins are ruthless enough to do it without batting an eye if they're re-elected. It would probably be the most tragic thing that could happen to our beloved state. But afterward, when the troops leave . . ." Here he explained that white resistance to the troops would be so adamant that upon their despairing withdrawal, "everything would be just like before, only the poor Nigras would lose all the friendship and goodwill they had."

Barrett's uncle is a cotton planter and head of the Citizens' Council in Lexington and his father is a founder. Don himself is "a sort of honorary member" because he "wanted to give my $5," though he is under the usually accepted age. Contemplating the possibility of Negro political control in the Delta through its 65 to 70 per cent Negro majority—"although it would *never* happen"—Barrett said such a regime "without white man's control would be chaos."

"If we turned politics over to them, we'd have another Congo. It's not wild like that under the patient, restraining hand of the white man, when they behave reasonably well.

"Do anything to us? I don't think so, no'm. I don't believe the Nigras, if they got control, would have any reason to hurt people who have nurtured and cared for them, but it would be chaos. Yes, out of their incompetence. The economy would collapse, and it would be like Reconstruction. You remember the Nigras in power in Reconstruction were voting themselves carriages and all kind of luxuries. It wouldn't be out of malice—they're a kindly people—but out of inability to run things. The Southern code of hospitality, gentleness, kindness—they've learned it and accepted it. . . .

"If the majority of Nigras with the vote there"—this was in reference to Charles City County, Va.—"haven't taken over, it's because they haven't got the initiative. But look at Memphis. Nigras are 32 per cent of the electorate. They're beginning to control politics, and Memphis is beginning to look like a dirty Northern city," he said in another spurt of disgust.

Barrett is also apprehensive about treatment of white women under black domination. "If the social system is thrown out of kilter, as moderates would do, there would be more danger than there is now under the patient hand of white leadership. I would certainly take up arms to protect our women. To me there is nothing more wonderful than a Southern lady. Gosh! It's really undefinable. But she's cultured, genteel, intelligent, beautiful—usually beautiful, anyway."

In defense of the social and economic system, Barrett would not eat with a Negro, or call one Mr. or Mrs. or Miss, because "it's not socially acceptable, it's not done—anymore than I'd cut more than one piece of steak at a time or tuck my napkin under my chin."

Nor would he betray his manners for distinguished Negroes or for different customs in other places. In Milwaukee, where he visited an aunt and "a wonderful Yankee uncle—the only good Yankee I know," he did not desist from giving his bus seat to standing ladies, in the Mississippi way, just because it was not the usual practice in Wisconsin.

As for celebrated and accomplished Negroes, Barrett says, "more power to 'em." He cited "Gaston in Birmingham"—a millionaire Negro banker and property owner. "You can see he obviously has a very high I.Q., is well-mannered and a fine man, I'm sure. Well, it's just a combination of genes that worked out that way. But the chances are 1 in 5,000 that his children would be like that."

There are "exceptional" Negroes in Lexington, who own stores, cafes and funeral businesses, but no professionals. "We are courteous and treat them with the respect due their education," he explained. "There's none of this pushing around or 'Get outa my way' for them in stores or anywhere—or for the lowest field hand either."

Barrett scoffs at the outsiders' notion that it's deprivation and "brutality" which makes Negroes migrate from the South.

"That's ridiculous. It's economic. The Negro definitely was necessary to farming 20 years ago. My uncle owns a plantation where he had 60 families chopping cotton, borrowing money, depending on him—you know, old-style sharecropping. Ten of the 15 left live there now because they love my uncle and they depend on him, although he just needs five of 'em. But he gives them Saturday-night spending money and everything and he could say, 'Fred, go up the hill and kill me a big snake,' or 'Go cut off your head,' and Fred would do it.

"They don't help *him*. They're an economic liability. He supports 10 families out of love and loyalty. He's a fine fellow, president of the Tchula Citizens' Council. The others left because they had to sell their small farms—with mechanization, the Nigras can't make a profit on a little farm—and had no place to live. Now you just see old grandfathers and little bitty children, pickaninnies. The young ones have gone to Chicago.

"My girl, I talked to her on the phone and this horrible thing had happened. Houston was dead. Houston drove their tractor and she just loved him. Mr. Foose's father—that's his name, Mary's father, Mr. Foose—and Houston's father were always on the place together. Houston's father had worked for Mr. Foose's father all that time, and they loved him.

"The Citizens' Council, Mr. Foose is a leader in it, is not like the Ku Klux Klan. We hate violence. But we are determined to keep our way of life," he declared with rapidly rising fervor. "Nobody can take it away from us, and I would die for it. I wouldn't do anything foolish, but we will not give up.

"People say Nigras are catching up—that's wonderful—but that's no justification for social change in 1963 for what might happen in 500 or 1,000 years."

Barrett is not much disturbed by the current Mississippi Negro drive to write in 15,000 or 20,000 Negro protest votes for Aaron Henry, state N.A.A.C.P. president, for governor, and the Rev. Ed King, a young, white civil-rights devotee, for lieutenant-governor, and to draw 200,000 disfranchised Negro votes in a straw election for Henry. Nor does he share outside dismay at intimidation of Negro voting aspirants—random violence, arrests of demonstrators, eviction of would-be voters from jobs and property, and a few killings.

"Federal right to vote? No, the Constitution gives the states the right to say who shall vote and who shall not. There's no such thing as the right to vote. It's a privilege, earned only after qualifications set up by the state have been met. Instead of reducing voting requirements, we ought to make them more strict. I believe in the poll tax. Our $2 poll tax goes straight to the schools, white and colored.

"I don't think there's any harm in a few qualified Negroes voting. But you can't open the floodgates. I don't condone violence, but the state has the right of police power to protect the health, morals and general welfare of the people. And when feelings are running high and the spark is there, they could set off a riot.

"I think the police were right in Greenwood and Jackson [scenes of summer disorders and mass arrests of Negroes seeking the vote and other civil rights]. And about these peaceful grievances, they should not trespass on private property."

Barrett went—"defending my state; no, not that, either, as an observer"—to the University of Mississippi upon the entrance of James Meredith to the university. He drove to Oxford with a friend, without his father's permission.

"I was close enough to the marshals to see what was happening," he related. "Some of the boys were armed, and one man was standing by the Y building shooting out street lights with a .22 rifle. The students were jeering and sneering and occasionally tossing a cigarette butt at the marshals. All of a sudden, McShane [Chief U.S. Marshal James Joseph McShane] said, 'Gas 'em!' and from a clear blue sky, a patrolman got hit in the head, from behind, and knocked down by a marshal throwing tear gas—that metal case hit him.

"Barnett [Gov. Ross Barnett] made a mistake. That Sunday, if he'd issued a call to white males of Mississippi to stand firm at the gate, why, you'd have seen 600,000 men mustered at the gate. I know all of Holmes County would have come, except a couple of scalawags.

"I didn't attack the marshals, and I was not armed, it was not my place to. But if Governor Barnett had called the Citizens' Councils and other responsible citizens, and had said, 'Come, it is Armageddon, get your gun,—well, I certainly *would.* Yes, *ma'am!*

"Oxford seemed to me a nightmare. I felt I was not in the United States, but in Budapest or a Warsaw ghetto. If that was American action, then God save us."

If whites and Negroes attend schools together, he wonders "what's to keep little white Mary from bringing home little black Johnny from school some day, and that leads to mixed dating and mixed marriages."

Would either of his sisters grow up to choose a Negro husband? "Heavenly days, no! But girls who haven't had the upbringing would if we change the social order."

He considers Cleve McDowell, the Negro recently expelled from the University of Mississippi for carrying a gun, as "more dangerous than Meredith. The way he behaved, like I've heard people say, 'he's a good Nigra, he just wants an education.' And that would lead to acceptance. He behaved like a nigger, he would open doors, he had good manners and he scuffed his feet and held his head down. So, he could be the leak in the dike, and then the dams burst.

"Of course, Meredith was the most segregated Nigra in the United States. He was ignored. Yes." (He laughed in appreciation of the placard rhymes which appeared on the campus: "Ignore the Nigger with Vigor" and "Nigger-free in '63.") "Ole Miss has never really been integrated."

Barrett was "not much impressed" by the Negro March on Washington. "It wasn't any different from what I see Saturday night in Lexington when they come to town to get drunk and cut up, except they're happier in Lexington." He smiled here at the remembered spectacle of Lexington police warning the tipsy Fred, "Now, Fred, how many times I got to tell you?" and at Fred's shuffling, laughing promise to stay sober.

He described Negro pleasure in Government " 'modities"—the surplus foods that they get on welfare—and the willingness of "many, many, many" simply to collect relief and " 'modities" rather than work. All the Negroes on the Barrett place "get real butter and cheese" from the welfare, and "we use oleo."

Barrett, a 96-average student in high school and on a scholarship at Ole Miss, would vote for Governor Barnett, "the most courageous leader of our time," for "dictator or anything." He is now more proud of being a Mississippian than an American, and laments our "Federal power, a crushing force, a rampage," under which we're "no longer the land of the free." He also deplores foreign policy which, with the United Nations, "is destroying the only pro-West governments in Africa. Katanga and the Union of South Africa, we stab them in the back."

He takes a grisly view of Federal aid to states and localities. His story is "not original," but he compares Federal aid to the starving hunter who whacked off part of his famished dog's tail, ate off the meat, and threw the bone to the beast. Whereupon the "whimpering dog," like recipients of Federal aid, gratefully "licked the hunter's hand."

For all his lordly and loving attachment to Negro friends, Barrett sees an eventual solution in the departure of all Negroes for the North "to live on welfare," since the planters and automated land no longer need them. He also believes the Delta will be "forever agrarian," though partly industrialized with small, imported industries employing whites in a prosperous blend of his beloved old way of life and new Yankee paychecks.

This, then, is the romantic tradition and reactionary passion with which the young segregationists of a dwindling old South face the nonviolent Negro revolution. In love with the life long gone, they stand embattled, fighting change with talk of old times, planter-rulers and good servants happy in subjection.

—MARGARET LONG,
"A Southern Teenager Speaks His Mind," 1963

22. Equal Rights: The Unending Struggle

Earl Warren

EDITORIAL NOTE: *The Deep South resisted desegregation with almost fanatical stubbornness, and the struggle for desegregation and for civil rights had to be fought out city by city and State by State. Negroes—and their white supporters—called for desegregation not only in schools and buses, but in public parks, swimming pools, athletic fields, in stores, restaurants, theaters. Almost every contest followed a familiar pattern. Negroes would exercise their right to equal access of public facilities; local or State authorities would arrest them on the charge of creating public disorder; then the case would go on appeal to the higher courts. In almost every instance the right of the Negro to exercise—or to agitate for the exercise of —his constitutional right, was vindicated, though often in vain, for few Southern communities were prepared to accept the judicial verdict. We give here two notable judicial decisions—the first, Wright* versus *Georgia, sustained the right of Negroes to use municipal parks; the second, Peterson* versus *Greenville, sustained the right of Negroes to service at lunch counters and struck down state ordinances requiring segregation in these and similar facilities.*

A. *Wright v. Georgia*

WARREN, C. J.: PETITIONERS, SIX YOUNG Negroes, were convicted of breach of the peace for peacefully playing basketball in a public park in Savannah, Georgia, on the early afternoon of Monday, January 23, 1961. The record is devoid of evidence of any activity which a breach of the peace statute might be thought to punish. Finding that there is no adequate state ground to bar review by this Court and that the convictions are violative of due process of law secured by the Fourteenth Amendment, we hold that the judgments below must be reversed.

Only four witnesses testified at petitioners' trial: the two arresting officers, the city recreational superintendent and a sergeant of police. All were prosecution witnesses. No witness contradicted any testimony given by any other witnesses. On the day in question the petitioners were playing in a basketball court at Daffin Park, Savannah, Georgia. The park is owned and operated by the city for recreational purposes, is about 50 acres in area, and is customarily used only by whites. A white woman notified the two police officer witnesses of the presence of petitioners in the park. They investigated, according to one officer, "because some colored people were playing in the park. I did not ask this white lady how old these people were. As soon as I found out these were colored people I immediately went there." The officer also conceded that "I have never made previous arrests in Daffin Park because people played basketball there. . . . I arrested these people for playing basketball in Daffin Park. One reason was because they were negroes. I observed the conduct of these people, when they were on the basketball court and they were doing nothing besides playing basketball, they were just normally playing basketball, and none of the children from the schools were there at that particular time." The other officer admitted that petitioners "were not necessarily creating any disorder, they were just 'shooting at the goal,' that's all they were doing, they wasn't disturbing anything." Petitioners were neat and well dressed. Nevertheless, the officers ordered the petitioners to leave the park. One petitioner asked one of the officers "by what authority" he asked them to leave; the officer responded that he "didn't need any orders to come out there. . . ." But he admitted that "it is [not] unusual for one to inquire 'why' they are being arrested." When arrested the petitioners obeyed the police orders and without disturbance entered the cruiser to be transported to police headquarters. No crowd assembled.

The recreational superintendent's testimony was confused and contradictory. In essence he testified that school children had preference in the use of the park's playground facilities but that there was no objection to use by older persons if children were not there at the time. No children were present at this time. The arrests were made at about 2 P.M. The schools released their students at 2:30 and, according to one officer, it would have been at least 30 minutes before any children could have reached the playground. The officer also stated that he did not know whether the basketball court was reserved for a particular age group and did not know the rules of the City Recreational Department. It was conceded at the trial that no signs were posted in the park indicating what areas, if any, were reserved for younger children at particular hours. In oral argument before this Court it was conceded that the regulations of the park were not printed.

The accusation charged petitioners with assembling "for the purpose of disturbing the public peace . . ." and not dispersing at the command of the officers. The jury was charged, with respect to the offense itself, only in terms of the accusation and the statute. Upon conviction five petitioners were sentenced to pay a fine of $100 or to serve five months in prison. Petitioner Wright was sentenced to pay a fine of $125 or to serve six months in prison.

Petitioners' principal contention in this Court is that the breach of the peace statute did not give adequate warning that their conduct violated that enactment in derogation of their rights under the Due Process Clause of the Fourteenth Amendment of the Constitution of the United States. . . .

Since there is some question as to whether the Georgia Supreme Court considered petitioners' claim of vagueness to have been properly raised in the demurrer we prefer to rest our jurisdiction upon a firmer foundation. We hold, for the reason set forth hereinafter, that there was no adequate state ground for the Georgia court's refusal to consider error in the denial of petitioners' motions for a new trial. . . .

Three possible bases for petitioners' convictions are suggested. First, it is said that failure to obey the command of a police officer constitutes a traditional form of breach of the peace. Obviously, however, one cannot be punished for failing to obey the command of an officer if that command is itself violative of the Constitution. The command of the officers in this case was doubly a violation of petitioners' constitutional rights. It was obviously based, according to the testimony of the arresting officers themselves, upon their intention to enforce racial discrimination in the park. For this reason the order violated the Equal Protection Clause of the Fourteenth Amendment. See New Orleans City Park Improvement Ass'n v. Detiege. . . . The command was also violative of petitioners' rights because, as will be seen, the other asserted basis for the order—the possibility of disorder by others—could not justify exclusion of the petitioners from the park. Thus petitioners could not constitutionally be convicted for refusing to obey the officers. If petitioners were held guilty of violating the Georgia statute because they disobeyed the officers, this case falls within the rule that a generally worded statute which is construed to punish conduct which cannot constitutionally be punished is unconstitutionally vague to the extent that it fails to give adequate warning of the boundary between the constitutionally permissible and constitutionally impermissible applications of the statute. . . .

Second, it is argued that petitioners were guilty of a breach of the peace because their activity was likely to cause a breach of the peace by others. The only evidence to support this contention is testimony of one of the police officers that "The purpose of asking them to leave was to keep down trouble, which looked like to me might start—there were five or six cars driving around the park at the time, white people." But that officer also stated that this "was [not] unusual traffic for that time of day." And the park was 50 acres in area. Respondent contends the petitioners were forewarned that their conduct would be held to violate the statute. . . . But it is sufficient to say again that a generally worded statute, when construed to punish conduct which cannot be constitutionally punished, is unconstitutionally vague. And the possibility of disorder by others cannot justify exclusion of persons from a place if they otherwise have a constitutional right (founded upon the Equal Protection Clause) to be present. . . .

Third, it is said that the petitioners were guilty of a breach of the peace because because a park rule reserved the playground for the use of younger people at the time. However, neither the existence nor the posting of any such rule has been proved. . . . The police officers did not inform them of it because they had no knowledge of any such rule themselves. Furthermore, it is conceded that there was no sign or printed regulation which would give notice of any such rule.

Under any view of the facts alleged to constitute the violation it cannot be maintained that petitioners had adequate notice that their conduct was prohibited by the breach of the peace statute. It is well established that a conviction under a criminal enactment which does not give adequate notice that the conduct charged is prohibited is violative of due process. . . .

—CHIEF JUSTICE EARL WARREN, Wright *v.* Georgia, 1963

B. *Peterson v. Greenville, 1963*

WARREN, C. J.: THE PETITIONERS WERE convicted in the Recorder's Court of the City of Greenville, South Carolina, for violating the trespass statute of that State. Each was sentenced to pay a fine of $100 or in lieu thereof to serve 30 days in jail. An appeal to the Greenville County Court was dismissed, and the Supreme Court of South Carolina affirmed. . . . We granted certiorari to consider the substantial federal questions presented by the record. . . .

The 10 petitioners are Negro boys and girls who, on August 9, 1960, entered the S. H. Kress store in Greenville and seated themselves at the lunch counter for the purpose, as they testified, of being served. When the Kress manager observed the petitioners sitting at the counter, he "had one of [his] . . . employees call the Police Department and turn off the lights and state the lunch counter closed." A captain of police and two other officers responded by proceeding to the store in a patrol car where they were met by other policemen and two state agents who had preceded them there. In the presence of the police and the state agents, the manager "announced that the lunch counter was being closed and would everyone leave" the area. The petitioners, who had been sitting at the counter for five minutes, remained seated and were promptly arrested. The boys were searched, and both boys and girls were taken to police headquarters.

The manager of the store did not request the police to arrest petitioners; he asked them to leave because integrated service was "contrary to local customs" of segregation at lunch counters and in violation of the following Greenville City ordinance requiring separation of the races in restaurants:

> It shall be unlawful for any person owning, managing or controlling any hotel, restaurant, cafe, eating house, boarding-house or similar establishment to furnish meals to white persons and colored persons in the same room, or at the same table, or at the same counter; . . .

The manager and the police conceded that the petitioners were clean, well dressed, unoffensive in conduct, and that they sat quietly at the counter which was designed to accommodate 59 persons. The manager described his establishment as a national chain store of 15 or 20 departments, selling over 10,000 items. He stated that the general public was invited to do business at the store and that the patronage of Negroes was solicited in all departments of the store other than the lunch counter.

Petitioners maintain that South Carolina has denied them right of free speech, both because their activity was protected by the First and Fourteenth Amendments and because the trespass statute did not require a showing that the Kress manager gave them notice of his authority when he asked them to leave. Petitioners also assert that they have been deprived of the equal protection of the laws secured to them against state action by the Fourteenth Amendment. We need decide only the last of the questions thus raised.

The evidence in this case establishes beyond doubt that the Kress management's decision to exclude petitioners from the lunch counter was made because they were Negroes. It cannot be disputed that under our decisions "private conduct abridging individual rights does no violence to the Equal Protection Clause unless to some significant extent the State in any of its manifestations has been found to have become involved in it. . . ."

It cannot be denied that here the City of Greenville, an agency of the State, has provided by its ordinance that the decision as to whether a restaurant facility is to be operated on a desegregated basis is to be reserved to it. When the State has commanded a particular result, it has saved to itself the power to determine that result and thereby "to a significant extent" has "become involved" in it, and, in fact, has removed that decision from the sphere of private choice. It has thus effectively determined that a person owning, managing or controlling an eating place is left with no choice of his own but must segregate his white and Negro patrons. The Kress management in deciding to exclude Negroes, did precisely what the city law required.

Consequently, these convictions cannot stand, even assuming, as respondent contends, that the manager would have acted as he did independently of the existence of the ordinance. The State will not be heard to make this contention in support of the convictions. For the convictions had the effect, which the State cannot deny, of enforcing the ordinance passed by the City of Greenville, the agency of the State. When a state agency passes a law compelling persons to discriminate against other persons because of race, and the State's criminal processes are employed in a way which enforces discrimination mandated by that law, such a palpable violation of the Fourteenth Amendment cannot be saved by attempting to separate the mental urges of the discriminators.

Reversed.

—Chief Justice Earl Warren, in Peterson *v.* Greenville, 1963

23. A Night of Terror in Plaquemine, Louisiana, 1963

James J. Farmer

EDITORIAL NOTE: *Many historians have concluded that the South is more given to violence than other sections of the country, and they ascribe this propensity not so much to the frontier tradition—just as strong, after all, in the West—as to the institution of slavery and the tradition of white superiority. "Slavery" wrote Thomas Jefferson in his* Notes on the State of Virginia, *provides "a perpetual exercise of the most boisterous of passions," and what was true of slavery proved no less true of the relations of whites and Negroes in the century after slavery's abolition. Outraged by Negro demands for equality, frustrated by the Federal courts which consistently sustained Negro demands and just as consistently reversed State courts when they sought to punish Negroes for sit-ins or demonstrations, and embittered by the disapproval of the rest of the country, Southerns took matters into their own hands. During the late fifties and the early sixties something like a reign of terror flourished in Mississippi, Louisiana, and Alabama. Scores of Negro churches were burned, hundreds of Negro leaders were attacked and many of them murdered, thousands of Negro demonstrators were arrested and jailed. James J. Farmer, founder and director of CORE (Congress of Racial Equality), and one of the most widely and deeply respected of Negro leaders, recalls here his experiences in Plaquemine, Louisiana, in the summer of 1963.*

I WENT DOWN to Plaquemine toward the end of August 1963 on the first day of what I innocently assumed would be a routine three-day trip. We staged a protest march into town after my speech. When the march was over, all the leaders, myself included, were arrested and taken off to jail in nearby Donaldsonville (which hospitably offered us its facilities in lieu of the already overcrowded Plaquemine jail).

We stayed in jail for a week and a half. As a result, I missed the March on Washington. The timing was unfortunate, but I felt that I really had no choice. Having cast my lot with the people of Plaquemine, I could not simply pull rank and walk out. Moreover, this was my opportunity to reaffirm publicly the insight that CORE had gained during the Freedom Rides of the previous year—that filling the jails could serve as a useful instrument of persuasion. So I sent a message to Washington, which was read by Attorney Floyd B. McKissick, CORE's national chairman, and remained in jail until all the local demonstrators were out. When we came out, the spirit of militancy was spreading in Plaquemine, and two days later a group of young people organized another demonstration, protesting segregation in public places as well as exclusion from the city. This time, however, the marchers did not even get into town. The chief of police stopped them halfway, arrested the leaders, and held the rest of the marchers where they were until state troopers arrived. The troopers came on horseback, riding like cowboys, and they charged into the crowd of boys and girls as if they were rounding up a herd of stampeding cattle. They were armed with billy clubs and cattle prods, which they used mercilessly. Many of the youngsters who fell under the blows were trampled by the horses. (The children of Selma, whose suffering at the hands of police appalled the nation two years later, were but a part of a spiritual community of brave Southern youngsters like these who for years have been deprived of national attention by inadequate press coverage.)

This gratuitous savagery inflicted upon their children immediately aroused the adults to a pitch of militancy much more intense than anything the organizational effort had been able to achieve. The ministers, who had previously hung back, united for the first time. (Only one minister, the Rev. Jetson Davis, had been active in the movement. It was his Plymouth Rock Baptist Church to which the injured boys and girls had fled for comfort and medical assistance.) Apathy or fear or whatever had caused their reluctance dissolved in outrage. The next morning, Sunday, every minister in the Negro quarter preached a sermon extolling freedom and condemning police brutality. After church, according to agreement, they led their congregations to Reverend Davis' church and organized a massive march in protest against the rout of the previous day. As the time approached for the march to begin, some of the ministers began to waver. One of them hesitated on his way to the front of the line. "Where's my wife?" he said, looking around fearfully. "I don't see my wife. I think I'd better just go on home." His wife was standing right behind him. "Man," she said, "if you don't get up there in the front of that line, you ain't got no wife."

He marched, all right, but his presence could not alter the course of events. This time when the troopers intercepted the marchers there was nothing impromptu about the confrontation. They did not even come on horseback; they came in patrol cars and the horses arrived in vans. The troopers mounted their horses and assembled their weapons as if the crowd of unarmed men and women before them were an opposing army; they charged into the mass as they had done the day before, flailing with billy clubs and stabbing with cattle prods. "Get up, nigger!" one would shout, poking a man with an electric prod and beating him to the ground with a club. "Run, nigger, run!"

I was waiting at the Plymouth Rock Church. I watched the Negroes come running back, those who could run, bleeding, hysterical, faint, some of the stronger ones carrying the injured. The nurse started to bandage the wounds and the rest of us began to sing "We Shall Overcome"; but the troopers rode roaring through the streets right up to the door of the church. The Freedom Rock Church, we call it now. They dismounted and broke into the church, yelling and hurling tear gas bombs in front of them—bomb after bomb, poisoning the air. The gas masks protecting the troopers' faces transformed them into monsters as they stood and watched our people growing more and more frantic, screaming with pain and terror, trampling on one another in their frenzied efforts to escape through the back door to the parsonage behind the church. When the people had finally escaped, the troopers set about destroying the empty church. They knocked out the windows, overturned the benches, laid waste everything they could reach, and flooded the gutted building with high-pressure hoses until Bibles and hymnals floated in the aisles.

Then they attacked the parsonage to which we had fled. They sent tear gas bombs smashing through the windows, until all the windows were shattered and almost everyone inside was blinded and choking. The screaming was unbearable. I caught sight of Ronnie Moore administering mouth-to-mouth resuscitation to a young woman. People writhed on the floor, seeking oxygen. A few managed to push through the rear door into the parsonage yard, but the troopers, anticipating them, had ridden around to the back with more bombs to force them in again. And then bombs thrown into the parsonage forced them back out into the yard. All these men and women, who just that morning had resolutely banded together to reach out for freedom and dignity, were reduced now to running from torment, helpless victims of a bitter game.

We tried to telephone for help, but the operators were not putting through any outgoing calls from the Negro section. Within the community, though, there was telephone service, and several calls got through to us in the parsonage. What had appeared to be random and mindless brutality proved to have had a mad purpose after all. It was a manhunt. Troopers were in the streets, kicking open doors, searching every house in the Negro community, overturning chairs and tables, looking under beds and in closets, yelling, "Come on out, Farmer, we know you're in there. Come on out, Farmer! We're going to get you." We could hear the screaming in the streets as the troopers on horseback resumed their sport with the cattle prods and billy clubs: "Get up, nigger! Run, nigger, run!" Holding their victims down with the cattle prod, they were saying, "We'll let you up, nigger, if you tell us where Farmer is." Two of our girls, hiding beneath the church, overheard one trooper saying to another, "When we catch that goddam nigger Farmer, we're gonna kill him."

Spiver Gordon, CORE field secretary in Plaquemine, who, people say, looks like me, told me later that he wandered out of the church into the street at this time. Sighting him, state troopers ran up shouting, "Here he is boys. We got Farmer. We got their m-----f------ Jesus." A trooper beckoned to a crowd of hoodlums who were watching nearby, many holding chains, ropes, clubs. "What post we gonna hang him from?" said one. After Spiver convinced them he wasn't me, he took a good lacing for looking like me. An officer said, "He ain't Farmer. You've beat him enough. Put him in the car and arrest him."

There seemed no prospect of aid from any quarter. We were all suffering intensely from the tear gas, and the troopers kept us running with the bombs. In desperation I sent two people creeping through the grass from the parsonage to a funeral hall half a block away to ask for refuge. The owners of the hall agreed to shelter us (although I doubt that they knew what they were taking on). So we crawled on our bellies through the grass, in twos, threes, fours, making use of guerrilla tactics that some remembered from the war but none of us had ever learned as a technique of non-violent demonstration, until we reached our new sanctuary. Night had fallen by the time all three hundred of us were safely inside, jammed together like straws in a broom into two rooms and a hallway. The sound of screaming still echoed in the streets as the troopers beat down another Negro ("Run, nigger, run!") or invaded another house. The telephones were still useless.

Very shortly the troopers figured out where we were. One of them—a huge, raging, red-faced man—kicked open the back door of the funeral home and screamed, "Come on out, Farmer. We know you're in there. We're gonna get you." I was in the front room. I could look down the hallway, over all the heads, right into his face: it was flushed and dripping with sweat; his hair hung over his eyes, his mouth was twisted. Another trooper burst through the door to stand beside him. "Farmer! Come out!"

I had to give myself up. I felt like a modern Oedipus who, unaware, brought down a plague upon the city. In this hall, their lives endangered by my presence, were three hundred people, many of whom had never even seen me before that day. I began to make my way into the hall, thinking that I would ask to see the warrant for my arrest and demand to know the charges against me. But before I could take three steps the men around me grabbed me silently and pulled me back into the front room, whispering fiercely, "We're not going to let you go out there tonight. That's a lynch mob. You go out there tonight, you won't be alive tomorrow morning."

The trooper, meanwhile, had discovered a large Negro in the back room. He shouted triumphantly: "Here he is, we got that nigger Farmer! Come on in, boys. We got him here."

"I'm not Farmer," the man said. A third trooper came in.

"That ain't Farmer," he said. "I know that nigger." They went through his identification papers. He wasn't Farmer.

Suddenly, to everyone's astonishment, a woman pushed her way through the crowd to the back room and confronted the troopers. It was the owner of the funeral home, a "Nervous Nellie," as they say, who had previously held herself apart from the movement. I can never know—she herself probably does not know—what inner revolution or what mysterious force generated in that crowded room plucked her from her caul of fear and thrust her forth to assert with such a dramatic and improbable gesture her new birth of freedom. A funeral hall is as good a place as any for a person to come to life, I suppose, and her action sparked a sympathetic impulse in everyone who watched as she planted herself in front of the first trooper and shook a finger in his face: "Do you have a search warrant to come into my place of business?"

The trooper stared down at her, confounded, and backed away. "No," he said.

"You're not coming into my place of business without a search warrant. I'm a taxpayer and a law-abiding citizen. I have a wake going on here."

I prayed inwardly that her valiant subterfuge would not prove to be a prophecy.

"This ain't no wake," the trooper said, looking around at the throng of angry, frightened people crushed together before him. "These people ain't at no wake."

"Well, you're not coming into my place of business without a search warrant." The accusing finger pushed him back to the door, where he muttered for a moment to his men outside, then turned and yelled, "All right. We got all the tear gas and all the guns. You ain't got nothin'. We'll give you just five minutes to get Farmer out here. Just five minutes, that's all." He slammed the door.

The door clanged in my ears like the door of a cell in death row. "I'll go out and face them," I said, but once again I was restrained. They would stick by me, these strangers insisted, even if they all had to die, but they would not let me out to be lynched. Someone standing near me pulled out a gun. "Mr. Farmer," he said, "if a trooper comes through that door, he'll be dead."

"If a trooper comes through that door, he may be dead," I conceded. "But what about the trooper behind him and all the ones behind that one? You'll only provoke them into shooting and we won't have a chance." Very reluctantly he allowed me to take the gun from him. It is hard for people to practice non-violence when they are looking death in the face. I wondered how many others were armed.

Then my own private thoughts engulfed me. Reverend Davis was leading a group in the Lord's Prayer; another group was singing "We Shall Overcome." I was certain I was going to die. What kind of death would it be? Would they mutilate me first? What does it feel like to die? Then I grew panicky about the insurance. Had I paid the last installment? How much was it? I couldn't remember. I couldn't remember anything about it. My wife and little girls—how would it be for them? Abbey was only two then—too young to remember; but Tami was four and a half, and very close to me—she would remember. Well, damn it, if I had to die, at least let the organization wring some use out of my death. I hoped the newspapers were out there. Plenty of them. With plenty of cameras.

I was terrified. The five minutes passed. Six. Seven. Eight. A knock at the front door. My lawyers from New Orleans, Lolis Elie and Robert Collins, identified themselves and squeezed in, breathless. New Orleans radio had broadcast the news that a manhunt was in progress in Plaquemine, and they had driven over immediately. The community, they said, was in a state of siege. Everywhere one looked one saw troopers, like an invading army. The two lawyers had crawled through the high grass to seek refuge in the graveyard, but when they got there the place came alive: there was a Negro behind every tombstone ("All find safety in the tomb," sang Yeats, in another context). Apparently everyone had counted on the dead to be more hospitable than the living. Apparently, also, everyone knew where I was, but no one was telling the white men. The troopers, it seemed, had been bluffing; they could not be wholly sure I was in the funeral home. It occurred to me that my physical safety, in some elusive way that had very little to do with me, had become a kind of transcendent symbol to all these people of the possibilities of freedom and personal dignity that existed for them. By protecting me, they were preserving their dreams. But did they understand, I wondered, that through their acts of courage during this desperate night they had taken the first great steps toward realizing these possibilities? Did they sense that they had gained at least some of that freedom for which they longed here, and now?

Just as the lawyers finished their story there was another knock at the door. For a moment I thought the troopers had come at last, until I remembered that troopers don't knock. The two men who entered were recently acquired friends from Plaquemine, and pretty rough characters in their own right: my neighbor from town, whom I shall call Fred, and Bill, a buddy of his, ex-Marines who, I knew, carried several guns in their car at all times. The troopers, they told me, had grown systematic. They had set up roadblocks on every street leading out of town. The men who had been waiting in the back had just driven off in the direction of the sheriff's office, presumably to get a search warrant. In short, if I did not get out right now, my life would not be worth a dime.

I told my lawyers to get in their car and try to drive out through the roadblocks. I thought the troopers might respect their identification as attorneys. If they got through, they were to call New York at once, call my wife and tell her I was all right, call Marvin Rich at CORE and have him get in touch with the FBI, call New Orleans and try to get some kind of federal protection. It was imperative that we make contact with the outside world.

Then Fred and Bill set forth their plan. The woman who owned the funeral home had two hearses. They would send the old one out as a decoy with just a driver, who would take it down the main streets, making sure it was spotted at every roadblock. If pursued, he would speed up. Meanwhile, we would try to escape in the second hearse which was waiting, its motor already running, in a garage which we could reach without going out of the house.

If there was something unsettling about the prospect of riding to safety in a hearse, it was nonetheless the logical conclusion to the macabre events of the day. And we could see no alternative. Fred and Bill led the way to the garage, forcing a passage through the sweating men and women who murmured phrases of encouragement and good wishes as we passed. I prayed that our departure would release them from danger, marveling once more at the courage and devotion shown by these strangers.

It was cool, briefly, in the garage, but the hearse was hot and stuffy again. Ronnie Moore, Reverend Davis, and I crawled into the back and crouched down—three restless, nervous men huddled together in a space meant for one motionless body. I thought I remembered that Huey Long had once escaped from someone in a hearse, and for a moment I almost felt like smiling. Someone climbed into the driver's seat and we were off, speeding down the back roads toward New Orleans. Fred and Bill, heavily armed (although I did not know that at the time), followed us in their car. We took a winding route with countless detours over very rough country roads which the Negroes knew more intimately than the whites. Although you can drive from Plaquemine to New Orleans in less than two hours by highway, it took us four and a half hours, despite the fact that we were going very fast and did not stop at all. Whenever a car approached we flattened out on the floor of the hearse until the road was clear again. Our grim destination was another funeral home; our only protection was blackness, a color which had never before promised immunity to Negroes in the South. At times during that wild ride I thought I was already dead. I don't know what the others thought. But when at last we climbed out of the hearse into the hot New Orleans night, we were, by the grace of God and the extraordinary courage of many ordinary men, still very much alive. And not yet entirely out of danger.

When we finally got in touch with the New Orleans CORE, we discovered that our story was already out. The two lawyers had passed the roadblocks and called the authorities in New Orleans, and the press had picked up the news immediately. They had also called my wife, before she had heard anything, to tell her not to worry: "Jim's all right."

"Oh," said Lula. "Why shouldn't he be?"

"There was a little trouble down in Plaquemine, but there's nothing to worry about now. He's out of danger." Whereupon Lula turned on the television set and learned that there was a house-to-house search reportedly going on in Plaquemine, Louisiana, for

CORE National Director, James Farmer . . . and, a little later, that James Farmer was reported missing in Plaquemine, Louisiana. She told me later that she turned off the news broadcast and took the children outside where the voices they would hear were less ominous. Shortly afterward, when she went to call the press to try to find out more, she found they were already waiting for her at the house.

In New York, though, they never carried the complete story. The next morning I held a press conference at the CORE headquarters in New Orleans. Newspaper and TV reporters carefully took down all the details, but what they wrote never got farther than New Orleans. But then the list of stories that the newspapers have overlooked in the South and elsewhere is endless.

A trial was scheduled for me the next day in Plaquemine. I was not exactly eager to return but I announced at the press conference that I intended to appear at the appointed time to be served with the warrant for my arrest and to hear the charges, whatever they might be. The FBI sent a man to New York to find out the details from our national office. Our people told him I was going back into Plaquemine the next day and asked if the FBI could guarantee my safety; our attorney, Lolis Elie, called the FBI regional office in New Orleans with the same request. To both requests, the response was the same: the FBI was an investigatory agency, not a protection agency; they could not guarantee my life. However, since the situation was an extraordinary one, they would see what they could do.

With this ambiguous support, Ronnie Moore, Reverend Davis, and I returned somewhat nervously to Plaquemine the next morning. The city police were waiting for us; as soon as we drove into town we saw a policeman in a squad car in front of us announce our arrival into his radio. To our relief FBI agents were everywhere, questioning people in the Negro section, the white section, and around the courthouse. Two agents came over to me as soon as I walked into the courtroom. But as it turned out the troopers had no warrant for my arrest, no charges against me. Nor could we take any action against them, for their name plates and badge numbers had been taped over during the manhunt. In fact, we learned that many of the men who had been riding that night were not even regular troopers: they were ordinary citizens deputized for the occasion.

The drama of Plaquemine ended there, but its consequences are still alive. A new Negro community grew out of that terrible night, aroused, unified, determined to act.

—JAMES J. FARMER, *Freedom—When?*, 1965

24. The Reverend Dr. Martin Luther King Jr. Writes a Letter from the Birmingham Jail

Martin Luther King, Jr.

EDITORIAL NOTE: *The hard core of resistance to desegregation in the South was the old "Deep South" of Alabama, Mississippi and Louisiana. During the sixties the people—and the authorities—of these states earned a melancholy reputation throughout the world by their readiness to resort to violence. And as Negro organizations made one city after another a kind of test-case, names like Bogalusa, Selma, McComb, and Plaquemine came to have reprehensible connotations. In the sixties no city earned itself a more shameful reputation than Birmingham, Alabama. In November 1962, however, the white citizens of Birmingham, tired of agitation and violence, had finally voted the notorious Sheriff "Bull" Connor out of office, and things took a turn for the better. The next spring, Martin Luther King Jr. and his followers determined to make a massive effort to desegregate Birmingham. They were met by a new wave of violence and lawlessness, worse than any that had gone before. Frightened, the authorities resorted to wholesale arrests of Negro demonstrators, including hundreds of children. When the Reverend Dr. King defied an injunction against further demonstrations, he was arrested and placed in solitary confinement. While in jail he penned this memorable letter to a group of clergymen who had taken him to task for "unwise and untimely" activities.*

April 16, 1963

MY DEAR FELLOW CLERGYMEN:*

WHILE CONFINED HERE in the Birmingham city jail, I came across your recent statement calling my present activities "unwise and untimely." Seldom do I pause to answer criticism of my work and ideas. If I sought to answer all the criticisms that cross my desk, my secretaries would have little time for anything other than such correspondence in the course of the day, and I would have no time for constructive work. But since I feel that you are men of genuine good will and that your criticisms are sincerely set forth, I want to try to answer your statement in what I hope will be patient and reasonable terms.

I think I should indicate why I am here in Birmingham, since you have been influenced by the view which argues against "outsiders coming in." I have the honor of serving as president of the Southern Christian Leadership Conference, an organization operating in every southern state, with headquarters in Atlanta, Georgia. We have some eighty-five affiliated organizations across the South, and one of them is the Alabama Christian Movement for Human Rights. Frequently we share staff, educational and financial resources with our affiliates. Several months ago the affiliate here in Birmingham asked us to be on call to engage in a nonviolent direct-action program if such were deemed necessary. We readily consented, and when the hour came we lived up to our promise. So I, along with several members of my

* AUTHOR'S NOTE: This response to a published statement by eight fellow clergymen from Alabama (Bishop C. C. J. Carpenter, Bishop Joseph A. Durick, Rabbi Hilton L. Grafman, Bishop Paul Hardin, Bishop Holan B. Harmon, the Reverend George M. Murray, the Reverend Edward V. Ramage and the Reverend Earl Stallings) was composed under somewhat constricting circumstances. Begun on the margins of the newspaper in which the statement appeared while I was in jail, the letter was continued on scraps of writing paper supplied by a friendly Negro trusty, and concluded on a pad my attorneys were eventually permitted to leave me. Although the text remains in substance unaltered, I have indulged in the author's prerogative of polishing it for publication.

staff, am here because I was invited here. I am here because I have organizational ties here.

But more basically, I am in Birmingham because injustice is here. Just as the prophets of the eighth century B.C. left their villages and carried their "thus saith the Lord" far beyond the boundaries of their home towns, and just as the Apostle Paul left his village of Tarsus and carried the gospel of Jesus Christ to the far corners of the Greco-Roman world, so am I compelled to carry the gospel of freedom beyond my own home town. Like Paul, I must constantly respond to the Macedonian call for aid.

Moreover, I am cognizant of the interrelatedness of all communities and states. I cannot sit idly by in Atlanta and not be concerned about what happens in Birmingham. Injustice anywhere is a threat to justice everywhere. We are caught in an inescapable network of mutuality, tied in a single garment of destiny. Whatever affects one directly, affects all indirectly. Never again can we afford to live with the narrow, provincial "outside agitator" idea. Anyone who lives inside the United States can never be considered an outsider anywhere within its bounds.

You deplore the demonstrations taking place in Birmingham. But your statement, I am sorry to say, fails to express a similar concern for the conditions that brought about the demonstrations. I am sure that none of you would want to rest content with the superficial kind of social analysis that deals merely with effects and does not grapple with underlying causes. It is unfortunate that demonstrations are taking place in Birmingham, but it is even more unfortunate that the city's white power structure left the Negro community with no alternative.

In any nonviolent campaign there are four basic steps: collection of the facts to determine whether injustices exist; negotiation, self-purification; and direct action. We have gone through all these steps in Birmingham. There can be no gainsaying the fact that racial injustice engulfs this community. Birmingham is probably the most thoroughly segregated city in the United States. Its ugly record of brutality is widely known. Negroes have experienced grossly unjust treatment in the courts. There have been more unsolved bombings of Negro homes and churches in Birmingham than in any other city in the nation. These are the hard, brutal facts of the case. On the basis of these conditions, Negro leaders sought to negotiate with the city fathers. But the latter consistently refused to engage in good-faith negotiation.

Then, last September, came the opportunity to talk with leaders of Birmingham's economic community. In the course of the negotiations, certain promises were made by the merchants—for example, to remove the stores' humiliating racial signs. On the basis of these promises, the Reverend Fred Shuttlesworth and the leaders of the Alabama Christian Movement for Human Rights agreed to a moratorium on all demonstrations. As the weeks and months went by, we realized that we were the victims of a broken promise. A few signs, briefly removed, returned; the others remained.

As in so many past experiences, our hopes had been blasted, and the shadow of deep disappointment settled upon us. We had no alternative except to prepare for direct action, whereby we would present our very bodies as a means of laying our case before the conscience of the local and the national community. Mindful of the difficulties involved, we decided to undertake a process of self-purification. We began a series of workshops on nonviolence, and we repeatedly asked ourselves: "Are you able to accept blows without retaliating?" "Are you able to endure the ordeal of jail?" We decided to schedule our direct-action program for the Easter season, realizing that except for Christmas, this is the main shopping period of the year. Knowing that a strong economic-withdrawal program would be the by-product of direct action, we felt that this would be the best time to bring pressure to bear on the merchants for the needed change.

Then it occurred to us that Birmingham's mayoralty election was coming up in March, and we speedily decided to postpone action until after election day. When we discovered that the Commissioner of Public Safety, Eugene "Bull" Connor, had piled up enough votes to be in the run-off, we decided again to postpone action until the day after the run-off so that the demonstrations could not be used to cloud the issues. Like many others, we waited to see Mr. Connor defeated, and to this end we endured postponement after postponement. Having aided in this community need, we felt that our direct-action program could be delayed no longer.

You may well ask: "Why direct action? Why sit-ins, marches and so forth? Isn't negotiation a better path?" You are quite right in calling for negotiation. Indeed, this is the very purpose of direct action. Nonviolent direct action seeks to create such a crisis and foster such a tension that a community which has constantly refused to negotiate is forced to confront the issue. It seeks so to dramatize the issue that it can no longer be ignored. My citing the creation of tension as part of the work of the nonviolent-resister may sound rather shocking. But I must confess that I am not afraid of the word "tension." I have earnestly opposed violent tension, but there is a type of constructive, nonviolent tension which is necessary for growth. Just as Socrates felt that it was necessary to create a tension in the mind so that individuals could rise from the bondage of myths and half-truths to the unfettered realm of creative analysis and objective appraisal, so must we see the need for nonviolent gadflies to create the kind of tension in society that will help men rise from the dark depths of prejudice and racism to the majestic heights of understanding and brotherhood.

The purpose of our direct-action program is to create a situation so crisis-packed that it will inevitably open the door to negotiation. I therefore concur with you in your call for negotiation. Too long has our beloved Southland been bogged down in a tragic effort to live in monologue rather than dialogue.

One of the basic points in your statement is that the action that I and my associates have taken in Birmingham is untimely. Some have asked: "Why didn't you give the new city administration time to act?" The only answer that I can give to this query is that the new Birmingham administration must be prodded about as much as the outgoing one, before it will act. We are sadly mistaken if we feel that the election of Albert Boutwell as mayor will bring the millennium to Birmingham. While Mr. Boutwell is a much more gentle person than Mr. Connor, they are both segregationists, dedicated to maintenance of the status quo. I have hope that Mr. Boutwell will be reasonable enough to see the futility of massive resistance to desegregation. But he will not see this without pressure from devotees of civil rights. My friends, I must say to you that we have not made a single gain in civil rights without determined legal and nonviolent pressure. Lamentably, it is an historical fact that privileged groups seldom give up their privileges voluntarily. Individuals may see the moral light and voluntarily give up their unjust posture; but, as Reinhold Niebuhr has reminded us, groups tend to be more immoral than individuals.

We know through painful experience that freedom is never voluntarily given by the oppressor; it must be demanded by the oppressed. Frankly, I have yet to engage in a direct-action campaign that was "well timed" in the view of those who have not suffered unduly from the disease of segregation. For years now I have heard the word. "Wait!" It rings in the ear of every Negro with piercing familiarity. This "Wait" has almost always meant "Never." We must come to see, with one of our distinguished jurists, that "justice too long delayed is justice denied."

We have waited for more than 340 years for our constitutional and God-given rights. The nations of Asia and Africa are moving with jetlike speed toward gaining political independence, but we still creep at horse-and-buggy pace toward gaining a cup of coffee at a lunch counter. Perhaps it is easy for those who have never felt the stinging darts of segregation to say, "Wait." But when you have seen vicious mobs lynch your mothers and fathers at will and drown your sisters and brothers at whim; when you have seen hate-filled policemen curse, kick and even kill your black brothers and sisters; when you see the vast majority of your twenty million Negro brothers smothering in an airtight cage of poverty in the midst of an affluent society; when you suddenly find your tongue twisted and your speech stammering as you seek to explain to your six-year-old daughter why she can't go to the public amusement park that has just been advertised on television, and see tears welling up in her eyes when she is told that Funtown is closed to colored children, and see ominous clouds of inferiority beginning to form in her little mental sky, and see her beginning to distort her personality by developing an unconscious bitterness toward white people; when you have to concoct an answer for a five-year-old son who is asking: "Daddy, why do white people treat colored people so mean?"; when you take a cross-country drive and find it necessary to sleep night after night in the uncomfortable corners of your automobile because no motel will accept you; when you are humiliated day in and day out by nagging signs reading "white" and "colored"; when your first name becomes "nigger," your middle name becomes "boy" (however old you are) and your last name becomes "John," and your wife and mother are never given the respected title "Mrs."; when you are harried by day and haunted by night by the fact that you are a Negro, living constantly at tiptoe stance, never quite knowing what to expect next, and are plagued with inner fears and outer resentments; when you are forever fighting a degenerating sense of "nobodiness"—then you will understand why we find it difficult to wait. There comes a time when the cup of endurance runs over, and men are no longer willing to be plunged into the abyss of despair. I hope, sirs, you can understand our legitimate and unavoidable impatience.

You express a great deal of anxiety over our willingness to break laws. This is certainly a legitimate concern. Since we so diligently urge people to obey the Supreme Court's decision of 1954 outlawing segregation in the public schools, at first glance it may seem rather paradoxical for us consciously to break laws. One may well ask: "How can you advocate breaking some laws and obeying others?" The answer lies in the fact that there are two types of laws: just and unjust. I would be the first to advocate obeying just laws. One has not only a legal but a moral responsibility to obey just laws. Conversely, one has a moral responsibility to disobey unjust laws. I would agree with St. Augustine that "an unjust law is no law at all."

Now, what is the difference between the two? How does one determine whether a law is just or unjust? A just law is a man-made code that squares with the moral law or the law of God. An unjust law is a code that is out of harmony with the moral law. To put it in the terms of St. Thomas Aquinas: An unjust law is a human law that is not rooted in eternal law and natural law. Any law that uplifts human personality is just. Any law that degrades human personality is unjust. All segregation statutes are unjust because segregation distorts the soul and damages the personality. It gives the segregator a false sense of superiority and the segregated a false sense of inferiority. Segregation, to use the terminology of the Jewish philosopher Martin Buber, substitutes an "I–it" relationship for an "I–thou" relationship and ends up relegating persons to the status of things. Hence segregation is not only politically, economically and sociologically unsound, it is morally wrong and sinful. Paul Tillich has said that sin is separation. Is not segregation an existential expression of man's tragic separation, his awful estrangement, his terrible sinfulness? Thus it is that I can urge men to obey the 1954 decision of the Supreme Court, for it is morally right; and I can urge them to disobey segregation ordinances, for they are morally wrong.

Let us consider a more concrete example of just and unjust laws. An unjust law is a code that a numerical or power majority group compels a minority group to obey but does not make binding on itself. This is *difference* made legal. By the same token, a just law is a code that a majority compels a minority to follow and that it is willing to follow itself. This is *sameness* made legal.

Let me give another explanation. A law is unjust if it is inflicted on a minority that, as a result of being denied the right to vote, had no part in enacting or devising the law. Who can say that the legislature of Alabama which set up that state's segregation laws was democratically elected? Throughout Alabama all sorts of devious methods are used to prevent Negroes from becoming registered voters, and there are some counties in which, even though Negroes constitute a majority of the population, not a single Negro is registered. Can any law enacted under such circumstances be considered democratically structured?

Sometimes a law is just on its face and unjust in its application. For instance, I have been arrested on a charge of parading without a permit. Now, there is nothing wrong in having an ordinance which requires a permit for a parade. But such an ordinance becomes unjust when it is used to maintain segregation and to deny citizens the First-Amendment privilege of peaceful assembly and protest.

I hope you are able to see the distinction I am trying to point out. In no sense do I advocate evading or defying the law, as would the rabid segregationist. That would lead to anarchy. One who breaks an unjust law must do so openly, lovingly, and with a willingness to accept the penalty. I submit that an individual who breaks a law that conscience tells him is unjust, and who willingly accepts the penalty of imprisonment in order to arouse the conscience of the community over its injustice, is in reality expressing the highest respect for law.

Of course, there is nothing new about this kind of civil disobedience. It was evidenced sublimely in the refusal of Shadrach, Meshach and Abednego to obey the laws of Nebuchadnezzar, on the ground that a higher moral law was at stake. It was practiced superbly by the early Christians, who were willing to face hungry lions and the excruciating pain of chopping blocks rather than submit to certain unjust laws of the Roman Empire. To a degree, academic freedom is a reality today because Socrates practiced civil disobedience. In our own nation, the Boston Tea Party represented a massive act of civil disobedience.

We should never forget that everything Adolf Hitler did in Germany was "legal" and everything the Hungarian freedom fighters did in Hungary was "illegal." It was "illegal" to aid and comfort a Jew in Hitler's Germany. Even so, I am sure that, had I lived in Germany at the time, I would have aided and comforted my Jewish brothers. If today I lived in a Communist country where certain principles dear to the Christian faith are suppressed, I would openly advocate disobeying that country's antireligious laws.

I must make two honest confessions to you, my Christian and Jewish brothers. First, I must confess that over the past few years I have been gravely disappointed with the white moderate. I have almost reached the regrettable conclusion that the Negro's great stumbling block in his stride toward freedom is not the White Citizens' Councilor or the Ku Klux Klanner, but the white moderate, who is more devoted to "order" than to justice; who prefers a negative peace which is the absence of tension to a positive peace which is the presence of justice; who constantly says: "I agree with you in the goal you seek, but I cannot agree with your methods of direct action;" who paternalistically believes he can set the timetable for another man's freedom; who lives by a mythical concept of time and who constantly advises the Negro to wait for a "more convenient season." Shallow understanding from people of good will is more frustrating than absolute misunderstanding from people of ill will. Lukewarm acceptance is much more bewildering than outright rejection.

I had hoped that the white moderate would understand that law and order exist for the purpose of establishing justice and that when they fail in this purpose they become the dangerously structured dams that block the flow of social progress. I had hoped that the white moderate would understand that the present tension in the South is a necessary phase of the transition from an obnoxious negative peace, in which the Negro passively accepted his unjust plight, to a substantive and positive peace, in which all men will respect the dignity and worth of human personality. Actually, we who engage in nonviolent direct action are not the creators of tension. We merely bring to the surface the hidden tension that is already alive. We bring it out in the open, where it can be seen and dealt with. Like a boil that can never be cured so long as it is covered up but must be opened with all its ugliness to the natural medicines of air and light, injustice must be exposed, with all the tension its exposure creates, to the light of human conscience and the air of national opinion before it can be cured.

In your statement you assert that our actions, even though peaceful, must be condemned because they precipitate violence. But is this a logical assertion? Isn't this like condemning a robbed man because his possession of money precipitated the evil act of robbery? Isn't this like condemning Socrates because his unswerving commitment to truth and his philosophical inquiries precipitated the act by the misguided populace in which they made him drink hemlock? Isn't this like condemning Jesus because his unique God-consciousness and never-ceasing devotion to God's will precipitated the evil act of crucifixion? We must come to see that, as the federal courts have consistently affirmed, it is wrong to urge an individual to cease his efforts to gain his basic constitutional rights because the quest may precipitate violence. Society must protect the robbed and punish the robber.

I had also hoped that the white moderate would reject the myth concerning time in relation to the struggle for freedom. I have just received a letter from a white brother in Texas. He writes: "All Christians know that the colored people will receive equal rights eventually, but it is possible that you are in too great a religious hurry. It has taken Christianity almost two thousand years to accomplish what it has. The teachings of Christ take time to come to earth." Such an attitude stems from a tragic misconception of time, from the strangely irrational notion that there is something in the very flow of time that will inevitably cure all ills. Actually, time itself is neutral; it can be used either destructively or constructively. More and more I feel that the people of ill will have used time much more effectively than have the people of good will. We will have to repent in this generation not merely for the hateful words and actions of the bad people but for the appalling silence of the good people. Human progress never rolls in on wheels of inevitability; it comes through the tireless efforts of men willing to be co-workers with God, and without this hard work, time itself becomes an ally of the forces of social stagnation. We must use time creatively, in the knowledge that the time is always ripe to do right. Now is the time to make real the promise of democracy and transform our pending national elegy into a creative psalm of brotherhood. Now is the time to lift our national policy from the quicksand of racial injustice to the solid rock of human dignity.

You speak of our activity in Birmingham as extreme. At first I was rather disappointed that fellow clergymen would see my nonviolent efforts as those of an extremist. I began thinking about the fact that I stand in the middle of two opposing forces in the Negro community. One is a force of complacency, made up in part of Negroes who, as a result of long years of oppression, are so drained of self-respect and a sense of "somebodiness" that they have adjusted to segregation; and in part of a few middle-class Negroes who, because of a degree of academic and economic security and because in some ways they profit by segregation, have become insensitive to the problems of the masses. The other force is one of bitterness and hatred, and it comes perilously close to advocating violence. It is expressed in the various black nationalist groups that are springing up across the nation, the largest and best-known being Elijah Muhammad's Muslim movement. Nourished by the Negro's frustration over the continued existence of racial discrimination, this movement is made up of people who have lost faith in America, who have absolutely repudiated Christianity, and who have concluded that the white man is an incorrigible "devil."

I have tried to stand between these two forces, saying that we need emulate neither the "do-nothingism" of the complacent nor the hatred and despair of the black nationalist. For there is the more excellent way of love and nonviolent protest. I am grateful to God that, through the influence of the Negro church, the way of nonviolence became an integral part of our struggle.

If this philosophy had not emerged, by now many streets of the South would, I am convinced, be flowing with blood. And I am further convinced that if our white brothers dismiss as "rabble-rousers" and "outside agitators" those of us who employ nonviolent direct action, and if they refuse to support our nonviolent efforts, millions of Negroes will, out of frustration and despair, seek solace and security in black-nationalist ideologies—a development that would inevitably lead to a frightening racial nightmare.

Oppressed people cannot remain oppressed forever. The yearning for freedom eventually manifests itself, and that is what has happened to the American Negro. Something within has reminded him of his birthright of freedom, and something without has reminded him that it can be gained. Consciously or unconsciously, he has been caught up by the *Zeitgeist,* and with his black brothers of Africa and his brown and yellow brothers of Asia, South America and the Caribbean, the United States Negro is moving with a sense of great urgency toward the promised land of racial justice. If one recognizes this vital urge that has engulfed the Negro community, one should readily understand why public demonstrations are taking place. The Negro has many pent-up resentments and latent frustrations, and he must release them. So let him march; let him make prayer pilgrimages to the city hall; let him go on freedom rides—and try to understand why he must do so. If his repressed emotions are not released in nonviolent ways, they will seek expression through violence; this is not a threat but a fact of history. So I have not said to my people: "Get rid of your discontent." Rather, I have tried to say that this normal and healthy discontent can be channeled into the creative outlet of nonviolent direct action. And now this approach is being termed extremist.

But though I was initially disappointed at being categorized as an extremist, as I continued to think about the matter I gradually gained a measure of satisfaction from the label. Was not Jesus an extremist for love: "Love your enemies, bless them that curse you, do good to them that hate you, and pray for them which despitefully use you, and persecute you." Was not Amos an extremist for justice: "Let justice roll down like waters and righteousness like an ever-flowing stream." Was not Paul an extremist for the Christian gospel: "I bear in my body the marks of the Lord Jesus." Was not Martin Luther an extremist: "Here I stand; I cannot do otherwise, so help me God." And John Bunyan: "I will stay in jail to the end of my days before I make a butchery of my conscience." And Abraham Lincoln: "This nation cannot survive half slave and half free." And Thomas Jefferson: "We hold these truths to be self-evident, that all men are created equal . . ." So the question is not whether we will be extremists, but what kind of extremists we will be. Will we be extremists for hate or for love? Will we be extremists for the preservation of injustice or for the extension of justice? In that dramatic scene on Calvary's hill three men were crucified. We must never forget that all three were crucified for the same crime—the crime of extremism. Two were extremists for immorality, and thus fell below their environment. The other, Jesus Christ, was an extremist for love, truth and goodness, and thereby rose above his environment. Perhaps the South, the nation and the world are in dire need of creative extemists.

I had hoped that the white moderate would see this need. Perhaps I was too optimistic; perhaps I expected too much. I suppose I should have realized that few members of the oppressor race can understand the deep groans and passionate yearnings of the oppressed race, and still fewer have the vision to see that injustice must be rooted out by strong, persistent and determined action. I am thankful, however, that some of our white brothers in the South have grasped the meaning of this social revolution and committed themselves to it. They are still all too few in quantity, but they are big in quality. Some—such as Ralph McGill, Lillian Smith, Harry Golden, James McBride Dabbs, Ann Braden and Sarah Patton Boyle—have written about our struggle in eloquent and prophetic terms. Others have marched with us down nameless streets of the South. They have languished in filthy, roach-infested jails, suffering the abuse and brutality of policemen who view them as "dirty nigger-lovers." Unlike so many of their moderate brothers and sisters, they have recognized the urgency of the moment and sensed the need for powerful "action" antidotes to combat the disease of segregation.

Let me take note of my other major disappointment. I have been so greatly disappointed with the white church and its leadership. Of course, there are some notable exceptions. I am not unmindful of the fact that each of you has taken some significant stands on this issue. I commend you, Reverend Stallings, for your Christian stand on this past Sunday, in welcoming Negroes to your worship service on a nonsegregated basis. I commend the Catholic leaders of this state for integrating Spring Hill College several years ago.

But despite these notable exceptions, I must honestly reiterate that I have been disappointed with the church. I do not say this as one of those negative critics who can always find something wrong with the church. I say this as a minister of the gospel, who loves the church; who was nurtured in its bosom; who has been sustained by its spiritual blessings and who will remain true to it as long as the cord of life shall lengthen.

When I was suddenly catapulted into the leadership of the bus protest in Montgomery, Alabama, a few years ago, I felt we would be supported by the white church. I felt that the white ministers, priests and rabbis of the South would be among our strongest allies. Instead, some have been outright opponents, refusing to understand the freedom movement and misrepresenting its leaders; all too many others have been more cautious than courageous and have remained silent behind the anesthetizing security of stained-glass windows.

In spite of my shattered dreams, I came to Birmingham with the hope that the white religious leadership of this community would see the justice of our cause and, with deep moral concern, would serve as the channel through which our just grievances could reach the power structure. I had hoped that each of you would understand. But again I have been disappointed.

I have heard numerous southern religious leaders admonish their worshipers to comply with a desegregation decision because it is the law, but I have longed to hear white ministers declare: "Follow this decree because integration is morally right and because the Negro is your brother." In the midst of blatant injustices inflicted upon the Negro, I have watched white churchmen stand on the sideline and mouth pious irrelevancies and sanctimonious trivialities. In the midst of a mighty struggle to rid our nation of racial and economic injustice, I have heard many ministers say: "Those are social issues, with which the gospel has no real concern." And I have watched many churches commit themselves to a completely other-worldly religion which makes a strange, un-Biblical distinction between body and soul, between the sacred and the secular.

I have traveled the length and breadth of Alabama, Mississippi and all the other southern states. On sweltering summer days and crisp autumn mornings I have looked at the South's beautiful churches with their lofty spires pointing heavenward. I have beheld the impressive outlines of her massive religious-education buildings. Over and over I have found myself asking: "What kind of people worship here? Who is their God? Where were their voices when the lips of Governor Barnett dripped with words of interposition and nullification? Where were they when Governor Wallace gave a clarion call for defiance and hatred? Where were their voices of support when bruised and weary Negro men and women decided to rise from the dark dungeons of complacency to the bright hills of creative protest?"

Yes, these questions are still in my mind. In deep disappointment I have wept over the laxity of the church. But be assured that my tears have been tears of love. There can be no deep disappointment where there is not deep love. Yes, I love the church. How could I do otherwise? I am in the rather unique position of being the son, the grandson and the great-grandson of preachers. Yes, I see the church as the body of Christ. But, oh! How we have blemished and scarred that body through social neglect and through fear of being nonconformists.

There was a time when the church was very powerful—in the time when the early Christians rejoiced at being deemed worthy to suffer for what they believed. In those days the church was not merely a thermometer that recorded the ideas and principles of popular opinion; it was a thermostat that transformed the mores of society. Whenever the early Christians entered a town, the people in power became disturbed and immediately sought to convict the Christians for being "disturbers of the peace" and "outside agitators." But the Christians pressed on, in the conviction that they were "a colony of heaven," called to obey God rather than man. Small in number, they were big in commitment. They were too God-intoxicated to be "astronomically intimidated." By their effort and example they brought an end to such ancient evils as infanticide and gladiatorial contests.

Things are different now. So often the contemporary church is a weak, ineffectual voice with an uncertain sound. So often it is an archdefender of the status quo. Far from being disturbed by the presence of the church, the power structure of the average community is consoled by the church's silent—and often even vocal—sanction of things as they are.

But the judgment of God is upon the church as never before. If today's church does not recapture the sacrificial spirit of the early church, it will lose its authenticity, forfeit the loyalty of millions, and be dismissed as an irrelevant social club with no meaning for the twentieth century. Every day I meet young people whose disappointment with the church has turned into outright disgust.

Perhaps I have once again been too optimistic. Is organized religion too inextricably bound to the status quo to save our nation and the world? Perhaps I must turn my faith to the inner spiritual church, the church within the church, as the true *ekklesia* and the hope of the world. But again I am thankful to God that some noble souls from the ranks of organized religion have broken loose from the paralyzing chains of conformity and joined us as active partners in the struggle for freedom. They have left their secure congregations and walked the streets of Albany, Georgia, with us. They have gone down the highways of the South on tortuous rides for freedom. Yes, they have gone to jail with us. Some have been dismissed from their churches, have lost the support of their bishops and fellow ministers. But they have acted in the faith that right defeated is stronger than evil triumphant. Their witness has been the spiritual salt that has preserved the true meaning of the gospel in these troubled times. They have carved a tunnel of hope through the dark mountain of disappointment.

I hope the church as a whole will meet the challenge of this decisive hour. But even if the church does not come to the aid of justice, I have no despair about the future. I have no fear about the outcome of our struggle in Birmingham, even if our motives are at present misunderstood. We will reach the goal of freedom in Birmingham and all over the nation, because the goal of America is freedom. Abused and scorned though we may be, our destiny is tied up with America's destiny. Before the pilgrims landed at Plymouth, we were here. Before the pen of Jefferson etched the majestic words of the Declaration of Independence across the pages of history, we were here. For more than two centuries our forebears labored in this country without wages; they made cotton king; they built the homes of their masters while suffering gross injustice and shameful humiliation—and yet out of a bottomless vitality they continued to thrive and develop. If the inexpressible cruelties of slavery could not stop us, the opposition we now face will surely fail. We will win our freedom because the sacred heritage of our nation and the eternal will of God are embodied in our echoing demands.

Before closing I feel impelled to mention one other point in your statement that has troubled me profoundly. You warmly commended the Birmingham police force for keeping "order" and "preventing violence." I doubt that you would have so warmly commended the police force if you had seen its dogs sinking their teeth into unarmed, nonviolent Negroes. I doubt that you would so quickly commend the policemen if you were to observe their ugly and inhumane treatment of Negroes here in the city jail; if you were to watch them push and curse old Negro women and young Negro girls; if you were to see them slap and kick old Negro men and young boys; if you were to observe them, as they did on two occasions, refuse to give us food because we wanted to sing our grace together. I cannot join you in your praise of the Birmingham police department.

It is true that the police have exercised a degree of discipline in handling the demonstrators. In this sense they have conducted themselves rather "nonviolently" in public. But for what purpose? To preserve the evil system of segregation. Over the past few years I have consistently preached that nonviolence demands that the means we use must be as pure as the ends we seek. I have tried to make clear that it is wrong to use immoral means to attain moral ends. But now I must affirm that it is just as wrong, or perhaps even more so, to use moral means to preserve immoral ends. Perhaps Mr. Connor and his policemen have been rather nonviolent in public, as was Chief Pritchett in Albany, Georgia, but they have used the moral means of nonviolence to maintain the immoral end of racial injustice. As T. S. Eliot has said: "The last temptation is the greatest treason: To do the right deed for the wrong reason."

I wish you had commended the Negro sit-inners and demonstrators of Birmingham for their sublime courage, their willingness to suffer and their amazing discipline in the midst of great provocation. One day the South will recognize its real heroes. They will be the James Merediths, with the noble sense of purpose that enables them to face jeering and hostile mobs, and with the agonizing loneliness that characterizes the life of the pioneer. They will be old, oppressed, battered Negro women, symbolized in a seventy-two-year-old woman in Montgomery, Alabama, who rose up with a sense of dignity and with her people decided not to ride segregated buses, and who responded with ungrammatical profundity to one who inquired about her weariness: "My feets is tired, but my soul is at rest." They will be the young high school and college students, the young ministers of the gospel and a host of their elders, courageously and nonviolently sitting in at lunch counters and willingly going to jail for conscience' sake. One day the South will know that when the disinherited children of God sat down at lunch counters, they were in reality standing up for what is best in the American dream and for the most sacred values in our Judaeo-Christian heritage, thereby bringing our nation back to those great wells of democracy which were dug deep by the founding fathers in their formulation of the Constitution and the Declaration of Independence.

Never before have I written so long a letter. I'm afraid it is much too long to take your precious time. I can assure you that it would have been much shorter if I had been writing from a comfortable desk, but what else can one do when he is alone in a narrow jail cell, other than write long letters, think long thoughts and pray long prayers?

If I have said anything in this letter that overstates the truth and indicates an unreasonable impatience, I beg you to forgive me. If I have said anything that understates the truth and indicates my having a patience that allows me to settle for anything less than brotherhood, I beg God to forgive me.

I hope this letter finds you strong in the faith. I also hope that circumstances will soon make it possible for me to meet each of you, not as an integrationist or a civil-rights leader but as a fellow clergyman and a Christian brother. Let us all hope that the dark clouds of racial prejudice will soon pass away and the deep fog of misunderstanding will be lifted from our fear-drenched communities, and in some not too distant tomorrow the radiant stars of love and brotherhood will shine over our great nation with all their scintillating beauty.

Yours for the cause of Peace and Brotherhood,
MARTIN LUTHER KING, JR.

—MARTIN LUTHER KING, *Why We Can't Wait,* 1964

25. "We Face a Moral Crisis" June, 1963

John F. Kennedy

EDITORIAL NOTE: *All through 1963 disorder mounted in Alabama. One crisis had come with the jailing of the Reverend Dr. Martin Luther King. A second was the murder of the Baltimore mail-carrier, William Moore, who had set out on a one-man "freedom walk" to Mississippi. A third came with the effort of Governor Wallace to defy and frustrate the federal court order requiring the University of Alabama to admit Negro students. "I am the embodiment of the sovereignty of this State" said Governor Wallace, "and I will be present to bar the entrance of any Negro who attempts to enroll at the University of Alabama." When the Governor attempted to carry out this plan, President Kennedy federalized the National Guard and moved them into Tuscaloosa to keep order, and to protect the rights of Negro students. That evening, June 11, the President broadcast an appeal to the nation to end the shame of racial discrimination.*

No President had been more deeply committed to the principle of equality than John F. Kennedy, and that commitment was strengthened by his sense of history and his respect for the opinions of mankind. He knew that the United States was in danger of forfeiting her moral leadership in the free world by her policies of racism. None of Kennedy's addresses was marked by a loftier eloquence or a deeper passion than his plea for an end to discrimination and the enactment of a fair and just civil rights bill.

THIS AFTERNOON, FOLLOWING a series of threats and defiant statements, the presence of Alabama National Guardsmen was required at the University of Alabama to carry out the final and unequivocal order of the United States District Court of the Northern District of Alabama.

That order called for the admission of two clearly qualified young Alabama residents who happened to have been born Negro.

That they were admitted peacefully on the campus is due in a good measure to the conduct of the students of the University of Alabama who met their responsibilities in a constructive way.

I hope that every American, regardless of where he lives, will stop and examine his conscience about this and other related incidents.

This nation was founded by men of many nations and backgrounds. It was founded on the principle that all men are created equal, and that the rights of every man are diminished when the rights of one man are threatened.

Today we are committed to a worldwide struggle to promote and protect the rights of all who wish to be free. And when Americans are sent to Vietnam or West Berlin we do not ask for whites only.

It ought to be possible, therefore, for American students of any color to attend any public institution they select without having to be backed up by troops. It ought to be possible for American consumers of any color to receive equal service in places of public accommodation, such as hotels and restaurants, and theaters and retail stores without being forced to resort to demonstrations in the street.

And it ought to be possible for American citizens of any color to register and to vote in a free election without interference or fear of reprisal.

It ought to be possible, in short, for every American to enjoy the privileges of being American without regard to his race or his color.

In short, every American ought to have the right to be treated as he would wish to be treated, as one would wish his children to be treated. But this is not the case.

The Negro baby born in America today, regardless of the section or the state in which he is born, has about one-half as much chance of completing high school as a white baby, born in the same place, on the same day; one-third as much chance of completing college; one-third as much chance of becoming a professional man; twice as much chance of becoming unemployed; about one-seventh as much chance of earning $10,000 a year; a life expectancy which is seven years shorter and the prospects of earning only half as much.

This is not a sectional issue. Difficulties over segregation and discrimination exist in every city, in every state of the Union, producing in many cities a rising tide of discontent that threatens the public safety.

Nor is this a partisan issue. In a time of domestic crisis, men of good will and generosity should be able to unite regardless of party or politics.

This is not even a legal or legislative issue alone. It is better to settle these matters in the courts than on the streets, and new laws are needed at every level. But law alone cannot make men see right.

We are confronted primarily with a moral issue. It is as old as the Scriptures and is as clear as the American Constitution. The heart of the question is whether all Americans are to be afforded equal rights and equal opportunities; whether we are going to treat our fellow Americans as we want to be treated.

If an American, because his skin is dark, cannot eat lunch in a restaurant open to the public; if he cannot send his children to the best public school available; if he cannot vote for the public officials who represent him; if, in short, he cannot enjoy the full and free life which all of us want, then who among us would be content to have the color of his skin changed and stand in his place?

Who among us would then be content with the counsels of patience and delay? One hundred years of delay have passed since President Lincoln freed the slaves, yet their heirs, their grandsons, are not fully free. They are not yet freed from the bonds of injustice; they are not yet freed from social and economic oppression.

And this nation, for all its hopes and all its boasts, will not be fully free until all its citizens are free.

We preach freedom around the world, and we mean it. And we cherish our freedom here at home. But are we to say to the world—and much more importantly to each other—that this is the land of the free, except for the Negroes; that we have no second-class citizens, except Negroes; that we have no class or caste system, no ghettos, no master race, except with respect to Negroes.

Now the time has come for this nation to fulfill its promise. The events in Birmingham and elsewhere have so increased the cries for equality that no city or state or legislative body can prudently choose to ignore them.

The fires of frustration and discord are burning in every city, North and South. Where legal remedies are not at hand, redress is sought in the streets in demonstrations, parades and protests, which create tensions and threaten violence—and threaten lives.

We face, therefore, a moral crisis as a country and a people. It cannot be met by repressive police action. It cannot be left to increased demonstrations in the streets. It cannot be quieted by token moves or talk. It is time to act in the Congress, in your state and local legislative body, and above all, in all of our daily lives.

It is not enough to pin the blame on others, to say this is a problem of one section of the country or another, or deplore the facts that we face. A great change is at hand, and our task, our obligation is to make that revolution, that change peaceful and constructive for all.

Those who do nothing are inviting shame as well as violence. Those who act boldly are recognizing right as well as reality.

Next week I shall ask the Congress of the United States to act, to make a commitment it has not fully made in this century to the proposition that race has no place in American life or law.

The Federal judiciary has upheld that proposition in a series of forthright cases. The Executive Branch has adopted that proposition in the conduct of its affairs, including the employment of Federal personnel, and the use of Federal facilities, and the sale of Federally financed housing.

But there are other necessary measures which only the Congress can provide, and they must be provided at this session.

The old code of equity law under which we live commands for every wrong a remedy. But in too many communities, in too many parts of the country wrongs are inflicted on Negro citizens and there are no remedies in law.

Unless the Congress acts their only remedy is the street.

I am, therefore, asking the Congress to enact legislation giving all Americans the right to be served in facilities which are open to the public—hotels, restaurants and theaters, retail stores and similar establishments. This seems to me to be an elementary right.

Its denial is an arbitrary indignity that no American in 1963 should have to endure, but many do.

I have recently met with scores of business leaders, urging them to take voluntary action to end this discrimination. And I've been encouraged by their response. And in the last two weeks over 75 cities have seen progress made in desegregating these kinds of facilities.

But many are unwilling to act alone. And for this reason nationwide legislation is needed, if we are to move this problem from the streets to the courts.

I'm also asking Congress to authorize the Federal Government to participate more fully in lawsuits designed to end segregation in public education. We have succeeded in persuading many districts to desegregate voluntarily. Dozens have admitted Negroes without violence.

Today a Negro is attending a state-supported institution in every one of our 50 states. But the pace is very slow.

Too many Negro children entering segregated grade schools at the time of the Supreme Court's decision nine years ago will enter segregated high schools this fall, having suffered a loss which can never be restored.

The lack of an adequate education denies the Negro a chance to get a decent job. The orderly implementation of the Supreme Court decision therefore, cannot be left solely to those who may not have the economic resources to carry their legal action or who may be subject to harassment.

Other features will also be requested, including greater protection for the right to vote.

But legislation, I repeat, cannot solve this problem alone. It must be solved in the homes of every American in every community across our country.

In this respect, I want to pay tribute to those citizens, North and South, who've been working in their communities to make life better for all. They are acting not out of a sense of legal duty but out of a sense of human decency. Like our soldiers and sailors in all parts of the world, they are meeting freedom's challenge on the firing line and I salute them for their honor—their courage.

My fellow Americans, this is a problem which faces us all, in every city of the North as well as the South.

Today there are Negroes unemployed, two or three times as many compared to whites, inadequate in education, moving into the large cities, unable to find work, young people particularly out of work, without hope, denied equal rights, denied the opportunity to eat at a restaurant or a lunch counter, or go to a movie theater, denied the right to a decent education, denied the right to attend a state university even though qualified.

It seems to me that these are matters which concern us all—not merely Presidents, or Congressmen, or Governors, but every citizen of the United States.

This is one country. It has become one country because all of us and all the people who came here had an equal chance to develop their talents.

We cannot say to 10 percent of the population that "you can't have that right. Your children can't have the chance to develop whatever talents they have, that the only way that they're going to get their rights is to go in the street and demonstrate."

I think we owe them and we owe ourselves a better country than that.

Therefore, I'm asking for your help in making it easier for us to move ahead and provide the kind of equality of treatment which we would want ourselves—to give a chance for every child to be educated to the limit of his talent.

As I've said before, not every child has an equal talent or an equal ability or equal motivation. But they should have the equal right to develop their talent and their ability and their motivation to make something of themselves.

We have a right to expect that the Negro community will be responsible, will uphold the law. But they have a right to expect the law will be fair, that the Constitution will be color blind, as Justice Harlan said at the turn of the century.

This is what we're talking about. This is a matter which concerns this country and what it stands for, and in meeting it I ask the support of all our citizens.

Thank you very much.

—JOHN F. KENNEDY, radio and television address, June 11, 1963

26. Tragedy in Birmingham

James Reston

EDITORIAL NOTE: *The summer of 1963 saw a brief abatement of the racial crisis in Birmingham, but trouble flared up again in the fall with the token desegregation of some public schools. On Sunday morning, September 15, came another crisis in the struggle, one which horrified the whole nation. That morning someone hurled a bomb into the Negro Baptist Church, destroying the church, killing four little girls and wounding fourteen others who were attending Sunday School. "This is the most distressing day in the history of Birmingham," said Sheriff Bailey, but no one was ever arrested for the murder, and Birmingham itself quickly closed ranks in self-defense and self-approval. When a young lawyer, Charles Morgan Jr., charged the whole of Birmingham with responsibility for the crime, he was ostracized and finally driven out of the city. The distinguished reporter for* The New York Times, *James Reston, here tries to explain the Birmingham state of mind.*

BIRMINGHAM, SEPT. 19. THE STRIKING THING about Birmingham to an outsider is that it seems so advanced industrially and so retarded politically. It has seized the scientific revolution and rejected the social revolution of our time. Accordingly, it is engaged in a remarkable and hazardous experiment: it is trying to back full speed into the future.

The visible and audible symbols of the city dramatize this paradox. It lies in a long valley surrounded by lovely flowering hills. Above the forest of smoking chimneys stands on a peak a vast stainless steel statue of Vulcan, like some hideous modernistic monster out of the German Ruhr.

Yet down below in the city the symbols are not of the fires of the future but of the fires of the past. The Confederate flag is painted on the cars and helmets of Gov. George Wallace's state troopers, now very much in evidence here, and the biggest clock in town booms out across the city from the tower of the Protective Life Insurance Company a few bars of "Dixie" before it strikes each hour.

Look to the industrial future, says the gleaming Vulcan. "Look away, look away, look away, Dixie Land,' chimes the clock.

THE HISTORICAL BACKGROUND

That Birmingham should have become the symbol of Southern defiance adds to the paradox, for it did not come out of the tradition of the old agrarian, slave-holding, plantation South. It was not even incorporated until December, 1871, in the decade after the War Between the States; it was populated from the North more than almost any Southern city, and its commercial and industrial ties now run to New York and Pittsburgh rather than to Atlanta or New Orleans.

Like most industrial cities it does have a tradition of putting private interests above public interests and it does have a history of violence. It was for many years an overgrown mining camp, populated by rough men from all sections of the country. Convict labor from the state prisons worked in the mines until the early 1920's, and National Guardsmen first went on strike patrol during the coal miners' walkout here in 1894.

Thus Birmingham is not like any other city in the country. Industrially it is ahead of much of the North; politically it is behind most of the urban South. It pays its Negroes better and in some ways treats them worse than most Southern towns, partly because it suffers from some of the worst aspects of both industrialization and segregation.

No generalization about Birmingham is safe, but its history does help suggest one possible explanation about the present attitude of many of its most influential leaders. This is not a city dominated by inherited wealth. More than in most Southern cities, Birmingham's commercial and industrial leaders are self-made men, with the self-made man's feeling that others can be just as successful too if they will only work.

Many white leaders here created their own fortunes, others are managers under pressure from Northern headquarters to produce the maximum at the minimum cost.

As human beings, they are probably no better or worse than business leaders in other cities, but there is something in the history and atmosphere of this place, some relationship between the idea of the supremacy of the dollar and the supremacy of the white man, that has made them feel they could hold out longer against social change.

It isn't that they wanted more than other white leaders in Atlanta and elsewhere, but merely that in this particular city they thought they could get away with demanding more.

THE COUNTER-PRESSURE

The result is that the leaders of Birmingham are trapped for the time being in the struggle. For the more they have delayed making concessions to Negro equality, the more the Federal Government has dramatized their dilemma, and the more the Negroes have demanded, and the more business the city has lost.

The death of the four Negro children in this week's bombing of a Negro church has merely brought all this to a head. It has shocked the community, but there is little evidence that it has changed the convictions of the white leaders about what they regard as the proper (separate) relations between the races.

They merely seem a little more convinced now that the continued uproar here is not good business, and Birmingham wants good business, even if it has to obey the Federal law to get it.

—JAMES RESTON, in *The New York Times,* September 20, 1963

27. Official Lawlessness in the South

Anthony Lewis

EDITORIAL NOTE: *The American constitutional system is full of inconsistencies. It is a system where fundamental rights are protected by the Constitution and the Bill of Rights, and guaranteed to every American by federal law and federal courts; it is, at the same time, a federal system, where responsibility for law enforcement is State and local. The federal government does not have any effective law enforcement agencies—the FBI disclaims that role—but depends almost entirely on local and state officials and, in the first instance, on State courts. Ours is, too, a "government of laws and not of men," but it is one where public opinion—which is mostly local opinion—profoundly conditions law enforcement. It is, finally, a system not only of formal checks and balances, but of built-in delays and frustrations. Thus it has always been possible for local minorities who feel strongly about some issue—The Fugitive Slave law, for example, or the rights of labor, or prohibition—to defeat and even nullify the will of national majorities. It should not surprise us that many Southern communities were able to frustrate the decision of the Court in Brown* v. *Topeka; after all, the South has been frustrating the clear meaning of the Fourteenth and Fifteenth Amendments for almost a century.*

This description of the workings of official nullification of the law in the Deep South comes from The New York Times*'s constitutional expert, Anthony Lewis.*

ON SEPTEMBER 19, 1963, twelve Negro residents of Clinton, Louisiana, wrote letters to the mayor and the district attorney requesting the appointment of a bi-racial committee on community relations. They suggested respectfully that such a committee could give "careful consideration of the many problems facing our community" and would help "to avoid civil domestic disturbances of racial tension." One of the writers was a seventy-five-year-old woman, a lifelong resident of the area; another was the husband of the superintendent of the local Negro schools.

The response came on December 3rd, when the twelve Negroes were arrested. The charge was intimidating public officials; bail was set at four thousand dollars each. Somehow the defendants managed to raise the money; but they must await trial.

In Itta Bena, Mississippi, a group of Negroes marched to the home of the deputy sheriff on the night of June 18, 1963, to ask for police protection against harassment of a voter-registration campaign. Fifty-seven were arrested and charged with disturbing the peace. After a night in jail, forty-five of them—all but those less than fifteen years old—were tried by a justice of the peace. They had no lawyer, and no evidence was introduced connecting any individual defendant with illegal action. It took just over an hour for the trial, conviction and sentences. Every man was given a sentence of six months in jail and a fine of five hundred dollars. (The fine amounted to five and one-half months more in jail, at the Mississippi rate of three dollars a day to work off fines, because these impoverished people could not pay.) Each woman was sentenced to four months and two hundred dollars.

To go free while they tried to appeal, the defendants had to produce appeal bonds—fixed at seven hundred and fifty dollars for the men, five hundred dollars for the women. They could not raise that money, and so they were imprisoned, some in the quarters and conditions of chain gangs. Two months later, at the urging of Attorney General Robert F. Kennedy, the National Council of the Churches of Christ in America put up the cash, a New York insurance company wrote a bond, and the defendants were released. At a new trial before a jury they were convicted again. They then appealed to a circuit court. If they lose there, they must go next to the Mississippi Supreme Court. Then they can seek review in the Supreme Court of the United States.

The events in Clinton and Itta Bena were not isolated incidents.

Again and again today Negroes in certain parts of the South find themselves caught up in the machinery of the criminal law because of entirely innocent acts—that is, acts that would be innocent anywhere else. A man appeals for help to an official, supposedly his public servant. The next thing he knows he is charged with a crime, arrested, convicted on no evidence of anything that constitutionally can be a crime, held on bail that is difficult or impossible for him to raise, forced to go through a long and frustrating and expensive legal process before someone—probably the Supreme Court—ends the lawless course of law.

The Clinton and Itta Bena cases illustrate a particularly disturbing aspect of southern resistance to change in race relations—corruption of the processes of law. Corruption is not too strong a word; it is used by a gentle man given to understatement, Burke Marshall, the head of the Justice Department's Civil Rights Division, who often gets appeals for help from persons caught up in this kind of southern justice. Not all of the South has forgotten this country's commitment to law; but in Mississippi, Alabama and sections of some other states today, men sworn to exalt the law ruthlessly and cynically misuse it in order to repress the Negro's demand for rights.

The cynicism can be so pervasive that it seems absurd and outrageous. Consider what has happened in the last few years to Aaron Henry, a Negro pharmacist in Clarksdale, Mississippi, and a local official of the Nationsl Association for the Advancement of Colored People. In 1961, after some freedom riders tried to desegregate the railroad waiting room in Clarksdale, the county prosecutor, Thomas Pearson, called Mr. Henry in for questioning about his asserted attempts to "disturb" existing race relations. In January, 1962, when Negroes held off buying from Clarksdale stores that discriminated against them, Mr. Henry was charged with a conspiracy in restraint of trade; the prosecution is still pending. In March of that year he was accused of an indecent assault on an itinerant eighteen-year-old white youth who had allegedly hitched a ride with him; he was convicted and sentenced to two months in jail, but the Supreme Court agreed to review the conviction the next term. Mr. Henry accused Prosecutor Pearson and the Clarksdale police chief, Benford Collins, of dreaming up that charge, and they promptly sued him for libel; a jury awarded them all they asked, forty thousand dollars, the Mississippi Supreme Court affirmed that judgment and the case is now pending in the U.S. Supreme Court. In June, 1962, Mr. Henry's wife was dismissed from her job as a local public-school teacher; she brought suit in a federal court, and the case is still pending. In March, 1963, Mr. Henry's home was bombed. Two men admitted the crime, but one was acquitted by a jury and the charge against the other was then dropped; the district attorney in charge of the prosecution complained in open court that Prosecutor Pearson had tried to persuade a witness not to testify against the arsonist. In June, 1963, Mr. Henry was convicted of "parading without a permit" when he picketed City Hall to protest segregation; that conviction is on appeal. After the bombing of his home, Mr. Henry obtained a permit for a revolver and hired a private watchman at his home. On the night of July 30, 1963, Police Chief Collins arrested the watchman for possession of a concealed weapon—the revolver, which he had left on the seat of a car parked in the driveway—and confiscated the revolver.

It is not only stubborn Negro leaders of civil-rights organizations who meet such tactics. "A very proper midwestern law professor," as he was once described, ran into them in the summer of 1963. He was Charles Oldfather of the University of Kansas, a white man who had never before imagined the world in which some southern Negroes live. His daughter Felicia, president of the student body at Carleton College, went down to Albany, Georgia, to help the Negro movement that summer. She was arrested and charged with "vagrancy," and Professor Oldfather went down to Albany to help her. He watched the trial and was surprised to find her convicted despite testimony that he was supporting her. Felicia decided to leave Albany, and Professor Oldfather drove her car over to the Negro section to pick up her belongings. This is what happened next, in his words: "As I was heading back downtown, I was motioned over to the curb by two officers in a county police car. After my driver's license was examined, I was instructed to get out of the car and to put my hands on the roof. I was frisked, my wrists were handcuffed behind my back and I was driven to the county jail in the police car. . . .

"Inquiry disclosed that I was being arrested for driving a car with a bad muffler, and that the car was impounded. . . . The arresting officer, when he had finished questioning me, walked across the room to a desk where he engaged another man in conversation. He punctuated the end of his conversation by taking a sap [blackjack] out of his hip pocket, slamming it onto the top of the desk and looking meaningfully at me."

When Professor Oldfather told the police that he was planning to leave Albany with his daughter, he was immediately released and the car returned to him. He is not likely to forget that in the year 1963, in the United States, he was arrested in handcuffs for supposedly driving a car with a faulty muffler.

Physical brutality is not only threatened by law-enforcement officials. John Frazier, a Negro college student from Greenville, Mississippi, took a bus from Atlanta to Greenville on August 26, 1960. He sat up front despite warnings from the driver. At several stops in Mississippi the driver got off. Then, at Winona, the sheriff and a deputy met the bus, and they said: "Nigger, we want to see you." According to Frazier's sworn testimony, the deputy began beating him with a blackjack and the sheriff with his fists, one of them saying: "You had no business sitting at the front of that bus. You know you are a Mississippi nigger, and that does not work here." Mr. Frazier lost consciousness during the beating and came to in a police car on the way to jail. There a doctor treated him. He was charged with disturbing the peace and resisting arrest. The next morning he was allowed to telephone a friend in Jackson to ask for a lawyer's help, but as he started to tell the story of what had happened the telephone was taken from his hand and he was beaten again. The doctor came back and stopped a nose bleed. Mr. Frazier was eventually tried, convicted and released on two thousand dollars' bond pending appeal.

When John Frazier took that bus ride, it had been the law of this country for fourteen years that racial segregation could not be practiced in interstate commerce. The sheriff who arrested him and the judge who convicted him knew that that was the law, but they were not interested. Like so many of their brethren in that part of the South they were dedicated to defeating that federal law and preserving the white supremacy called for by the unconstitutional statutes and customs of Mississippi.

Law in these instances has become the instrument of the ruling class in a caste system. It has become, really, the Marxist idea of law, as officially defined by the Soviet Union in 1938: "Law is a combination of the rules of behavior established or sanctioned by state authority, reflecting the will of the ruling class—rules of behavior whose application is assured by the coercive power of the state for the purpose of protecting, strengthening and developing relationships and procedures suitable and beneficial to the ruling class."

It is important to recognize that defiance of federal law is not just an occasional aberration by an occasional southern police officer. There are places where there is a wholesale perversion of justice, from bottom to top, from police force to supreme court.

The police, for example. On May 8, 1963, a gasoline bomb was thrown into the home of a leading Negro citizen of Holmes County, Mississippi, who headed a voter-registration campaign. The next day he and his common-law wife were arrested and charged with arson of their own home; four student workers were charged with the same crime, and one with obstructing the investigation by photographing the burned house. Eventually the arson charges were dismissed for lack of evidence—there never had been any. By then the man and his wife had gone through a formal marriage ceremony some months earlier. But the local grand jury that looked into the fire indicted them for unlawful cohabitation. Although they were advised that this charge could not legally apply so far back in time, they decided it would be easier to plead guilty and pay a hundred-dollar fine.

And mayors. In Ruleville, Mississippi, on August 6, 1963, Mayor Charles Dorrough arrested three Negro student voting workers because they were accompanying frightened local Negroes to the polls. The mayor was acting in the capacity of police chief, and the formal charge he placed was conspiracy to commit an unstated offense. The students were taken to the town hall, tried by the mayor in his capacity as police magistrate, convicted, given a sentence of thirty days and a fine of one-hundred dollars each. At the "trial" the mayor commented that there was no need to take any testimony, since everyone knew what had happened. The cases were then appealed.

And voting registrars. Among others there is the story, told in

Chapter 8, of John Hardy—the student who was pistol-whipped by the registrar when he tried to help two Negroes register in Walthall County, Mississippi.

And prosecutors. In Americus, Georgia, on August 8, 1963, four student civil-rights workers, white and Negro, were charged with "insurrection" under a Georgia statute that the Supreme Court had held unconstitutional in 1937. Because this offense was punishable by death, they were denied bail. After they had been in jail two months, the prosecutor, Stephen Pace, stated frankly that he had brought the charge in the hope not of obtaining constitutional convictions but of discouraging civil-rights activities. He said: "The basic reason for bringing these charges was to deny the defendants, or ask the court to deny them, bond. We were in hopes that by holding these men, we would be able to talk to their lawyers and talk to their people and convince them that this type of activity is not the right way to go about it." The defendants stayed in jail until a federal court ordered them released in January, 1964.

And judges. Judge Durwood T. Pye of Atlanta conducted a series of trials in 1963 and 1964 of persons charged with trespass for sit-in demonstrations. He sentenced Ashton Jones, a sixty-seven-year-old white minister from California, to a year and a half in prison and a thousand-dollar fine for helping some Negroes attempt to gain entry to a white church. Then Judge Pye set bail at twenty thousand dollars. The Georgia Supreme Court found that excessive and ordered it reduced to five thousand dollars. Mr. Jones's wife came from California with five thousand dollars, but Judge Pye refused to accept cash, saying only Georgia real estate would do for bond. After Mr. Jones had been in prison seven months, a white Atlanta woman pledged her property for the bail and he was released.

Judge Pye also gave an eighteen-month sentence—six in the common jail and twelve on the public works—to an eighteen-year-old white girl, Mardon Walker of Connecticut College for Women. She was convicted of trespass after a sit-in attempt at a restaurant. Despite the Georgia Supreme Court's bail ruling in the Reverend Walker's case, he fixed her bond at fifteen thousand dollars. Two citizens of Atlanta put that up.

The prosecutions of freedom riders in Jackson, Mississippi, show how an entire local system of courts can work with lawless law-enforcement officials to make federal rights virtually meaningless. In 1961, three hundred and three persons were arrested in Jackson for trying to use the interstate bus terminal on a desegregated basis. Everyone knew that segregation in the terminal was unlawful; in addition to the constitutional decisions of the Supreme Court as to any state-enforced racial discrimination, the Interstate Commission had issued specific rules against terminal segregation. The freedom riders who tried to exercise these rights were charged with breach of the peace. Eventually, as anyone must have known, the charges could not stand because there was simply no evidence to support them. But the Mississippi court system made it clear that anyone who really wanted to enforce his federal rights would have to go all the way to the Supreme Court of the United States—and that it would take a long time, and much expense and trouble, to get there.

The authorities insisted that every one of the arrested persons have a separate trial, although there was no legally relevant difference in the facts of the cases. This meant that, instead of a single test case, every defendant had to retain a lawyer and personally return to Jackson for a trial—and then, if he persisted, a new trial on appeal. Counsel mostly had to be brought from far away also, for no white lawyer in Mississippi will handle a civil-rights case and there are only four Negro lawyers who will. The Mississippi courts also fixed bail of fifteen hundred dollars in most cases, a total of $372,000 for the group. The three hundred and four licensed Mississippi surety companies refused to write bail bonds.

Fifty-six of the defendants gave up in the face of these tactics, accepted suspended sentences and paid two-hundred-dollar fines for their crime of believing that federal law applied in Mississippi. The others fought on. Most drew sentences of four months in jail and a five-hundred-dollar fine. Their cases had to go through the city court, county court, circuit court and supreme court of Mississippi. On June 13, 1964, the first twenty-nine petitioned the Supreme Court of the United States. They were able to do so at last because their convictions had been affirmed by the Mississippi Supreme Court in an opinion saying that no "abject surrender" of racial customs "should be expected, much less demanded."

Among state supreme courts, Alabama's has a particularly notable record for cynical disregard of federal law. For more than six years it prevented a final ruling on the right of the National Association for the Advancement of Colored People to operate in Alabama—and during that time the N.A.A.C.P. was barred by a "temporary" restraining order from doing business in the state. The ground advanced by the state for ousting the association, that it had not signed a registration form and paid a ten-dollar fee, was found patently unconstitutional by the Supreme Court of the United States in June, 1964. But that was the fourth Supreme Court decision required in the case, and there was no assurance that more may not be needed. Once the Alabama Supreme Court threw out an N.A.A.C.P. appeal on the ground that the wrong form of writ had been used. The U.S. Supreme Court found that ground frivolous, but the Alabama court at first refused to follow the ruling, saying the Supreme Court had been misinformed. A second Supreme Court decision was followed by years of delay, a third warning from Washington and, finally, the first hearing for the N.A.A.C.P. in Alabama. The state supreme court then again refused to pass on the merits of the case, finding this time that the association's lawyers had written their brief in the wrong order. When the case was argued before the U.S. Supreme Court, the lawyer for Alabama found himself embarrassedly unable to explain his own court's decision.

And governors. Again and again such southern governors as George Wallace of Alabama have told their people that federal law need not be obeyed, that decisions of the highest court in the land are not binding, that there is some "legal" way to resist laws one does not like. They have made lawlessness respectable.

And legislators. The legislatures of several southern states attempted to deal with federal measures against racial discrimination by passing transparently invalid statutes purporting to make the exercise of federal rights a state crime. A Mississippi statute declared it a crime to make false statements to any federal official; it was left to state law-enforcement processes to decide what was "false," and the statute added that the assertedly false statement need not be "material" to be punished. When Mississippi officials invoked this statute against two Negroes who testified in the federal courts about voting discrimination, the Justice Department moved to block the state prosecution as an unconstitutional attempt at intimidation.

And all state officials, it must be remembered—legislators and governors and prosecutors and judges—are bound by oath to support the Constitution of the United States.

—Anthony Lewis in *The New York Times, Portrait of a Decade: The Second American Revolution*, 1964

28. Official Lawlessness: A Documentary Record

EDITORIAL NOTE: *The Southern Regional Council, a biracial organization of liberal Southerners dedicated to ameliorating the racial tensions of the South, collected these affidavits from victims of official lawlessness in several Southern states during the crisis of the sixties. These, and scores of others, were published in the SRC's official journal,* New South.

DOCUMENT NO. 20:

ON FRIDAY NIGHT, October 27, 1961, a group of Negroes were at a Negro cafe in Birmingham, Ala. One of them reportedly made the remark that if the colored women were not intercoursing with the policemen, the nigger men were pimping with them. The owner of the cafe reportedly called the police, and two policemen soon came . . . They lined up all the Negroes around the wall of the cafe and stationed a police dog at the door . . . and told him to sit there and watch. Then they tried to find out who made the statement. They threatened to turn the dog loose on all the Negroes if they did not tell who made the statement about the policemen.

Kennon Travis was not there, but somehow his name was brought up, and the policemen went to his home looking for him. Mr. Phillip Travis, Sr. and Mrs. Travis tell what happened after that.

On Oct. 28, 1961, at about 2:00 in the morning, a Birmingham policeman . . . knocked on my door and asked if my son Kennon (19) was home. I said he was. The officer said he wanted him. I asked him if he had a warrant, and he said he didn't need no damn warrant. But [the] officer . . . broke open the screen door, broke open the front door, and came in with his pistol in his hand and said "Where's the boy?" I was in my pajamas and my wife was also. She did not have a chance even to put on her house coat. Kennon came to a room door in the front room and said, "Here I am." The officer then struck him on the head with his gun. When he struck him he said, "Nigger you make a damn good speech." I told the officers not to hit him, and he turned toward me with his pistol pointed at me. I grabbed the gun and when I saw that he was trying to point the pistol at my chest, I pushed his hand toward the ceiling and we began to scuffle. We scuffled across the dining room. My oldest son Phillip, Jr. (24) was awakened by the noise and came to see what was happening. By this time [another] officer . . . came in and fired his pistol toward the floor. Then he struck Phillip Jr. on the head with his pistol, opening a bloody wound. Phillip had not said or done anything at all. While I was struggling to keep Officer Jones from shooting me. Officer King struck me on the head with his pistol, knocking me unconscious. I fell down by the dining room table. Then while I was unconscious on the floor the [first] officer . . . backed away and shot me. The bullet entered my upper right thigh and came out through my left buttock.

Kennon got our rifle because he said they have killed my father. My wife made him put it down and made him go out and get into the police car. But when she tried to come back into the house, the officer cursed her and refused to allow her to enter *her own home,* so she had to go across the street to a neighbor's house in her night clothes . . . [he] called more policemen and soon there were about seven more police cars at the scene.

The officers took away my two oldest sons and my daughter. She had seen everything and had said she was going to call our lawyer and tell him everything. Then they decided to take her for questioning. Neither I nor my wife knew where they were taking them, nor why. Then around 5:00 a.m. they came and took my wife away to the City Hall in Birmingham. She saw that they had brought them there also. We have three other young children at the house aged 10, 12, and 14, and they were awakened by the noise and saw everything.

They can never forget such a scene. The house was one bloody mess.

I was taken to a hospital. After the ambulance left, my wife was allowed to come back into the house. They beat Kennon in the police car and knocked him unconscious. I had to have 14 stitches in my head and had to be hospitalized with a gunshot wound. All this happened on my birthday. Though holes had been knocked into my two sons' heads, they were not given medical attention.

I was not arrested at the time. But at the trial on Nov. 14, I was arrested and charged with interferring with an officer. Phillip Jr. was charged with interfering with an officer. Kennon was charged with disorderly conduct, resisting arrest, and presenting firearms.

I have never had any trouble with the law before in my life. But I could not stand by and watch an officer attack my son for no reason whatever. On July 1, this year, [the same] officer came to our house late at night, walked in and got Kennon out of bed. My wife and I wanted to know what they wanted with him, and he said that they just wanted to talk to him out in the car. But when they got him in the car, they took him away and beat him. So I would not let them take him out again unless they had a warrant. My son Phillip served his country for three years and nine months in the U.S. Air Force, but not to preserve racial injustice. We have filed a complaint with the F.B.I.

PHILLIP TRAVIS
MRS. MARGARET TRAVIS
VERNA TRAVIS
KENNON TRAVIS
PHILLIP TRAVIS, JR.

DOCUMENT NO. 25:

On Monday morning, May 28, 1962, at around 2:30 a.m., I was at a filling station located at 16th Street and 4th Ave. North in Birmingham. An officer came by on a motorcycle and asked whose car I was in. I said it was mine. He said, "boy, who you done robbed?" I said, "Nobody." He called other policemen and two

Birmingham policemen in uniform . . . came to the filling station and picked me up. They took me to a place on 9th Alley and 16th Street North. They parked their car between a railroad car and a fence. They asked me about old times. They talked threateningly. One of them said they had it all set up to kill me, but I did not walk into it. They asked me where I lived. When I told them they contradicted me and started beating me. They beat me all over the car. One of them jammed the car door against me, pinning me in the car. While he held the door against me, the other one beat me with his stick. I was able to block most of the head blows. He asked me did it feel good. He beat me on my arms and shoulders with his stick, and he must have struck me at least twenty solid blows. He asked me did that feel good. They kicked me all over the body and tried to kick me between the legs. They pinned me on the trunk of the car and then knocked me over to the other side of the car. They threw me under a boxcar on the tracks and one of them kicked me hard in the side. They slammed me against the fence and punched me in the body with their night sticks. One of my eyes were badly damaged . . .

Then they took me to jail and one of them hit me as I was going from the car to the jailhouse. Before they took me to jail, one of them asked the other, "What charge shall we put on this ________?" The other one said he didn't know. They both decided they would charge me with grand larceny from person. This was what they charged me with at the jail. They did not take me to the hospital . . .

That morning at the jail I passed out. I was taken to University Hospital in Birmingham that same morning at around 11:00. The doctor had to go into my chest with a needle. Every time I breathed, it made a bubbling sound in my chest. After he drew something out of my chest with a needle, I could breathe better.

I was released from the hospital on Tuesday, May 29, to go back to the jail. And that same Tuesday night at 9:40, *I was released from jail with no charges!* . . .

I am a veteran, having served in the armed forces from 1942 to 1948. On Friday morning, June 1, my eye and head pained me so that I went back to University Hospital. But they refused to treat me because I would not sign to pay the bills. I went to the V.A. Hospital and they found that I had three broken ribs. They sent me back to University Hospital and I am being treated there now. A muscle of my right eye was dislocated, causing me to have double vision. I am to undergo brain surgery at University Hospital on June 29.

WILLIE E. BOYD

DOCUMENT NO. 26:

On Thursday, March 1, 1962, at around 9:00 p.m., I was sitting in a cafe located on Ave. D and 18th Street in Ensley. (It has since been torn down.) An officer in uniform, of the Birmingham Police Department, came in and stood in the front of the cafe looking around. I was drinking a beer, but I was not drunk. Then the officer . . . came over to me and tapped me on the shoulder and said, "Come here boy." He asked for my driver's license. I showed it to him. Then he said, "Let's go outside." I said I didn't see why I should go outside because I was only having a beer. He did not say I was under arrest and he did not say why he wanted me to go outside. I have never had an officer ask for my driver's license unless I was in an automobile. I don't know why he bothered me.

I refused to go outside and he didn't say anything more but started shooting. If he had said I was under arrest, I would have gone with him. But he just asked me to come outside with him, and when I asked why I should go outside, he started shooting. I did not put my hands on him. He shot me in the side, shoulder, and wrist. I fell to the floor and was later taken to the hospital. I gave this statement to Rev. Oliver on April 5 while I was in the hospital. I have also given substantially the same story to the FBI.

I was charged with resisting arrest, assault and battery, and public drunkenness. On May 24, 1962, I was tried before Judge Ross Bell at the City Hall in Ensley. Even though two witnesses testified that I was not drunk and was not resisting arrest, and only the officer testified that I was drunk and resisting arrest, I was found guilty on both counts. The assault and battery charge was dropped. My hospital bill came to $1400.00, and $1200.00 of it was covered by insurance. But even though an insurance company paid most of my bill, I was still found guilty by the judge, and I am now trying to get enough money to pay a lawyer to appeal my case.

JIM MCCRORY

DOCUMENT NO. 64:

My name is Bennie J. Luchion. I am from New Orleans. I have been in Gadsden since May, 1963. I am a field worker for the Southern Christian Leadership Conference. I have been arrested six times in Etowah County seeking freedom in Alabama.

On June 15, 1963 I participated in a sit-in at Snellgrove Drug Store in Gadsden. When the police came to arrest me, I went limp and laid on the floor. An officer stood on my neck. I was taken to the city jail and was punched in the face and head by an officer . . . I fell to the floor and was kicked in the stomach.

On June 18, 1963, while being arrested again in Gadsden, I went limp. An officer pinned me against a police car and pushed a cattle prod to the base of my spine and held it there while the shock continued to go through my body. Then as I was getting into the car, I was prodded again. They took me to jail where they prodded me again and dragged me on the elevator.

On another occasion when I was in jail at Camp Gadsden, they wanted to separate me from the other prisoners and take me to the County Jail, but I refused. Then they came and applied the prod to my genitals and then took me back to the County Jail. That night at the County Jail officers came and took out Nathaniel Gaston and worked him over with the prods. Then one of the officers recognized me and said, "There's Bennie that gave us much trouble at Camp Gadsden." They called me out. I had been washing my socks and my hands were wet and also the front of my shirt and pants. I was prodded, pushed to the floor and pinned against an iron door. Because I was wet and up against an iron door, it was by far the most terrible experience I have been through so far. I managed to get hold of both prods and I held them off my stomach, but they began beating me with flashlights. I finally broke away and ran back into the cell and they did not come after me again.

One day in July 1963 I was canvassing for voter registration in Attalla, Alabama, and was picked up along with about five others and taken to the City Hall in Attalla. The Police Chief tried to make me say who I was and where I was from, but I would not say. He stomped on my toes and kicked my shins but still I would not say. Then he got out a brand new prod and applied it to me several times, but I took it. I began to get weaker and dizzy, but I tried to take it. Then when he put it to my genitals I said to him, "What about your God?" He stopped but threatened to put the Klan on me. We were not released till dark, and for about two days I was in a daze as the result of the prod treatment given to me by the Police Chief.

On August 3, 1963 during the march to the Coliseum, I was prodded many times in the rectum. These are a few of the brutalities I have experienced in the last several months in Etowah County. I have had to undergo special medical treatment as a result of the brutalities.

BENNIE J. LUCHION

DOCUMENT NO. 65:

My name is Willie James Grayer. I was born and reared in Gadsden. I have been arrested several times in Gadsden for protesting segregation. I have been prodded more times than I can remember.

On Friday, July 19, 1963 I went to the Court House in Gadsden to find out what a friend of mine was charged with. An officer on the outside stopped me and asked me what I was doing downtown. He asked if I wanted to go home or go to jail. I said it didn't make any difference. He told me to go home and said to go down Forest Avenue away from the downtown section. He refused to let me enter the Court House which I helped to pay for. I left, but I went toward town. Then he and another policeman came in a police car and picked me up and took me to jail. While still in the car, they used a cattle prod on me between my legs. They took me inside. As we were going up on the elevator they asked me about another person, but I said I did not know him. They said I was one of them damn smart niggers and that I was lying. Then they stopped the elevator between the third and fourth floors and beat me with their fists and they used the prods on me again, on my stomach, on my neck, on my genitals. That night my genitals swole up. I got out the next day, but since then I have suffered pain there from time to time and occasional bleeding. I have had medical attention and have been assured that I would get over it. But it was a very painful thing to have to suffer for the cause of freedom. I am not discouraged.

WILLIE JAMES GRAYER

DOCUMENT NO. 68:

My name is James Eddie Steele (20). I live at 1116 Coosa St. I was born and reared in Birmingham, and have completed two years of study at Alabama State College in Montgomery. I stayed out of college during the current term in order to have money to return to school.

On the evening of May 24, 1964 I went to visit my girl friend, Gloria Cauthen, at her home at 3928 No. 29th Ave. . . . At around 20 minutes or quarter to eleven, I left her house to go home. I had to take the car to my mother so she could go to work. I got in my car and drove off, going east on 29th Ave. I did not notice any police car following me. I turned right at Bethel Baptist Church and drove three short blocks to the intersection of 33rd St. and Vanderbilt Road. There is a speed breaker within that short distance. When I got to Vanderbilt Road and stopped at the intersection, a police car drove up beside me with the red light flashing. They told me to get out with my hands up. I did so. They searched me and told me to get into the police car. I did so. They asked for my driver's license which I gave to them. They asked whose car I had and where I was going, which I told them.

Then they asked if I knew I was going 90 miles an hour. This was impossible in the short distance I drove. I said I was not doing 90 miles an hour. They accused me of calling them a liar, and one of them struck me in the mouth with his fist. I asked why they were giving me a ticket for nothing. They said I was calling them a lie and one of them struck me in the eye with his fist. They gave me a choice of going to jail or accepting a ticket, but I insisted that I had not done anything, and I did not sign the ticket. . . . I was struck again, and one of them said, "Nigger, you're going to jail." I was jerked out of the car and both of them beat me with their fists and drove their knees into my body. I heard a voice say, "Don't beat him any more." They handcuffed my hands behind me and shoved me into their car. One of them got in the back and one in the front. They called for help. I called out of the car for someone to call my mother.

When the sergeant came, one of the officers who beat me told the sergeant that I grabbed him, and I told the sergeant I did not grab him. A crowd had gathered and the police forced them back. I was crying and calling for my mother. The officer in the back, annoyed at this, cursed me and threatened my life. My mother did come and I called her, but the officers would not allow her to get near me. I attempted to lean out the window to call mother, but one of the officers that came to the scene pushed me back down in the car. I heard one of the officers say to my mother that she would get the same thing if she did not stop hollering. When the wrecker came up, I asked why they were pulling in my car. They said that there was nobody to drive it. I said my mother could drive it. They said, "She's gone off hollering."

I pleaded with them not to beat me and asked . . . [one officer, by name] if he had a heart, and if he had a son or brother, and would he want anybody to beat them for nothing. He remarked, "How did that nigger know my name?" I said I saw it on the ticket. He accused me of threatening him, but I said I was not threatening him but just asked if he had a heart. He said he was going to get me for that. I said I did not care if they killed me because they had beat me enough already. He said he was going to see how much I could take.

They drove away with me. When they got near the ball diamond on Huntsville Road, the officer . . . asked me for his night stick. He was in the back seat with me. He began beating me with the stick and saying I made an ass of him before the sergeant saying I did not grab him. He beat me for asking if he had a son or a brother, talking to me as he landed each blow. He beat me all over my head and face. He said, "Nigger you won't want to live." I said yes I want to live and was pleading for mercy. But they had none. When I would lean down to avoid the blows in my face, the officer would strike upward hitting me in the face with the stick. When I would rise up from the under blows, he would come down into my face with the stick. I was crying and hollering and pleading but he kept beating me. He hit one place on the back of my head about ten times. Each blow seemed to make everything go black with pain. My hands were still handcuffed behind me. A car came by and he stopped beating me until the car passed.

Then the officer in the front said it was his time to beat me, so he got in the back and continued beating me while the other one drove. He beat me mostly in the body. They called me vile names and told me to get out of town after the trial tomorrow night.

They took me to Hillman Hospital. They jerked me out of the car, cursing me. I fell down outside the hospital and they cursed and jerked me up again. Again inside the hospital I collapsed and they cursed me again. I was on the floor crying and hollering. I asked them to take the cuffs off. They said they would not take them off as long as I was crying and hollering.

At the hospital I was given medical treatment and a bill for $100.00 for treatment. Then I was taken to jail. My parents got me out on bond after about 45 minutes and took me to Caraway Methodist Hospital where I stayed two weeks.

I lost my glasses and a shoe and some money and my driver's license. I have not seen any of these since they stopped me and beat me. They charged me with resisting arrest, speeding, assault and battery, and disorderly conduct.

James Eddie Steele

—*The New South*, June 1964

29. A Student Crusade to Mississippi, 1964

Elizabeth Sutherland, Editor

EDITORIAL NOTE: *The violence with which the people of the deep South reacted to the agitation of Negroes and their white associates approached a form of guerrilla warfare. As the federal government appeared unable to enforce the rights of Negroes, and the FBI appeared, as often as not, allied with the forces of repression, the Negroes took things into their own hands, though mostly with a philosophy of "non-violence." In this crusade against discrimination and for the vindication of political rights, they were supported by—in some cases guided by—various organizations in the North. Among these one of the most interesting and effective was the Student Nonviolent Coordinating Committee which drew chiefly from the colleges of New England and the Middle West. During the summer of 1964 some 650 members of this Committee volunteered for service in Mississippi. Many Southern whites were outraged at this "invasion" by what they considered Northern radicals and "Communists," bent on stirring up racial trouble, and responded by providing trouble of their own. Mrs. Sutherland, one of the Secretaries of the Committee, has collected and edited some of the letters which students wrote home to their parents during this "freedom summer."*

Mileston, July 23

DEAR MOM, DAD AND SHARI,

WE'VE BEEN LEARNING a little about conditions on some local plantations.

One plantation worker secretly left the plantation to come and ask us for help. He gets up at 3:30 A.M. and works on a tractor until dusk—for $5 a day, six days a week. His wife picks cotton for $2.50 a day. Two years ago he borrowed $250 from his plantation owner; since then, his "owner" has taken $10 a week out of his pay and hasn't stopped. A year and a half ago, when the debt had been paid, he asked the "owner" how much he still owed, he was told $100, and got the same answer ten weeks later (with the $10 a week still being deducted). He asked once too often, because the next week, after his boss discovered that he attended citizenship classes, the boss came to him with a note saying he owed $650. His boss and a local deputy sheriff are co-owners of the plantation . . .

Love,

Joel

Columbus

When the men from town here are drunk, they come up to the house saying, "I'm not scared of anything, hear." By the next day they are crawling again. The fear in their faces is pathetic. Last night a drunk man latched on to us. He kept talking about two things: he fought hard in Korea (shell shock and two lost toes, he has) and when he returned, the same people he was fighting for treated him like a dog; his wife died three months before. He took us to see his home ("it's open to you anytime"). There were three people there, his child, his mother-in-law, and her husband. The adults were all staggering drunk. There's not much recreation for Negroes except drinking and screwing, empty as life can be. The father-in-law was drunk but he was still *terrified.* You should see the faces, the eyes, of the men who are broken. The mother-in-law started talking: "sit down, god-darned it, I want to talk to you. The white people treat us colored folk so *bad.* There's nothing we can do. They killed those three boys, they'll kill us all. What can we do?" I wish I could remember what all she said. She was so drunk she didn't "Yasuh" us and she swore at us. That was good, because she told the truth (what she really felt) and for a white man to get this from a Mississippi Negro is exceptional . . .

Some of the proud Negroes among us say we are trying to save the black man's body and the white man's soul. But we have to save both souls. Many of these people are so smashed and whip-lashed by the treatment they've gotten that they're lost . . . This is the worst thing about segregation, it breaks people, it makes boys ("hey, boy, come here") out of men. The men are often so pitifully weak—unable to decide anything or to do anything. Another problem is that when the people get stronger, they often release against whites all the anger which they've repressed . . .

We are frustrated by the dozens of beaten down people we meet every day. Yesterday when we were in the rural areas of Lowndes county, we talked about Freedom registration to one woman in a terrible house who said "I can't sign no paper." Lester then asked her "how will the pay for jobs and the homes ever get better unless we get together. Negroes have to do something to get something." She said, "I ain't no Negro, I'm a nigger. The Boss Man, he don't say nothing but nigger girl to me. I'm just a nigger, I can't sign no paper."

Mileston, July 6

Dear Mom and Dad,

Mileston, where I'm staying, is in the flat Delta section of Holmes County. The Negro farms here were once part of huge plantations. In 1939 the federal government confiscated the land when the plantation owners failed to pay back taxes, and the land was divided up among Negro families who had applied for it. Land reform (on a miniscule scale) has had an enormous effect on the people . . .

Last year Hollis Watkins, a SNCC staff member, began a voter registration drive here. He got about 14 Negroes to go to the court house with the intention of registering to vote. Sheriff Smith greeted the party with a six shooter drawn from his pocket, and said "Okay, who's first?" Most of the Negroes remained cautiously quiet. After several seconds a man who had never before been a leader stepped up to the Sheriff, smiled and said, "I'm first, Hartman Turnbow." All registration applications were permitted to be filled out and all were judged illiterate. The next week, Turnbow's house was bombed with Molotov cocktails. When the Turnbows left the burning house, they were shot at, and they shot back until the attackers fled. A couple of days later, Mr. Turnbow, Hollis Watkins, Robert Moses and a couple of other people were arrested for arson; Turnbow was accused of having bombed his own house which wasn't insured. Sheriff Smith was the one witness against them. Mr. Turnbow was convicted in a Justice of Peace Court, but the conviction was overruled in a federal district court . . .

The Negro people we are living with have enormous hope and are extremely practical about achieving their goals. This community is an oasis of hope in a desert of broken minds: the plantation sharecroppers who have little reason for hope . . .

Love,

Joel

July 18

. . . Four of us went to distribute flyers announcing the meeting. I talked to a woman who had been down to register a week before. She was afraid. Her husband had lost his job. Even before we got there a couple of her sons had been manhandled by the police. She was now full of wild rumors about shootings and beatings, etc. I checked out two of them later. They were groundless. This sort of rumor-spreading is quite prevalent when people get really scared. . . .

At 6 P.M. we returned to Drew for the meeting, to be held in front of a church (they wouldn't let us meet inside, but hadn't told us not to meet outside). A number of kids collected and stood around in a circle with about 15 of us to sing freedom songs. Across the street perhaps 100 adults stood watching. Since this was the first meeting in town, we passed out mimeoed song sheets. Fred Miller, Negro from Mobile, stepped out to the edge of the street to give somebody a sheet. The cops nabbed him. I was about to follow suit so he wouldn't be alone, but Mac's policy [Charles McLaurin, SNCC project director] was to ignore the arrest. We sang on mightily "Ain't going to let no jailing turn me around." A group of girls was sort of leaning against the cars on the periphery of the meeting. Mac went over to encourage them to join us. I gave a couple of song sheets to the girls. A cop rushed across the street and told me to come along. I guess I was sort of aware that my actions would get me arrested, but felt that we had to show these girls that we were not afraid. I was also concerned with what might happen to Fred if he was the only one.

. . . The cop at the station was quite scrupulous about letting me make a phone call. I was then driven to a little concrete structure which looked like a power house. I could hear Fred's courageous, off-key rendition of a freedom song from inside and joined him as we approached. He was very happy to see me. Not long thereafter, four more of our group were driven up to make their calls . . .

The Drew jail consists of three small cells off a wide hall. It was filthy, hot and stuffy. A cop came back to give us some toilet paper. We sang songs for a while, and yelled greetings to Negroes who drove by curiously. One of the staff workers had been in jail 106 times. I asked the cop if he could open another cell as there were not enough beds accessible to us. He mumbled something about how that would be impossible and left. They hadn't confiscated anything and one of the guys had a battered copy of *The Other America,* so we divided up the chapters. I got the dismal one on the problems of the aged . . . To be old and forgotten is certainly a worse sentence than mine (I wouldn't recommend that book for those planning to do time) . . .

Well, the night was spent swatting mosquitoes. An old Negro couple walked by in front of the jail and asked how we were doing. They said they supported us and the old lady said, "God bless you all." This, in the context of a tense town with a pretty constant stream of whites in cars driving by. . . .

Batesville

The police gave us a hard time. All the time trumping up traffic violations. We were riding in a Volkswagen going 35 mph with the car in *third* gear. We were ticketed for going 110 mph. By-by $17 We are hard pressed for money.

Holly Springs, July 21

Dear Mom and Dad,

Harry and I went down to Canton to Harry's trial on a charge of blocking traffic with a truck load of books. A girl who is working in Canton also went to trial on a charge of running a stop sign on a corner where there is no stop sign. She paid a fine of $21 and Harry paid $23 . . .

The cops waited for Harry and me to leave town. As we were going north we saw two police cars pass us heading south. They were only a few minutes apart. Then about five minutes later two cars went around me and a cop came up behind. I had been careful not to go more than 55 mph in a 65 zone. The cop stopped me and said I had been going 75. When I told him I wasn't going that fast he got mad, took my driver's license and told me to follow him.

We went north to a gas station in Pickens where he called a judge to come hold trial . . . The cop said "Let me warn you about this judge, he's a real hanger. See that tree outside? He's hanged 15 guys from that tree. You can still see some little pieces of rope." He made several other remarks about hanging but it didn't scare us very much; we just looked at him.

He also asked what we thought of Goldwater. Harry is from New York. The cop said "Goldwater sure ran that nigger-loving Rockefeller crying back to New York, didn't he."

When the judge came in the cop pointed at me [a white] and said "This nigger here has broken the laws of the sovereign State of Mississippi." The judge didn't ask me to plead guilty or not guilty; he just asked if I had anything to say. I told him I was only going 55 and that two cars had passed me just before I was stopped. The cop said I was "passing everything on the road and was slowing down to 75 when I caught him." The judge said one of us was a liar, and that since he had known this policeman for a long time and since I was the first person ever to doubt his word, I must be wrong. So the fine was $27 or nine days in jail.

This wasn't enough though. When I had paid the fine I asked for my driver's license. The first cop told me the second cop had it. When I asked the second cop he said I had tried to run him off the road earlier that day. He told me to follow him back to Canton. When we got there I was charged with reckless driving and sent to jail on a $100 bond . . .

Enough,
Larry

Laurel, August 24

Dear Family,

Saturday afternoon, several of us were invited out to a farm 6 miles from town for a day of picnicking, swimming, relaxation and V.R. work out in the country . . . Bill Haden, a white COFO worker from Oregon, a local Negro and myself were sitting along the edge of the lake about 400 yards from the farmhouse singing some songs and playing the guitar. Just after finishing the last verse of Dylan's "Who Killed Davy Moore," we saw two whites coming towards us down the path from the farmhouse. Since we were expecting other people from the COFO office to be joining us, we didn't think anything strange about this. When they got somewhat closer and I didn't recognize them, I asked Bill if he knew who they were. He didn't know. A few seconds later, the younger man (about 5 feet 10, 200 lbs.) came up to me and asked me if I knew Dixie. I told him, I wasn't sure, to which he responded, "Well, you'd better be sure, and quick." I told him, "Well, sit down. Maybe we could work it out together." He told me just to play it. I've never learned a song quite so fast in all my life.

Apparently, he didn't appreciate my efforts, because the next thing I know, the guitar was out of my hands, kicked, and thrown out into the lake. Almost simultaneously, about 15 other rednecks, about 25–55 yrs. in age, emerged from the trees and brush surrounding the lake. The other man, who had first come up, began beating me with the big wooden club. I saw that it would be impossible for me to run around the edge of the lake back to the house without being further attacked and beaten. So, since I was born for the water, home I went. After I was 15 or 25 feet out, he pulled a pistol from beneath his shirt and began firing in my direction. Ten or twelve of the other men began shooting in the direction of the house and the fleeing COFO worker with pistols, rifles and shotguns.

When the bullets began hitting the water, not five feet from my head, I thought it was time to make a submarine exit. Coming up about a hundred and fifty feet further out, the bullets were splattering even beyond me, perhaps 30–40 feet. Since I didn't see any men at the other side of the lake, I was hoping to swim there, get out, and try and make it to the house. About ten minutes later, as I got out of the lake, two men came towards me out of the brush. The man in front had a forked tire iron and the man behind him had a steel chain.

Since old freedom fighters never give up, I again tried to humanize with the cat, asking him, "Wouldn't you like to sit down so we can talk this thing over? Although we might have our differences. . . ." While I was saying this, I was gradually taking a few steps back toward the lake, just in case he did not respond positively. Well, he didn't. Menacing the tire iron, he ordered me to get over to where the rest of the men were and not get wise. For a few more seconds, I tried to reason with him . . . Just about at that moment, one of them comes from the brush around the lake with his club. He swings it at me across the back and the man with the tire iron hits me across the knee while I think the man with the chain hit me across the ribs and back. Deciding that it was better to be a live chicken than a dead duck, I got the hell out of there. By some miracle, I was able to make it through the brush, barbed wire and all the shooting (by now from both sides) up to the farmhouse.

When I arrived, the COFO office had already been notified and I got on the phone immediately to the FBI in Laurel. After about five minutes, an FBI agent called back and wanted to know what was going on. I told him that the Civil War was reoccurring and would he *please* come on out—with the rest of the Federal Gov't. He wanted to know if we had notified the local police and sheriff's office. I told him we had, but they refused to be of any assistance. I then asked him if he could not protect us, would he be so kind as to come out and take pictures down by the lake of the man who had been firing on us? We exchanged a few more words, and I went to lie down on the floor. I vaguely remember the sheriff arriving maybe a half hour or 40 minutes later and taking the names of everybody in the house. We asked him if he would give us protection back to Laurel or at least ride with us. He replied, "I didn't carry you trouble-makers out here and I'm sure not going to take you back." With this, he left us. About 15–20 minutes later, the ambulance arrived and we were taken to Jones County Community Hospital. . . .

That's all for now, take care, don't worry,

Love,
Dave

Greenwood, July 11

. . . At the police station the insidious relation between the local law officials and the local law-breakers grew more obvious. A police officer was playing with a knife, rubbing his thumb over its edge. He pointed the knife at a girl, a co-worker, and said that he kept it sharp for "niggers like you." He then pushed her around. My assailant, still present, started in on one of the white workers, accusing him of being a "nigger-lover," and suggested to the officer that he castrate the boy. A bit later, he and my assailant both drove a Negro boy home who had been in jail.

We finally started to leave the station late that night, but we couldn't because all four of our car tires had been slashed. The Negro boy who had been driven home by them later told us that as they passed our car, one said, "There's the car those bastards are driving." We have good reason to suspect that the law enforcer, and the attacker, slashed the tires.

The man who beat me is now free. He paid a $25 fine. He is a friend of the judge's, of the police, and a member of the Citizens' Council. It is amazing that he was even fined. He probably would not have been one month ago. Still, it is no comfort to me. He is free, he is angry. He knows that he can get away with much worse. The FBI would not arrest him . . . I have no local protection. I have no Federal protection . . .

July 26–27

A real hum-dinger of an evening. More about Jake and Silas McGhee, the two brothers who have been integrating the movie theatre. You know that the FBI made the first arrest under the Civil Rights Act in connection with the beating of Silas.

Well, they went down again tonight. After the film was over, they called and asked if we could come pick them up. Nothing doing as yet, but they didn't like to try it alone. By the time we sent an all-Negro car down there, a mob of over 100 people had gathered, and the situation was really bad. We were on the phone all the time with one of the brothers. He described the movements of the crowd, and told us that the theatre manager was demanding that they get out, since the theatre was about to close for the night. The police were there, but refused to give them any protection. He couldn't see too well whether our car had pulled up yet. Then, with 3 of us listening on different extensions, he told us that he was going to shoot his way out. It was really tense for a few minutes, as we pleaded with him. He promised to hold out until our car arrived.

Bob Zellner and Phil M. and I jumped into another car to see if we could find out anything. We rode with windows up and doors locked tight. We got to the theatre and found it deserted. Whatever had happened—had already happened. Bob leaned out of the window and asked in his deep Southern accent where were the goddamn niggers at. Nobody knew. . . .

We found out that they had been picked up by our car after finally getting a police escort from the theatre. As they got in the car, the police stepped back, and as if on signal, the mob rushed the car, and a coke bottle was thrown through a window—the glass from the window and the bottle cutting both brothers over the eye. They went straight to the Leflore County Hospital and were treated promptly.

Another car went down to the hospital to see if everybody was all right. That car was shot at on the way, but finally managed to get safely to the hospital.

The situation was at this time fairly bad. Cars full of whites were riding up and down in front of the hospital. Five guns were seen, .22's and .38 pistols. Later, the mother of the brothers came with their older brother, Clarence, an army man with 12 years of army experience behind him (Korean War paratrooper) in full uniform. All were holed up at the hospital.

We were very afraid the hospital would demand that they leave the place [since the two younger brothers had been discharged after treatment]. We gave our people instructions not to leave unless they got a full escort and guarantees of safety. The local police refused outright, and the Highway Patrol said it would look in on the case.

We were on the phones like mad, talking to FBI, congressmen, trying to get the Pentagon to rescue the soldier in uniform, and so on. On the phone from the hospital, the soldier told us that if we didn't get him out in 30 minutes, he was taking his family out any way he could.

By this time, the FBI had finally decided to do something. Not on their own, of course, but after many, many phone calls, and many protestations on their part that they did not protect people. Two agents came over here to see the broken car window, and to see if they could get any fingerprints from the bits of coke bottle. At least 6 agents later showed up at the hospital, very hostile but taking statements like mad.

Meanwhile, we were getting a steady stream of information from the hospital. It seems that one of the kids was beaten on his way from the theatre to the car. With a policeman standing right beside him. The cops told them that they got themselves into it, and they had to get themselves out. This while in the middle of a mob, and while one of the kids was being beaten right and left.

The Hiway Patrol and the sheriff both sent people down to the hospital and Chief Larry also went down. The soldier had been convinced to stick it out, and not try to get out the back way. The sheriff finally agreed to escort them, but said that they would have to come over to the other side of the hospital and come out that way. To get to the other side, you have to cross the driveway where the white cars were moving around. No dice. Our people said they wouldn't move until they had a car in front and one in back and were escorted to their cars out *their* door. Finally they got an escort—and are home safe. They were headed off by a white car on the way back, but the police went over and cleared them out—the first positive action by the police during the whole incident. . . .

—Elizabeth Sutherland, Editor, *Letters From Mississippi*, 1965

30. The End of the Poll-Tax: The Twenty-Fourth Amendment, 1964

EDITORIAL NOTE: *With ratification by the thirty-eighth State, South Dakota, the Twenty-Fourth Amendment went into effect January 23, 1964.*

THE RIGHT OF citizens of the United States to vote in any primary or other election for President or Vice-President, or for Senator or Representative in Congress, shall not be denied or abridged by the United States or any other state by reason of failure to pay any poll tax or other tax.

—The Constitution of the United States

31. The Civil Rights Act of 1964

EDITORIAL NOTE: *The Civil Rights Act of 1964, passed with the compelling support of the new President, Lyndon B. Johnson, will doubtless prove to have been the most far-reaching piece of legislation since the Wagner Act and the Tennessee Valley Authority Act, and the most controversial since the income tax amendment. In addition to the provisions given below, the law contains sections prohibiting discrimination in employment, together with lengthy provisions for its own enforcement.*

AN ACT TO enforce the constitutional right to vote, to confer jurisdiction upon the district courts of the United States to provide injunctive relief against discrimination in public accommodations, to authorize the Attorney General to institute suits to protect constitutional rights in public facilities and public education, to extend the Commission on Civil Rights, to prevent discrimination in federally assisted programs, to establish a Commission on Equal Employment Opportunity, and for other purposes. . . .

TITLE I—VOTING RIGHTS

SEC. 101 (2). No person acting under color of law shall—

(a) in determining whether any individual is qualified under State law or laws to vote in any Federal election, apply any standard, practice, or procedure different from the standards, practices, or procedures applied under such law or laws to other individuals within the same county, parish, or similar political subdivision who have been found by State officials to be qualified to vote; . . .

(c) employ any literacy test as a qualification for voting in any Federal election unless (i) such test is administered to each individual wholly in writing; and (ii) a certified copy of the test and of the answers given by the individuals is furnished to him within twenty-five days of the submission of his request made within the period of time during which records and papers are required to be retained and preserved pursuant to title III of the Civil Rights Act of 1960. . . .

TITLE II—INJUNCTIVE RELIEF AGAINST DISCRIMINATION IN PLACES OF PUBLIC ACCOMMODATION

Sec. 201. (a). All persons shall be entitled to the full and equal enjoyment of the goods, services, facilities, privileges, advantages, and accommodations of any place of public accommodation, as defined in this section, without discrimination or segregation on the ground of race, color, religion, or national origin.

(b) Each of the following establishments which serves the public is a place of public accommodation within the meaning of this title if its operations affect commerce, or if discrimination or segregation by it is supported by State action:

(1) any inn, motel, or other establishment which provides lodging to transient guests, other than an establishment located within a building which contains not more than five rooms for rent or hire and which is actually occupied by the proprietor of such establishment as his residence;

(2) any restaurant, cafeteria, lunch room, lunch counter, soda fountain, or other facility principally engaged in selling food for consumption on the premises . . . ;

(3) any motion picture house, theater, concert hall, sports arena, stadium or other place of exhibition or entertainment. . . .

(d) Discrimination or segregation by an establishment is supported by State action within the meaning of this title if such discrimination or segregation (1) is carried on under color of any law, statute, ordinance, or regulation; or (2) is carried on under color of any custom or usage required or enforced by officials of the State or political subdivision thereof. . . .

SEC. 202. All persons shall be entitled to be free, at any establishment or place, from discrimination or segregation of any kind on the ground of race, color, religion, or national origin, if such discrimination or segregation is or purports to be required by any law, statute, ordinance, regulation, rule, or order of a State or any agency or political subdivision thereof. . . .

SEC. 206. (a) Whenever the Attorney General has reasonable cause to believe that any person or group of persons is engaged in a pattern or practice of resistance to the full enjoyment of any of the rights secured by this title, the Attorney General may bring a civil action in the appropriate district court of the United States by filing with it a complaint . . . requesting such preventive relief, including an application for a permanent or temporary injunction, restraining order or other order against the person or persons responsible for such pattern or practice, as he deems necessary to insure the full enjoyment of the rights herein described.

TITLE VI—NONDISCRIMINATION IN FEDERALLY ASSISTED PROGRAMS

SEC. 601. No person in the United States shall, on the ground of race, color, or national origin, be excluded from participation in, be denied the benefits of, or be subjected to discrimination under any program or activity receiving Federal financial assistance.

—U. S. Public Law, 88–352, 1964

32. President Johnson Asks Congress to Redeem the Fifteenth Amendment

Lyndon B. Johnson

EDITORIAL NOTE: *Notwithstanding a long series of Civil Rights Acts and Supreme Court decisions, the South continued to resist, by delay, by cunning, and by force, the implementation of the Fifteenth Amendment. The clash of Negroes attempting to vote with Southern officials determined to frustrate the exercise of the franchise by Negroes, came to a head in Selma, Alabama, in March 1965, with something like a reign of terror. The following week, on March 15, 1965, President Johnson went before a joint session of Congress to urge the immediate passage of a tougher Voting Rights act.*

REMARKS OF THE PRESIDENT TO A JOINT SESSION OF CONGRESS, MARCH 15, 1965

I SPEAK TONIGHT for the dignity of man and the destiny of democracy.

I urge every member of both parties, Americans of all religions and of all colors, from every section of this country, to join me in that cause.

At times history and fate meet at a single time in a single place to shape a turning point in man's unending search for freedom. So it was at Lexington and Concord. So it was a century ago at Appomattox. So it was last week in Selma, Alabama. There, long-suffering men and women peacefully protested the denial of their rights as Americans. Many were brutally assaulted. One good man, a man of God, was killed. There is no cause for pride in what has happened in Selma. There is no cause for self-satisfaction in the long denial of equal rights of millions of Americans. But there is cause for hope and for faith in our democracy in what is happening here tonight. For the cries of pain and the hymns and protests of oppressed people, have summoned into convocation all the majesty of this great government of the greatest nation on earth.

Our mission is at once the oldest and the most basic of this country: to right wrong, to do justice, to serve man. . . . Rarely in any time does an issue lay bare the secret heart of America itself. Rarely are we met with a challenge, not to our growth or abundance, or our welfare or our security, but rather to the values and the purposes and the meaning of our beloved nation.

The issue of equal rights for American Negroes is such an issue. And should we defeat every enemy, and should we double our wealth and conquer the stars and still be unequal to this issue, then we will have failed as a people and as a nation.

For with a country as with a person, "What is a man profited, if he shall gain the whole world, and lose his own soul?"

There is no Negro problem. There is no Southern problem. There is no Northern problem. There is only an American problem. And we are met here tonight as Americans, not as Democrats or Republicans, we are met here as Americans to solve that problem.

This was the first nation in the history of the world to be founded with a purpose. The great phrases of that purpose still sound in every American heart, North and South: "All men are created equal" —"government by consent of the governed"—"give me liberty or give me death." Those are not just clever words. Those are not just empty theories. In their name Americans have fought and died for two centuries, and tonight around the world they stand there as guardians of our liberty, risking their lives.

Those words are a promise to every citizen that he shall share in the dignity of man. This dignity cannot be found in a man's possessions. It cannot be found in his power or in his position. It really rests on his right to be treated as a man equal in opportunity to all others. It says that he shall share in freedom, he shall choose his leaders, educate his children, provide for his family according to his ability and his merits as a human being.

To apply any other test—to deny a man his hopes because of his color or race, or his religion, or the place of his birth—is not only to do injustice, it is to deny America and to dishonor the dead who gave their lives for American freedom.

Our fathers believed that if this noble view of the rights of man was to flourish, it must be rooted in democracy. The most basic right of all was the right to choose your own leaders. The history of this country in large measure is the history of expansion of that right to all of our people.

Many of the issues of civil rights are very complex and most difficult. But about this there can and should be no argument. Every American citizen must have an equal right to vote. There is no reason which can excuse the denial of that right. There is no duty which weighs more heavily on us than the duty we have to ensure that right.

Yet the harsh fact is that in many places in this country men and women are kept from voting simply because they are Negroes.

Every device of which human ingenuity is capable has been used to deny this right. The Negro citizen may go to register only to be told that the day is wrong, or the hour is late, or the official in charge is absent. And if he persists and if he manages to present himself to the registrar, he may be disqualified because he did not spell out his middle name or because he abbreviated a word on the application. And if he manages to fill out an application he is given a test. The registrar is the sole judge of whether he passes this test. He may be asked to recite the entire constitution, or explain the most complex provisions of state laws. And even a college degree cannot be used to prove that he can read and write.

For the fact is that the only way to pass these barriers is to show a white skin.

Experience has clearly shown that the existing process of law cannot overcome systematic and ingenious discrimination. No law that we now have on the books—and I have helped to put three of them there—can ensure the right to vote when local officials are determined to deny it.

In such a case our duty must be clear to all of us. The Constitution says that no person shall be kept from voting because of his race or his color. We have all sworn on oath before God to support and to defend that Constitution. We must now act in obedience to that oath.

Wednesday I will send to Congress a law designed to eliminate illegal barriers to the right to vote. . . .

This bill will strike down restrictions to voting in all elections—Federal, State, and local—which have been used to deny Negroes the right to vote. This bill will establish a simple, uniform standard which cannot be used, however ingenious the effort, to flout our Constitution. It will provide for citizens to be registered by officials of the United States government if the State officials refuse to register them. It will eliminate tedious, unnecessary lawsuits which delay the right to vote. Finally, this legislation will ensure that properly registered individuals are not prohibited from voting. . . .

To those who seek to avoid action by their national government in their own communities, who want to and who seek to maintain purely local control over elections, the answer is simple.

Open your polling places to all your people.

Allow men and women to register and vote whatever the color of their skin.

Extend the rights of citizenship to every citizen of this land.

There is no constitutional issue here. The command of the Constitution is plain.

There is no moral issue. It is wrong to deny any of your fellow Americans the right to vote in this country.

There is no issue of states rights or national rights. There is only the struggle for human rights.

I have not the slightest doubt what will be your answer.

But the last time a President sent a civil rights bill to the Congress it contained a provision to protect voting rights in Federal elections. That civil rights bill was passed after eight long months of debate. And when that bill came to my desk from the Congress for my signature, the heart of the voting provision had been eliminated.

This time, on this issue, there must be no delay, or no hesitation or no compromise with our purpose.

We cannot, we must not refuse to protect the right of every American to vote in every election that he may desire to participate in. And we ought not, we must not wait another eight months before we get a bill. We have already waited a hundred years and more and the time for waiting is gone. . . .

Even if we pass this bill, the battle will not be over. What happened in Selma is part of a far larger movement which reaches into every section and state of America. It is the effort of American Negroes to secure for themselves the full blessings of American life.

Their cause must be our cause too. Because it is not just Negroes, but really it is all of us, who must overcome the crippling legacy of bigotry and injustice. And we shall overcome.

As a man whose roots go deeply into Southern soil I know how agonizing racial feelings are. I know how difficult it is to reshape the attitudes and the structure of our society.

But a century has passed, more than a hundred years, since the Negro was freed. And he is not fully free tonight.

It was more than a hundred years ago that Abraham Lincoln, the great President of the Northern party, signed the Emancipation Proclamation, but emancipation is a proclamation and not a fact.

A century has passed, more than a hundred years since equality was promised. And yet the Negro is not equal.

A century has passed since the day of promise. And the promise is unkept.

The time of justice has now come. I tell you that I believe sincerely that no force can hold it back. It is right in the eyes of man and God that it should come. And when it does, I think that day will brighten the lives of every American.

For Negroes are not the only victims. How many white children have gone uneducated, how many white families have lived in stark poverty, how many white lives have been scarred by fear because we wasted our energy and our substance to maintain the barriers of hatred and terror.

So I say to all of you here and to all in the nation tonight, that those who appeal to you to hold on to the past do so at the cost of denying you your future.

This great, rich, restless country can offer opportunity and education and hope to all—all black and white, all North and South, sharecropper, and city dweller. These are the enemies—poverty, ignorance, disease. They are enemies, not our fellow man, not our neighbor, and these enemies too, poverty, disease and ignorance, we shall overcome.

Now let none of us in any section look with prideful righteousness on the troubles in another section or the problems of our neighbors. There is really no part of America where the promise of equality has been fully kept. In Buffalo as well as in Birmingham, in Philadelphia as well as in Selma, Americans are struggling for the fruits of freedom.

This is one nation. What happens in Selma or in Cincinnati is a matter of legitimate concern to every American. But let each of us look within our own hearts and our own communities, and let each of us put our shoulder to the wheel to root out injustice wherever it exists.

The real hero of this struggle is the American Negro. His actions and protests, his courage to risk safety and even to risk his life, have awakened the conscience of this nation. His demonstrations have been designed to call attention to injustice, designed to provoke change, designed to stir reform. He has called upon us to make good the promise of America. And who among us can say that we would have made the same progress were it not for his persistent bravery, and his faith in American democracy.

—President Lyndon B. Johnson, Address to the Congress, March 15, 1965

33. The Voting Rights Act of 1965

EDITORIAL NOTE: *After prolonged debate and a stubborn filibuster, the Administration bill passed the Congress by large majorities: 333 to 48 in the House, 77 to 19 in the Senate. This bill outlawed devices to frustrate the Negro vote, and provided for enforcement through federal election examiners and the Courts. Under its provisions, Negro registration increased substantially throughout most of the South, though only moderately in such recalcitrant states as Mississippi, Alabama and South Carolina.*

AN ACT TO enforce the fifteenth Amendment to the Constitution of the United States, and for other purposes.

Sec. 2. No voting qualification or prerequisite to voting, or standard, practice, or procedure shall be imposed or applied by any State or political subdivision to deny or abridge the right of any citizen of the United States to vote on account of race or color.

Sec. 4 (a) To assure that the right of citizens of the United States to vote is not denied or abridged on account of race or color, no citizen shall be denied the right to vote in any Federal, State, or local election because of his failure to comply with any test or device in any State with respect to which the determinations have been made under subsection (b) or in any political subdivision with respect to which such determinations have been made as a separate unit, unless the United States District Court for the District of Columbia in an action for a declaratory judgment brought by such State or subdivision against the United States has determined that no such test or device has been used during the five years preceding the filing of the action for the purpose or with the effect of denying or abridging the right to vote on account of race or color.

If the Attorney General determines that he has no reason to believe that any such test or device has been used during the five years preceding the filing of the action for the purpose or with the effect of denying or abridging the right to vote on account of race or color, he shall consent to the entry of such judgment.

(b) The provisions of subsection (a) shall apply in any State or in any political subdivision of a state which (1) the Attorney General determines maintained on November 1, 1964, any test or device, and with respect to which (2) the Director of the Census determines that less than 50 per centum of the persons of voting age residing therein were registered on November 1, 1964, or that less than 50 per centum of such persons voted in the presidential election of November 1964.

(c) The phrase "test or device" shall mean any requirement that a person as a prerequisite for voting or registration for voting (1) demonstrate the ability to read, write, understand, or interpret any matter, (2) demonstrate any educational achievement or his knowledge of any particular subject, (3) possess good moral character, or (4) prove his qualifications by the voucher of registered voters of members of any other class.

(d) For purposes of this section no State or political subdivision shall be determined to have engaged in the use of tests or devices for the purpose or with the effect of denying or abridging the right to vote on account of race or color if (1) incidents of such use have been few in number and have been promptly and effectively corrected by State or local action, (2) the continuing effect of such incidents has been eliminated, and (3) there is no reasonable probability of their recurrence in the future.

(2) No person who demonstrates that he has successfully completed the sixth primary grade in a public school in, or a private school accredited by, any State or territory, the District of Columbia, or the Commonwealth of Puerto Rico in which the predominant classroom language was other than English, shall be denied the right to vote in any Federal, State, or local election because of his inability to read, write, understand, or interpret any matter in the English language, except that in States in which State law provides

that a different level of education is presumptive of literacy, he shall demonstrate that he has successfully completed an equivalent level of education in a public school in, or a private school accredited by, any State or territory, the District of Columbia, or the Commonwealth of Puerto Rico in which the predominant classroom language was other than English.

August 6, 1965

—Appendix to South Carolina *v.* Katzenbach, 1966

34. The Right to Vote: The Unending Struggle

A. *Anderson v. Martin*

EDITORIAL NOTE: *With grandfather clauses and all-white party primaries outlawed, and poll taxes prohibited by constitutional amendment, Southern States resorted to new techniques to prevent Negroes from voting. One of the most overt was the Louisiana requirement that in all elections the race of the candidate be designated on the ballot. A unanimous court held this a violation of the Equal Protection Clause of the Fourteenth Amendment.*

CLARK, J.: APPELLANTS, RESIDENTS OF East Baton Rouge, Louisiana, are Negroes. Each sought election to the School Board of that parish in the 1962 Democratic Party primary election. Prior to the election they filed this suit against the Secretary of State of Louisiana seeking to enjoin the enforcement of Act 538 of the 1960 Louisiana Legislature . . . which requires the Secretary to print, in parentheses, the race of each candidate opposite his name on all ballots. Asserting that the statute violated, *inter alia*, the Fourteenth and Fifteenth Amendments, appellants sought both preliminary and permanent injunctions and a temporary restraining order. A United States district judge denied the motion for a temporary restraining order and a three-judge court was convened. After a hearing on the merits, the preliminary injunction was denied with one judge dissenting. Thereafter the appellants sought to amend their complaint so as to show that the primary election had been held and that both appellants had been defeated because of the operation and enforcement of the statute here under attack. They further alleged that they "intend to be candidates in the next duly constituted democratic primary election for nomination as members of the East Baton Rouge Parish School Board. . . ." Leave to amend was denied by the district judge and the three-judge court thereafter denied the request for a permanent injunction. We have concluded that the compulsory designation by Louisiana of the race of the candidate on the ballot operates as a discrimination against appellants and is therefore violative of the Fourteenth Amendment's Equal Protection Clause. In view of this we do not reach appellants' other contentions.

At the outset it is well that we point out what this case does not involve. It has nothing whatever to do with the right of a citizen to cast his vote for whomever he chooses and for whatever reason he pleases or to receive all information concerning a candidate which is necessary to a proper exercise of his franchise. It has to do only with the right of a State to require or encourage its voters to discriminate upon the grounds of race. In the abstract, Louisiana imposes no restriction upon anyone's candidacy nor upon an elector's choice in the casting of his ballot. But by placing a racial label on a candidate at the most crucial stage in the electoral process—the instant before the vote is cast—the State furnishes a vehicle by which racial prejudice may be so aroused as to operate against one group because of race and for another. This is true because by directing the citizen's attention to the single consideration of race or color, the State indicates that a candidate's race or color is an important —perhaps paramount—consideration in the citizen's choice, which may decisively influence the citizen to cast his ballot along racial lines. Hence in a State or voting district where Negroes predominate, that race is likely to be favored by a racial designation on the ballot, while in those communities where other races are in the majority, they may be preferred. The vice lies not in the resulting injury but in the placing of the power of the State behind a racial classification that induces racial prejudice at the polls.

As we said in NAACP *v.* Alabama . . . : "The crucial factor is the interplay of governmental and private action. . . ." Here the statute under attack prescribes the form and content of the official ballot used in all elections in Louisiana. The requirement that "[e]very application for or notification or declaration of candidacy, and every certificate of nomination and every nomination paper filed . . . shall show for each candidate named therein, whether such candidate is of the Caucasian race, the Negro race or other specified race" was not placed in the statute until 1960. Prior to that time the primary election ballot contained no information on the candidates other than their names; nor did the general election ballot, which only grouped the named candidates according to their respective political party. The 1960 amendment added "race" as the single item of information other than the name of the candidate. This addition to the statute in the light of "private attitudes and pressures" towards Negroes at the time of its enactment could only result in that "repressive effect" which "was brought to bear only after the exercise of governmental power." . . .

Nor can the attacked provision be deemed to be reasonably designed to meet legitimate governmental interests in informing the electorate as to candidates. We see no relevance in the State pointing up the race of the candidate as bearing upon his qualifications for office. Indeed, this factor in itself "underscores the purely racial character and purpose" of the statute. . . .

The State contends that its Act is nondiscriminatory because the labeling provision applies equally to Negro and white. Obviously, Louisiana may not bar Negro citizens from offering themselves as candidates for public office, nor can it encourage its citizens to vote for a candidate solely on account of race. . . . And that which cannot be done by express statutory prohibition cannot be done by indirection. Therefore, we view the alleged equality as superficial. Race is the factor upon which the statute operates and its involvement promotes the ultimate discrimination which is sufficient to make it invalid. . . . The judgment is therefore reversed.

Reversed.

—Justice Tom Clark, Opinion in Anderson *v.* Martin, 1964

B. *Louisiana v. the United States*

EDITORIAL NOTE: *After the Court had outlawed "grandfather" clauses and White Primary arrangements, and Congress had outlawed the poll tax, there remained only the literacy test as an effective weapon for denying the vote to the Negro. The great virtue of the literacy test, in the eyes of Southern voting registrars, was that no one could pass it if it was rigorously administered. Applicants could be asked not only to read but to "explain" the Constitution of the State and of the United States. Even judges of the Supreme Court cannot always explain to the satisfaction of everyone the meaning of such esoteric clauses as "due process of law," or "obligation of contract." It was to outlaw such malpractices as are cited in this decision that Congress finally prohibited literacy tests.*

BLACK, J.: THE COMPLAINT CHARGED that the defendants by following and enforcing unconstitutional state law had been denying and unless restrained by the court would continue to deny Negro citizens of Louisiana the right to vote, in violation of 42 U.S.C. § 1971(a) and the Fourteenth and Fifteenth Amendments to the United States Constitution. . . .

The complaint alleged, and the District Court found, that beginning with the adoption of the Louisiana Constitution of 1898, when approximately 44% of all the registered voters in the State were Negroes, the State had put into effect a successful policy of denying Negro citizens the right to vote because of their race. . . .

Louisiana, in 1921, adopted a new constitution replacing the repudiated "grandfather clause" with what the complaint calls an "interpretation test," which required that an applicant for registration be able to "give a reasonable interpretation" of any clause in the Louisiana Constitution or the Constitution of the United States. From the adoption of the 1921 interpretation test until 1944, the District Court's opinion stated, the percentage of registered voters in Louisiana who were Negroes never exceeded one percent. Prior to 1944 Negro interest in voting in Louisiana had been slight, largely because the State's white primary law kept Negroes from voting in the Democratic Party primary election, the only election that mattered in the political climate of that State. In 1944, however, this Court invalidated the substantially identical white primary law of Texas and with the explicit statutory bar to their voting in the primary removed and because of a generally heightened political interest, Negroes in increasing numbers began to register in Louisiana. The white primary system had been so effective in barring Negroes from voting that the "interpretation test" as a disfranching devise had been ignored over the years. Many registrars continued to ignore it after 1944, and in the next dozen years the proportion of registered voters who were Negroes rose from two-tenths of one percent to approximately 15% by March 1956. This fact, coupled with this Court's 1954 invalidation of laws requiring school segregation, prompted the State to try new devices to keep the white citizens in control. The Louisiana Legislature created a committee which became known as the "Segregation Committee" to seek means of accomplishing this goal. The chairman of this committee also helped to organize a semiprivate group called the Association of Citizens Councils, which thereafter acted in close cooperation with the legislative committee to preserve white supremacy. The legislative committee and the Citizens Councils set up programs, which parish voting registrars were required to attend, to instruct the registrars on how to promote white political control. The committee and the Citizens Councils also began a wholesale challenging of Negro names already on the voting rolls, with the result that thousands of Negroes, but virtually no whites, were purged from the rolls of voters. Beginning in the middle 1950's registrars of at least 21 parishes began to apply the interpretation test. In 1960 the State Constitution was amended to require every applicant thereafter to "be able to understand" as well as "give a reasonable interpretation" of any section of the State or Federal Constitution "when read to him by the registrar." The State Board of Registration in cooperation with the Segregation Committee issued orders that all parish registrars must strictly comply with the new provisions.

The interpretation test, the court found, vested in the voting registrars a virtually uncontrolled discretion as to who should vote and who should not. Under the State's statutes and constitutional provisions the registrars, without any objective standard to guide them, determine the manner in which the interpretation test is to be given, whether it is to be oral or written, the length and complexity of the sections of the State or Federal Constitution to be understood and interpreted, and what interpretation is to be considered correct. There was ample evidence to support the District

Court's finding that registrars in the 21 parishes where the test was found to have been used had exercised their broad powers to deprive otherwise qualified Negro citizens of their right to vote; and that the existence of the test as a hurdle to voter qualification has in itself deterred and will continue to deter Negroes from attempting to register in Louisiana.

Because of the virtually unlimited discretion vested by the Louisiana laws in the registrars of voters, and because in the 21 parishes where the interpretation test was applied that discretion had been exercised to keep Negroes from voting because of their race, the District Court held the interpretation test invalid on its face and as applied, as a violation of the Fourteenth and Fifteenth Amendments to the United States Constitution and of 42 U.S.C. § 1971(a). . . .

There can be no doubt from the evidence in this case that the District Court was amply justified in finding that Louisiana's interpretation test, as written and as applied, was part of a successful plan to deprive Louisiana Negroes of their right to vote. This device for accomplishing unconstitutional discrimination has been little if any less successful than was the "grandfather clause" invalidated by this court's decision in Guinn *v.* United States, supra, 50 years ago, which when that clause was adopted in 1898 had seemed to the leaders of Louisiana a much preferable way of assuring white political supremacy. The Governor of Louisiana stated in 1898 that he believed that the "grandfather clause" solved the problem of keeping Negroes from voting "in a much more upright and manly fashion" than the method adopted previously by the States of Mississippi and South Carolina, which left the qualification of applicants to vote "largely to the arbitrary discretion of the officers administering the law." A delegate to the 1898 Louisiana Constitutional Convention also criticized an interpretation test because the "arbitrary power, lodged with the registration officer, practically places his decision beyond the pale of judicial review; and he can enfranchise or disfranchise voters at his own sweet will and pleasure without let or hindrance."

But Louisianans of a later generation did place just such arbitrary power in the hands of election officers who have used it with phenomenal success to keep Negroes from voting in the State. The State admits that the statutes and provisions of the state constitution establishing the interpretation test "vest discretion in the registrars of voters to determine the qualifications of applicants for registration" while imposing "no definite and objective standards upon registrars of voters for the administration of the interpretation test." And the District Court found that "Louisiana * * * provides no effective method whereby arbitrary and capricious action by registrars of voters may be prevented or redressed." The applicant facing a registrar in Louisiana thus has been compelled to leave his voting fate to that official's uncontrolled power to determine whether the applicant's understanding of the Federal or State Constitution is satisfactory. As the evidence showed, colored people, even some with the most advanced education and scholarship, were declared by voting registrars with less education to have an unsatisfactory understanding of the Constitution of Louisiana or of the United States. This is not a test but a trap, sufficient to stop even the most brilliant man on his way to the voting booth. The cherished right of people in a country like ours to vote cannot be obliterated by the use of laws like this, which leave the voting fate of a citizen to the passing whim or impulse of an individual registrar.

—JUSTICE HUGO BLACK in Louisiana *v.* U.S., 1965

C. *South Carolina v. Katzenbach*

EDITORIAL NOTE: *August 6, 1965, Congress passed a Voting Rights Act designed to plug up various loopholes in previous voting rights acts, notably some of the variations on literacy tests in which Southern officials customarily indulged. This Act can be found in full in the appendix to the decision of the Court in South Carolina* v. *Katzenbach. Seven Southern states sought an injunction against the enforcement of this act on the ground that it violated the Constitution. The decision of the Court was unanimous except for a partial dissent by Justice Black.*

WARREN, C. J.: BY LEAVE OF the Court, South Carolina has filed a bill of complaint, seeking a declaration that selected provisions of the Voting Rights Act of 1965 violate the Federal Constitution, and asking for an injunction against enforcement of these provisions by the Attorney General. . . .

Recognizing that the questions presented were of urgent concern to the entire country, we invited all of the states to participate in this proceeding as friends of the court. A majority responded by submitting or joining in briefs on the merits, some supporting South Carolina and others the Attorney General. . . .

The Voting Rights Act was designed by Congress to banish the blight of racial discrimination in voting, which has infected the electoral process in parts of our country for nearly a century. The act creates stringent new remedies for voting discrimination where it persists on a pervasive scale, and in addition the statute strengthens existing remedies for pockets of voting discrimination elsewhere in the country. Congress assumed the power to prescribe these remedies from Section 2 of the 15th Amendment, which authorizes the national legislature to effectuate by "appropriate" measures the constitutional prohibition against racial discrimination in voting.

We hold that the sections of the act which are properly before us are an appropriate means for carrying out Congress's constitutional responsibilities and are consonant with all other provisions of the Constitution. We therefore deny South Carolina's request that enforcement of these sections of the act be enjoined.

[1]

The constitutional propriety of the Voting Rights Act of 1965 must be judged with reference to the historical experience which it reflects. Before enacting the measure, Congress explored with great care the problem of racial discrimination in voting.

The House approved the act by a vote of 328–74, and the measure passed the Senate by a margin of 79–18.

Two points emerge vividly from the voluminous legislative history of the act contained in the committee hearings and floor debates.

First: Congress felt itself confronted by an insidious and pervasive evil which had been perpetuated in certain parts of our country through unremitting and ingenious defiance of the Constitution.

Second: Congress concluded that the unsuccessful remedies which it had prescribed in the past would have to be replaced by sterner and more elaborate measures in order to satisfy the clear commands of the 15th Amendment.

According to the results of recent Justice Department voting suits, [discriminatory application of voting tests] is now the principal method used to bar Negroes from the polls. Discriminatory administration of voting qualifications has been found in all eight Alabama cases, in all nine Louisiana cases, and in all nine Mississippi cases which have gone to final judgment. Moreover, in almost all of these cases, the courts have held that the discrimination was pursuant to a widespread "pattern or practice."

White applicants for registration have often been excused altogether from the literacy and understanding tests or have been given easy versions, have received extensive help from voting officials, and have been registered despite serious errors in their answers.

Negroes, on the other hand, have typically been required to pass difficult versions of all the tests, without any outside assistance and without the slightest error. The good morals requirement is so vague and subjective that it has constituted an open invitation to abuse at the hands of voting officials. Negroes obliged to obtain vouchers from registered voters have found it virtually impossible to comply in areas where almost no Negroes are on the rolls.

In recent years, Congress has repeatedly tried to cope with the problem of facilitating case-by-case litigation against voting discrimination. The Civil Rights Act of 1957 authorized the Attorney General to seek injunctions against public and private interference with the right to vote on racial grounds. . . . The Civil Rights Act of 1960 . . . gave the Attorney General access to local voting records, and authorized courts to register voters in areas of systematic discrimination. Title I of the Civil Rights Act of 1964 expedited the hearing of voting cases before three-judge courts and outlawed some of the tactics used to disqualify Negroes from voting in Federal elections.

The previous legislation has proved ineffective for a number of reasons. Voting suits are unusually onerous to prepare, sometimes requiring as many as 6,000 man-hours spent combing through registration records in preparation for trial. Litigation has been exceedingly slow, in part because of the ample opportunities for delay afforded voting officials and others involved in the proceedings.

Even when favorable decisions have finally been obtained, some of the states affected have merely switched to discriminatory devices not covered by the Federal decrees or have enacted difficult new tests designed to prolong the existing disparity between white and Negro registration. Alternatively, certain local officials have defied and evaded court orders or have simply closed their registration offices to freeze the voting rolls. The provision of the 1960 law authorizing registration by Federal officers has held little impact on local maladministration because of its procedural complexities.

[2]

The Voting Rights Act of 1965 reflects Congress's firm intention to rid the country of racial discrimination in voting. The heart of the Act is a complex scheme of stringent remedies aimed at areas where voting discrimination has been most flagrant. . . .

The first of the remedies, contained in Section 4(a), is the suspension of literacy tests and similar voting qualifications for a period of five years from the last occurrence of substantial voting discrimination.

Section 5 prescribes a second remedy, the suspension of all new voting regulations pending review by Federal authorities to determine whether their use would perpetuate voting discrimination.

The third remedy . . . is the assignment of Federal examiners by the Attorney General to list qualified applicants who are thereafter entitled to vote in all elections.

Other provisions of the act prescribe subsidiary cures for persistent voting discrimination. Section 8 authorizes the appointment of Federal poll-watchers in places to which Federal examiners have already been assigned.

Section 10(d) excuses those made eligible to vote . . . from paying accumulated past poll taxes for state and local elections.

Section 12(e) provides for balloting by persons denied access to the polls in areas where Federal examiners have been appointed.

The remaining remedial portions of the Act are aimed at voting discrimination in any area of the country where it may occur.

[3]

These provisions of the Voting Rights Act of 1965 are challenged on the fundamental ground that they exceed the powers of Congress and encroach on an area reserved to the states by the Constitution.

Has Congress exercised its powers under the 15th Amendment in an appropriate manner with relations to the states?

The ground rules for resolving this question are clear. The language and purpose of the 15th Amendment, the prior decisions construing its several provisions, and the general doctrines of constitutional interpretation, all point to one fundamental principle. As against the reserved powers of the states, Congress may use any rational means to effectuate the constitutional prohibition of racial discrimination in voting.

We therefore reject South Carolina's argument that Congress may appropriately do no more than to forbid violations of the 15th Amendment in general terms—that the task of fashioning specific remedies or of applying them to particular localities must necessarily be left entirely to the courts. Congress is not circumscribed by any such artificial rules under Section 2 of the 15th Amendment. In the oft-repeated words of Chief Justice Marshall, referring to another specific legislative authorization in the Constitution, "this power, like all others vested in Congress, is complete in itself, may be exercised to its utmost extent, and acknowledges no limitations, other than prescribed in the Constitution."

[4]

Congress exercised its authority under the 15th Amendment in an inventive manner when it enacted the Voting Rights Act of 1965. First: The measure prescribes remedies for voting discrimination which go into effect without any need for prior adjudication. This was clearly a legitimate response to the problem, for which there is ample precedent under other constitutional provisions.

Second: The Act intentionally confines these remedies to a small number of states and political subdivisions which in most instances were familiar to Congress by name. This, too, was a permissible method of dealing with the problem. Congress had learned that substantial voting discrimination presently occurs in certain sections of the country, and it knew no way of accurately forecasting whether the evil might spread elsewhere in the future.

In acceptable legislative fashion, Congress chose to limit its attention to the geographic areas where immediate action seemed necessary. The doctrine of the equality of states, invoked by South Carolina, does not bar this approach, for that doctrine applies only to the terms upon which states are admitted to the union, and not to the remedies for local evils which have subsequently appeared.

We now consider the related question of whether the specific states and political subdivisions within Section 4(b) of the Act were an appropriate target for the new remedies. South Carolina contends that the coverage formula is awkwardly designed in a number of respects and that it disregards various local conditions, which have nothing to do with racial discrimination. These arguments, however, are largely beside the point.

To be specific, the new remedies of the Act are imposed on three states—Alabama, Louisiana, and Mississippi—in which Federal courts have repeatedly found substantial voting discrimination. Section 4(b) of the act also embraces two other states—Georgia and South Carolina—plus large portions of a third state—North Carolina —for which there was more fragmentary evidence of recent voting discrimination mainly adduced by the Justice Department and the Civil Rights Commission. All of these areas were appropriately subjected to the new remedies. In identifying past evils, Congress obviously may avail itself of information from any probative source.

The areas listed above, for which there was evidence of actual voting discrimination, share two characteristics incorporated by Congress into the coverage formula: the use of tests and devices for voter registration, and a voting rate in the 1964 Presidential election at least 12 points below the national average. Tests and devices are relevant to voting discrimination because of their long history as a tool for perpetrating the evil; a low voting rate is pertinent for the obvious reason that widespread disenfranchisement must inevitably affect the number of actual voters.

Accordingly, the coverage formula is rational in both practice and theory. . . .

We now arrive at consideration of the specific remedies prescribed by the Act for areas included within the coverage formula. South Carolina assails the temporary suspension of existing voting qualifications. The record shows that in most of the states covered by the Act, including South Carolina, various tests and devices have been instituted with the purpose of disenfranchising Negroes, have been framed in such a way as to facilitate this aim, and have been administered in a discriminatory fashion for many years. Under these circumstances, the 15th Amendment has clearly been violated.

The Act suspends literacy tests and similar devices for a period of five years from the last occurrence of substantial voting discrimination. This was a legitimate response to the problem, for which there is ample precedent in 15th Amendment cases.

Underlying the response was the feeling that states and political subdivisions which had been allowing white illiterates to vote for years could not sincerely complain about "dilution" of their electorates through the registration of Negro illiterates. Congress knew that continuance of the tests and devices in use at the present time, no matter how fairly administered in the future, would freeze the effect of past discrimination in favor of unqualified white registrants. Congress permissibly rejected the alternative of requiring a complete re-registration of all voters, believing that this would be too harsh on many whites who had enjoyed the franchise for their entire adult lives.

The Act suspends new voting regulations pending scrutiny by Federal authorities to determine whether their use would violate the 15th Amendment. This may have been an uncommon exercise of Congressional Power, as South Carolina contends, but the Court has recognized that exceptional conditions can justify legislative measures not otherwise appropriate.

Congress knew that some of the states covered by Sec. 4(b) of the Act had resorted to the extraordinary strategem of contriving new rules of various kinds for the sole purpose of perpetuating voting discrimination in the face of adverse Federal decrees. Congress had reason to suppose that these states might try similar maneuvers in the future, in order to evade the remedies for voting discrimination contained in the Act itself. Under the compulsion of these unique circumstances, Congress responded in a permissibly decisive manner. . . .

The Act authorizes the appointment of Federal Examiners to list qualified applicants who are thereafter entitled to vote, subject to an expeditious challenge procedure. This was clearly an appropriate response to the problem, closely related to remedies authorized in prior cases.

After enduring nearly a century of widespread resistance to the 15th Amendment, Congress has marshalled an array of potent weapons against the evil, with authority in the Attorney General to employ them effectively. Many of the areas directly affected by this development have indicated their willingness to abide by any restraints legitimately imposed upon them.

We here hold that the portions of the Voting Rights Act properly before us are a valid means for carrying out the commands of the 15th Amendment. Hopefully, millions of nonwhite Americans will now be able to participate for the first time on an equal basis in the Government under which they live.

We may finally look forward to the day when truly "the right of citizens of the United States to vote shall not be denied or abridged by the United States or by any state on account of race, color, or previous condition of servitude."

The bill of complaint is dismissed.

—Chief Justice Earl Warren,
in South Carolina *v.* Katzenbach, 1966

35. The Dark Ghetto of Harlem

Kenneth B. Clark

EDITORIAL NOTE: *More than any other public institution, the school was the focal point of racial tensions. It had been the Supreme Court decision in Brown* v. *Board of Education of Topeka which had set off a chain-reaction of racial tensions and conflict throughout the South. Outraged Southerners responded with—among many others—the* tu quoque *argument: look to your own schools, they said to the North. And quite rightly, too, for in most large cities in the North, schools were in fact segregated. Needless to say, this segregation was not by law but by fact, and reflected a parallel segregation in housing. From New York's Harlem to Los Angeles' Watts, circumstances had created Negro ghettos, ghettos none the less restrictive or odious because they were the by-products of economic and social malpractices. What should be done? Should desegregation be achieved by transporting Negro and white children out of their own neighborhoods to distant schools? Should it be achieved by prohibiting segregation in housing and by an energetic effort to provide Negro housing in heretofore white neighborhoods? Or should Northern cities strive rather to lift the standards of the Negro schools? Even were this done, might it not still be said that segregation—no matter how arrived at—was inherently unequal? Kenneth Clark, a distinguished Negro psychologist and founder of the famous HARYOU experiment, here describes the ghetto schools of Harlem.*

THE PUBLIC SCHOOLS in America's urban ghettos also reflect the oppressive damage of racial exclusion. School segregation in the South had, for generations, been supported by law; in the North, segregation has been supported by community custom and indifference. It is assumed that children should go to school where they live, and if they live in segregated neighborhoods, the schools are, as a matter of course, segregated. But the educational crisis in the ghettos is not primarily, and certainly not exclusively, one of the inequitable racial balance in the schools. Equally serious is the inferior quality of the education in those schools. Segregation and inferior education reinforce each other. Some persons take the position that the first must go before the second does; others, that the reverse is true. What is clear is that the problem of education in the urban ghetto seems to be a vicious cycle: If children go to school where they live and if most neighborhoods are racially segregated, then the schools are necessarily segregated, too. If Negroes move into a previously white community and whites then move away or send their children to private or parochial schools, the public schools will continue to be segregated. If the quality of education in Negro schools is inferior to that in white schools, whites feel justified in the fear that the presence of Negroes in their own school would lower its standards. If they move their own children away and the school becomes predominantly Negro, and therefore receives an inferior quality of education, the pattern begins all over again. The cycle of systematic neglect of Negro children must be broken, but the powerlessness of the Negro communities and the fear and indifference of the white community have combined so far to keep the cycle intact.

The central questions that lie behind the entire network of problems are these: Are Negroes such—in terms of innate incapacity *or* environmental deprivation—that their children are less capable of learning than are whites, so that any school that is permitted to became integrated necessarily declines in quality? Or has inferior education been systematically imposed on Negroes in the nation's ghettos in such a way as to compel poor performance from Negro children—a performance that could be reversed with quality education? The answer to these questions is of fundamental importance because the flight of white from the urban public school system in many American cities is based on the belief that the first is true and the second false. If the first is false and the second true— and the centers of power in the white community can be convinced of that fact—one of the basic injustices in American life could be corrected.

THE PUBLIC SCHOOLS: A SEGREGATED SYSTEM?

Unless firm and immediate steps are taken to reverse the present trend, the public school system in the Northern cities of America will become predominantly a segregated system, serving primarily Negroes. It will, in addition, become a school system of low academic standards, providing a second-class education for underclassed children and thereby a chief contributor to the perpetuation of the "social dynamite" which is the cumulative pathology of the ghetto.

In Chicago, 37 percent of the elementary schools (compared with 22 percent in New York) and 18 percent of the high schools (compared with 2 percent in New York) are now segregated; 48.3 percent of the pupils in Chicago are now Negro. In Cleveland, 60 percent of the elementary schools and 58 percent of the high schools are segregated, white or Negro. In Detroit, more than 40 percent of public school children are Negro. In Philadelphia, more than half of the public school children are now Negro. By 1963 the Washington, D.C., public schools, which ten years ago had been one-third Negro, had become more than three-quarters Negro; by 1970, more than nine out of ten children in the public schools in the nation's capital may be Negro.

In the public schools of Manhattan as a whole, 73 percent of the children are already nonwhites. Ninety percent of school age children in Harlem are in public schools; only two-thirds of the children in the rest of Manhattan are—the others have moved into private or parochial schools. Despite the fact that segregation has been illegal in the public school system of New York State since 1902, virtually all the 31,469 children in Harlem's schools (twenty elementary schools, four junior high schools, and no high schools) are Negro. Only two of the elementary schools have less than 89.9 percent Negro enrollment; and all the junior high schools are at least 91.4 percent Negro. This means that the bulk of the community's children in elementary and junior high schools are educated in *de facto* segregated schools although the city's Board of Education has an official policy of full integration.

The trend toward school segregation, in fact, is accelerating. Seventy-eight New York schools below high school became segregated between 1958 and 1963. Open enrollment and the free choice transfer policy, allowing parents to seek the transfer of their children to nonsegregated schools, have done little to improve the situation—less than 3 percent of the nonwhite students moved to other schools. Many whites point to this apathy on the part of Negroes as evidence that Negro families in general prefer segregated neighborhood schools to unsegregated distant schools. *Any* parent prefers a neighborhood school, all things being equal and often when not all is equal, and no public school desegregation plan that demands voluntary individual decisions is ever accepted by the majority of Negro or white parents. Yet even if more students did transfer out of the ghetto few, if any, whites would move into the ghetto, and while the schools of the ghetto themselves would probably decline in population, they would remain segregated.

The pairing system, often called the Princeton Plan, which merges the populations of two nearby elementary schools, one predominantly Negro and the other predominantly white, also offers little chance of success in complex urban residential patterns and school systems. The New York City Board of Education proposed in 1964 that twenty-one such pairings be made. If all were introduced at once—though the board responded to further reflection and to community pressures by reducing the proposed twenty-one to four—segregation in the city would be reduced by only 1 percent. If twenty schools a year were so paired, an unlikely move, the school system would still be one-quarter segregated in 1970. Sprawling, densely populated cities are not manageable, peaceful suburban communities like Princeton, and because the plan works in one area is no guarantee it will work in another.

In 1963, 45 percent of New York's nonwhite children attended segregated junior highs. The Board of Education proposals to change the system of feeding students from elementary schools into junior highs would reduce this percentage only slightly. At this rate, and providing that the city's population did not itself change, the junior high schools of New York would be desegregated by about 2010.

On the other hand, efforts to desegregate the twenty-five schools dominated now by nonwhites would make a difference in a single decade. If important efforts to achieve school integration are not adopted, segregation in the public schools will increase from the 22 percent of the elementary schools in 1963 to 38 percent in 1975; from 19 to 29 percent of the junior high schools; from 2 to 6 percent of the high schools. The schools by 1980 would be three-quarters Negro and Puerto Rican in the city as a whole and in Manhattan would probably exceed 90 percent, though the proportion may be expected to stabilize at that point.

One of the remedies suggested has been long-distance transportation of elementary school pupils, or "busing." This plan seems to offer immediate desegregation, but in many cases it would lead to bad education and, in the end, therefore, to even more segregation. Whites would pull out of the public school system even more rapidly than they are presently doing. In Brooklyn, for example, if real integration were the goal, about 70,000 Negro and Puerto Rican children, under eleven, would have to be transported twice a day, some of them ten miles away. In Manhattan, where schools have an even higher proportion of Negro and Puerto Rican children, even longer travel time would fail to bring about meaningful integration. As the Allen Commission Report said:

> It should be obvious, but does not always appear to be, that integration is impossible without white pupils. No plan can be acceptable, therefore, which increases the movement of white pupils out of the public schools. Neither is it acceptable, however, unless it contributes to desegregation.

—Kenneth B. Clark, *Dark Ghetto,* 1965

36. Watts

Arna Bontemps & Jack Conroy

EDITORIAL NOTE: *The years 1964 and 1965 had seen Negro unrest flare into violence in Philadelphia, Cleveland, New York's Harlem and Brooklyn, and—somewhat surprisingly—Rochester. These outbreaks gave notice that the crisis of Negro discontent was just as urgent in the North as in the South, and potentially even more dangerous. The explosion in Watts—a derelict section of greater Los Angeles—in the summer of 1965 was a portent of what might be expected everywhere in the North unless the public officials and the white population of Northern cities recognized Negro claims for equality—or even for simple justice—in housing, employment, education, and law enforcement. Officials, from the chief of police and the Mayor up to the highest state officials, proved themselves ineffectual in handling the immediate violence and, worse, obtuse in their incomprehension of fundamental crisis. A commission of inquiry threw only the dimmest light on the problem, and a year after the outbreak the situation in Watts shows no perceptible improvement.*

BY 1965 WATTS had a population density of 27.3 per acre, compared with a Los Angeles County average of 7.4. Two thirds of its residents had not completed high school, and the school dropout rate was more than twice the city average. Restless, bitter, disillusioned boys aimlessly roamed the streets. Boredom, frustration and despair hung in the air like a heavy pall. Justifying their surveillance by the existence of a very high crime rate in Watts, the police were always watching and often apprehending and frisking Wattsians. Most of those supervised were from the South, where the typical lawman is a contemptuous oppressor and natural enemy. "Every time I stop to look at something I feel a white cop's eyes boring into my back," one black citizen complained, "and I see them everywhere I go."

Civil Rights workers would refer to the 205 police officers in Watts, only five of them Negroes, as an "occupying power." An image of "Whitey"—any white man—as the principal architect of the district's misfortunes grew larger and larger. A constant target of Negro organizations was Los Angeles Police Chief William H. Parker, who frequently lectured on the subject: "Man Is by Nature a Predatory Animal Who Must Be Restrained." Negroes contended that he displayed more zeal in restraining them than he did in handling white lawbreakers, and that he sanctioned police brutality toward dark-skinned Angelenos.

James Tolbert, a Negro attorney who once lived in Watts and served five years as a probation officer, offered this comment:

> The key word in Watts is hopelessness. The trouble is that the hero there is the bad guy, not the good guy. The feeling too often is that "I had rather be a delinquent than be nothing."

Against such a background the long-predicted happening took place just as the hot day of August 11, 1965, was drawing to a close. Shortly after seven P.M. Lee Minikus and Bob Lewis, state highway patrolmen, stopped an automobile at the intersection of Avalon and One Hundred Sixteenth Streets. They ordered the driver, a twenty-one-year-old Negro named Marquette Frye, to step out, and when he did they accused him of drunken driving. The ensuing events have been described in a dozen different ways by as many eyewitnesses. One story is that Frye's pregnant mother heard the ruckus and emerged from her nearby home to reprimand Marquette for being drunk. Another is that she was pleading with Marquette to submit peaceably to the officers. At any rate, there followed an argument participated in by Frye, his mother, his older brother (who was with him in the car) on one side and the policemen on the other. The officers claimed that Frye struggled and had to be restrained. Negro spectators did not see it that way. They maintained that the cops had beaten Frye before throwing him in the police car, and to make matters worse, had stomped his pregnant mother. The upshot was that all three Fryes were driven off to jail.

As always is the case, a curious crowd had gathered. One of the policemen is reported to have held the onlookers at bay, saying something like: "Get back, you niggers! Clear out of here, you niggers!" Squad cars with flashing lights and screaming sirens began to arrive in dozens, and soon there were seventy-five policemen with menacing guns. Only one of these was a Negro, and he is credited with making some ineffectual efforts to restore calm and order. One thing is certain: all hell broke loose. Angry, shouting Negroes began throwing rocks or anything else handy, smashing windows, and manufacturing Molotov cocktails out of Coke bottles filled with gasoline. These they hurled into buildings, usually those housing white-owned businesses. Often, before the establishment was put to the torch, desirable merchandise was hauled away. There was no such thing as a leader, unless you could call the one who first kicked in a window a leader. Once the breach was made, others quickly followed. Television sets, furniture, and even refrigerators were hauled away in coaster wagons and shopping carts. Foodstuff was not neglected, and liquor was high on the loot priority list. "That man been robbin' me for years, now I'm gettin' some of it back" was a frequent excuse.

Negro shopkeepers hastily posted such signs as "Blood Brother," "Colored-Owned Business," or simply "Blood." The rioters sometimes spared these places, though not always. In the course of the six-day disorders, 1,000 fires were reported by the Fire Department, 300 being of major proportions. Entire blocks were reduced to smoking ruins resembling those of bombed-out cities in World War II. A conservative estimate of the property damage placed it at over $40,000,000.

During the first day of rioting more than 1,500 people, mostly young Negroes, were ranging the streets, throwing rocks and other missiles into store windows and stoning the cars of passing motorists who appeared to be white. On several occasions light-skinned Negroes were accorded the same treatment.

By Friday, the mob was in complete control. More than a thousand city policemen, deputy sheriffs, and State highway patrolmen were helpless. "Burn, baby, burn," the theme song of a popular Negro disc jockey called "the mighty Montague," took on a ghastly literalness. "Get Whitey! Get Whitey!" was another often-shouted slogan as white pedestrians and motorists were set upon and beaten, none fatally. After unaccountable hesitation, Mayor Samuel W. Yorty asked Lieutenant Governor Glenn Anderson (in charge while Governor Edmund G. Brown was vacationing in Europe) to send in the National Guard. There was further delay as Anderson also displayed some indecisiveness, but on Saturday the guardsmen moved into the battle zone. Eventually there were 12,500 of them. They sealed off the area, imposing a quarantine appropriate for the black death or the bubonic plague. Severe restrictions were placed upon Negroes going in and out of Watts, even doctors being submitted to a search. It was easy enough to get out, but hard to get back in. Food shortages became grave. Negroes who had taken no part in the rioting were embittered. Many had huddled in their living rooms, watching on television the hell-raising going on only a block or so away.

Included in the loot from raided stores had been a number of rifles and revolvers. A certain amount of sporadic sniping took place, usually from rooftops. Police cars searching for a sniper threw a floodlight on a Negro housewife sitting on her front lawn. Blinded by the glare and enraged at the intrusion, she shouted:

> I ain't out in the street, dammit! Dammit, don't bother me in my house! Y'all ain't right! That's the trouble! Y'all ain't right!

Another woman was compelled to get out of her house and stay in her front yard while guardsmen searched for a sniper they thought had fired from the roof. It didn't seem right to her, either, and she lamented:

> You shot into a house full of babies. I love my black babies as much as you love your white ones, and all I see around me is white faces with guns.

When all the hysterical talk about Negroes with guns simmered down, it was learned that of the thirty-four known dead in the riot, only three were white. And only one of the white casualties could have been shot by a Negro. Law-enforcement officers consistently referred to the rioters as "terrorists," but it was disclosed that the lawmen themselves knew a little about terrorism. The rioters were terrorists, all right, but their terrorism rarely had lethal consequences. It was aimed at Whitey's property more than at his life. One elderly Negro gentleman, who remembered Watts before the deluge of migrants came, shook his head sadly and said:

> These youngsters goin' around, hopped up tree-top tall on goof balls and whiskey, playin' the scare-Whitey game! They scare him all right, but they scare the livin' daylights out of me, too. And they scare theirselves plenty, you bet your boots.

Observers began to wonder about Chief Parker's riot control program, of which he had often boasted. The conventional methods of riot control—tear and nausea gas, fire hose, etc.—were never put into use. The wide streets of Watts lent themselves to such tactics. Instead, the police—and later the guardsmen—relied largely upon clubs and firearms. Flashing red lights on police cars and ambulances and screaming sirens added to the pandemonium, whereas in other cities it has been considered wise practice to eliminate such provocations of excitement. Nicholas Von Hoffman of the Chicago *Daily News,* one reporter who observed things for himself and did not rely upon police say-so or canned press releases, had a number of questions to ask.

He pointed out that the 664 Los Angeles city policemen sent into action chalked up two thirds of the slain, while the 12,500 National Guardsmen in the same area could be credited with only about four casualties. Very often the familiar question, "Who's in charge here?" seemed to be unanswerable. Von Hoffman quoted a white reporter as remarking: "On Thursday night, clearly no one was in command. I saw police going up and down beating people with their sticks and smashing car windows."

When uneasy calm descended upon Watts, everybody seemed to be affected with a case of psychic hangover. Most Negroes, young and old, walked about silently, either sullen or sad. There was no more communication between them and the white power structure than there had been before the holocaust. As for the men on top, mutual recriminations and accusations began to fly about as thickly as the brickbats had. Everybody wanted to get in the act, as Jimmy Durante complains. Governor Brown, flying hastily home from Greece, could see no employment opportunity or voting privilege significance in the situation. He went on:

> The riot took place in a scene of broken families and broken hearts, of lonely children and aimless adults, of frustration and poverty. . . . It is a tragedy that must not become a prophecy for this or any other great city in America.

With this in mind, he appointed an eight-man commission, headed by John A. McCone (formerly director of the Central Intelligence Agency), to investigate the riots, with subpoena powers "to make sure that all of us have access to the whole truth." The function of the investigatory commission, he said in a television speech, would be ". . . to probe deeply for the immediate and underlying causes of the Los Angeles riots and to recommend means to prevent their recurrence." Later on, he was to say in San Francisco that statements by Chief Parker had "hurt the whole cause of race relations in Los Angeles." One of these, undoubtedly, was Parker's exultant crowing that "We're on top now and they're on the bottom," referring to the rioters.

As for Parker, he could see no blemish or flaw in his conduct or that of his men. There had been too much handling of Negroes with "kid gloves" in the recent past, he concluded. Replying to accusations that police brutality not only had helped to precipitate the riot but had contributed to its prolongation, he made it plain that he was not going to suffer "in silence under such criticism" as did "the average police chief in America." Then he made a revelation:

> We have learned that a large proportion of the rioters in custody have criminal records. The feeling of the rioters has been to gloss over Negro crime and blame mistreatment by police.

Mayor Yorty concurred, and cited a favorite bête noire (albeit it was red-hued!). He dismissed the charges of police brutality by identifying them as ". . . part of a big lie technique shouted all over the world by Communists, dupes, and demagogues, irrespective of race."

Evangelist Billy Graham, surverying still smoldering Watts from the vantage point of a helicopter, envisioned "a dress rehearsal for revolution" instigated by "sinister forces trying to set race against race and class against class with the ruthless objective of overthrowing the government." This led the *Christian Century* in its September 1, 1965, issue to inquire editorially:

> What sinister forces, Mr. Graham? Are you implying with the John Birch Society that the Negro's rebellion is communist-inspired, communist-directed? Or do you mean by "sinister forces" the centuries-old rapaciousness of the white man, the white Christian's cold indifference to the plight of his Negro brother, the inactivity of genteel churches, the bitter despair which the Negro sucks from his legacy of abuse? Don't you know that it was your ancestors and ours who set race against race, class against class? If you believe that the nation is being ruined by sinister forces, name them.

Municipal Court Judge Loren Miller, a Negro attorney noted for his civil rights activities and for his incisive articles in the *Nation* and elsewhere, thought that the overwhelming vote for Proposition 14 in the November 1964 election had something to do with the hedged-in, wanting-to-bust-out feeling that had stirred discontent among the Wattsians, who felt that they were being enclosed within four walls. Proposition 14 had the effect of nullifying all fair housing legislation that had given Negroes a measure of at least legal protection. "The people distrust the police, and the police distrust the people," Judge Miller added. "They move in a constant atmosphere of hate."

Saul D. Alinsky, a community organizer whose work in the Chicago "Back of the Yards" neighborhood brought him international attention, offered—from his home in Carmel—two "conditions of reconstruction." The first was to give Police Chief Parker his walking papers. The second was to retire "that un-Christian, prehistoric muttonhead" James Francis Cardinal McIntyre, archbishop of the Los Angeles diocese. Alinsky elaborated: "I would recommend Parker to be security chief in Disneyland. And Cardinal McIntyre would be apostolic delegate to Taiwan, with the hope that we would then follow John Foster Dulles' suggestion and unleash him on the Chinese mainland."

Mayor Yorty had no power to implement the second recommendation, and he vigorously spurned the first. Dr. Martin Luther King, after a ninety-minute conference with Governor Brown, reported that the governor, too, defended Parker's conduct, but acknowledged that "his zeal for law enforcement could be misinterpreted as prejudice." Dr. King had said in Miami before he came to Los Angeles:

> I strongly deplore the violence. It is absolutely wrong, socially detestable and self-defeating. On the other hand, I equally deplore the continuation of ghetto life that millions of Negroes have to live in. They are in hopeless despair, and they feel they have no stake in society.

Alinsky's indictment of Cardinal McIntyre was not the only one. Civil rights leaders and liberal-minded Roman Catholic laymen and clergymen had previously assailed him for his censure and punishment of priests and nuns who had taken part in civil rights activities or had even spoken favorably of them. In 1964 Father William DuBay addressed an open letter to Pope Paul VI requesting that Cardinal McIntyre be dethroned. Late in the same year, Father John Coffield asked for and received a three-year leave of absence from his pastorate at Ascension Church so that he might go to Chicago to work in a Negro parish and to study psychology at the University of Chicago. He said frankly that the Cardinal's stricture on the race question had influenced his decision to leave Los Angeles.

Harlem Congressman Adam Clayton Powell, Jr., never at a loss for words, had some strong ones:

> In Los Angeles, the incinerating fuel for last week's explosion had been smoldering for years—police brutality. The arrogance of Police Chief Parker in refusing to heed the pleas of responsible Negro leadership steadily worsened the situation. More recently, the refusal of the Mayor to evolve a comprehensive anti-poverty program to siphon off many of that community's unemployed further was regarded as a kick in the stomach by many Negroes.

Ex-President Eisenhower, in characteristically muddled syntax, used these words to reprove the rioters:

> This kind of senseless violence—I don't care what the condition of these people who started it—they have made the conditions far worse. They have burned their homes and stores. They have cost an immeasurable amount of money that could have been spent in their favor.

Senator Robert F. Kennedy (D.-N.Y.) was moved to retort when he heard of Ike's homily:

> It is pointless to tell Negroes living in Northern slums to obey the law. To these Negroes, the law is their enemy. . . . By and large, white politicians in the North are completely out of touch with the ferment and hatred that exists among slum Negroes. They have traditionally done business with a small coterie of Negro leaders who, until 1962, could be depended upon to deliver the Negro vote as a bloc in return for a few political jobs and specified sums of money.

And what of the "terrorists" themselves? A few were still bellicose, but more were chastened and repentant. "It seemed like fun at first," one boy confessed, "throwing rocks at Whitey's big new cars. We didn't aim to hurt anybody, just mess up the cars. At least, not at first. Then it seemed like the stuff we took was just there for us. If we didn't take it, somebody else would. But then it got not to be so much fun at all but just trouble." Other contrite rioters recalled that some of the "Whitey" merchants hadn't been "devils" after all, but had occasionally done a kindness for them. But if the window is already broken, and the stuff you really need or want is just lying there for the taking, you got to be strong not to jump in and get your share.

The McCone commission issued a 101-page report in December 1965. It named unemployment as the most distressing problem in Watts, and deplored the "sickness in the center of our city." There were recommendations for job training programs, a more wholesome home life for children, and a "strengthened" police commission. Very few personal references were made, though Acting Governor Anderson was mildly chided for not calling in national guard troops soon enough. This dire warning was sounded:

> So serious and so explosive is the situation that, unless it is checked, the August riots may seem by comparison to be only a curtain raiser to what could blow up one day in the future.

—Arna Bontemps & Jack Conroy, *Anyplace But Here,* 1966

37. "The Barriers to Freedom Are Tumbling Down," 1965

Lyndon B. Johnson

EDITORIAL NOTE: *When Lyndon B. Johnson moved into the White House in November 1963, he took up the crusade for civil rights launched by President Kennedy. As Senator from Texas and as Vice President, Johnson had worked quietly but zealously for civil rights legislation. The first truly Southern President for almost a hundred years, he not only knew and understood the South, but was trusted by Southerners. He was, too, immensely skilled in the ways of politics: if it cannot be said that he imposed his will on the Congress, it can be said that he was successful in persuading Congress to accept his version of the popular will. Johnson not only carried through the Civil Rights Act of 1964 and the Voting Rights Act of 1965, but put the full power of his administration behind their enforcement. His speech at Howard University on June 4, 1965, contains the most eloquent statement of his philosophy.*

. . . THE BARRIERS TO . . . freedom are tumbling down. Freedom is the right to share, share fully and equally, in American society—to vote, to hold a job, to enter a public place, to go to school. It is the right to be treated in every part of our national life as a person equal in dignity and promise to all others.

But freedom is not enough. You do not wipe away the scars of centuries by saying: Now you are free to go where you want, or do as you desire, and choose the leaders you please.

You do not take a person who, for years, has been hobbled by chains and liberate him, bring him up to the starting line of a race and then say, "you are free to compete with all the others," and still justly believe that you have been completely fair.

Thus it is not enough just to open the gates of opportunity. All our citizens must have the ability to walk through those gates.

This is the next and the more profound stage of the battle for civil rights. We seek not just freedom but opportunity. We seek not just legal equity but human ability—not just equality as a right and a theory, but equality as a fact and equality as a result.

For the task is to give twenty million Negroes the same chance as every other American to learn and grow, to work and share in society, to develop their abilities—physical, mental and spiritual, and to pursue their individual happiness.

To this end equal opportunity is essential, but not enough, not enough. Men and women of all races are born with the same range of abilities. But ability is not just the product of birth. Ability is stretched or stunted by the family you live with, and the neighborhood you live in, by the school you go to and the poverty or the richness of your surroundings. It is the product of a hundred unseen forces playing upon the little infant, the child, and finally the man.

This graduating class at Howard University is witness to the indomitable determination of the Negro American to win his way in American life.

The number of Negroes in schools of higher learning has almost doubled in fifteen years. The number of nonwhite professional workers has more than doubled in ten years. The median income of Negro college women tonight exceeds that of white college women. And there are also the enormous accomplishments of distinguished individual Negroes—many of them graduates of this institution, and one of them the first lady ambassador in the history of the United States.

These are proud and impressive achievements. But they tell only the story of a growing middle class minority, steadily narrowing the gap between them and their white counterparts.

But for the great majority of Negro Americans—the poor, the unemployed, the uprooted and the dispossessed—there is a much grimmer story. They still, as we meet here tonight, are another nation. Despite the court orders and the laws, despite the legislative victories and the speeches, for them the walls are rising and the gulf is widening.

Here are some of the facts of this American failure.

Thirty-five years ago the rate of unemployment for Negroes and whites was about the same. Tonight the Negro rate is twice as high.

In 1948 the 8 percent unemployment rate for Negro teenage boys was actually less than that of whites. By last year that rate had grown to 23 percent, as against 13 percent for whites unemployed.

Between 1949 and 1959, the income of Negro men relative to white men declined in every section of this country. From 1952 to 1963 the median income of Negro families compared to white actually dropped from 57 percent to 53 percent.

In the years 1955 through 1957, 22 percent of experienced Negro workers were out of work at some time during the year. In 1961 through 1963 that proportion had soared to 29 percent.

Since 1947 the number of white families living in poverty has decreased 27 percent while the number of poorer nonwhite families decreased only 3 per cent.

The infant mortality of nonwhites in 1940 was 70 percent greater than whites. Twenty-two years later it was 90 percent greater.

Moreover, the isolation of Negro from white communities is increasing, rather than decreasing as Negroes crowd into the central cities and become a city within a city.

Of course Negro Americans as well as white Americans have shared in our rising national abundance. But the harsh fact of the matter is that in the battle for true equality too many are losing ground every day.

We are not completely sure why this is. We know the causes are complex and subtle. But we do know the two broad basic reasons. And we do know that we have to act.

First, Negroes are trapped—as many whites are trapped—in inherited, gateless poverty. They lack training and skills. They are shut in slums, without decent medical care. Private and public poverty combine to cripple their capacities.

We are trying to attack these evils through our poverty program, through our education program, through our medical care and our other health programs and a dozen more of the Great Society programs that are aimed at the root causes of this poverty.

We will increase, and we will accelerate, and we will broaden this attack in years to come until this most enduring of foes finally yields to our unyielding will. But there is a second cause—much more difficult to explain, more deeply grounded, more desperate in its force. It is the devastating heritage of long years of slavery; and a century of oppression, hatred, and injustice.

For Negro poverty is not white poverty. Many of its causes and many of its cures are the same. But there are differences—deep, corrosive, obstinate differences—radiating painful roots into the community, and into the family, and the nature of the individual.

These differences are not racial differences. They are solely and simply the consequence of ancient brutality, past injustice, and present prejudice. They are anguishing to observe. For the Negro they are a constant reminder of oppression. For the white they are a constant reminder of guilt. But they must be faced and they must be dealt with and they must be overcome, if we are ever to reach the time when the only difference between Negroes and whites is the color of their skin.

Nor can we find a complete answer in the experience of other American minorities. They made a valiant and a largely successful effort to emerge from poverty and prejudice.

The Negro, like these others, will have to rely mostly on his own efforts. But he just can not do it alone. For they did not have the heritage of centuries to overcome, and they did not have a cultural tradition which had been twisted and battered by endless years of hatred and hopelessness, nor were they excluded—these others—because of race or color—a feeling whose dark intensity is matched by no other prejudice in our society.

Nor can these differences be understood as isolated infirmities. They are a seamless web. They cause each other. They result from each other. They reinforce each other.

Much of the Negro community is buried under a blanket of history and circumstance. It is not a lasting solution to lift just one corner of that blanket. We must stand on all sides and we must raise the entire cover if we are to liberate our fellow citizens.

One of the differences is the increased concentration of Negroes in our cities. More than 73 per cent of all Negroes live in urban areas compared with less than 70 per cent of the whites. Most of these Negroes live in slums. Most of these Negroes live together—a separated people.

Men are shaped by their world. When it is a world of decay, ringed by an invisible wall, when escape is arduous and uncertain, and the saving pressures of a more hopeful society are unknown, it can cripple the youth and it can desolate the man.

There is also the burden that a dark skin can add to the search for a productive place in society. Unemployment strikes most swiftly and broadly at the Negro, and this burden erodes hope. Blighted hope breeds despair. Despair brings indifference to the learning which offers a way out. And despair, coupled with indifference, is often the source of destructive rebellion against the fabric of society.

There is also the lacerating hurt of early collision with white hatred or prejudice, distaste or condescension. Other groups have felt similar intolerance. But success and achievement could wipe it away. They do not change the color of a man's skin. I have seen this uncomprehending pain in the eyes of the little Mexican-American schoolchild that I taught many years ago. But it can be overcome. But, for many, the wounds are always open.

Perhaps most important—its influence radiating to every part of life—is the breakdown of the Negro family structure. For this, most of all, white America must accept responsibility. It flows from centuries of oppression and persecution of the Negro man. It flows from the long years of degradation and discrimination, which have attacked his dignity and assaulted his ability to provide for his family.

This, too, is not pleasant to look upon. But it must be faced by those whose serious intent is to improve the life of all Americans.

Only a minority—less than half—of all Negro children reach the age of 18 having lived all their lives with both of their parents. At this moment, tonight, little less than two-thirds are at home with both of their parents. Probably a majority of all Negro children receive Federally-aided public assistance sometime during their childhood.

The family is the cornerstone of our society. More than any other force it shapes the attitude, the hopes, the ambitions, and the values of the child. And when the family collapses it is the children that are usually damaged. When it happens on a massive scale the community itself is crippled.

So, unless we work to strengthen the family, to create conditions under which most parents will stay together—all the rest: schools, and playgrounds, and public assistance, and private concern, will never be enough to cut completely the circle of despair and deprivation.

There is no single easy answer to all of these problems. Jobs are part of the answer. They bring the income which permits a man to provide for his family. Decent homes in decent surroundings and a chance to learn—an equal chance to learn—are part of the answer. Welfare and social programs better designed to hold families together are part of the answer. Care for the sick is part of the answer. An understanding heart by all Americans is another big part of the answer. And to all these fronts—and a dozen more—I will dedicate the expanding efforts of the Johnson Administration.

—President Lyndon B. Johnson, Address at Howard University, 1965

38. The Emergence of Black Power

Stokely Carmichael

EDITORIAL NOTE: *Historically it is not defeat and desperation that encourage extremism and violence, but success and hope. The legal end to segregation, the enactment of two federal Civil Rights bills, the growing power of the Negro at the polls—all this bred impatience with the slow progress toward racial equality, and especially with the moderate, non-violent techniques of the older white and Negro civil rights groups. In 1965 and 1966 violence flared out in many Southern communities and then, not surprisingly, in the North. What* was *unexpected and, to many, shocking was the emergence of a philosophy of Black Power. In its more extreme form, that philosophy was espoused by the Black Muslims. Their most famous spokesman, Malcolm X, became disillusioned with their severely militant philosophy and, at the time of his murder in 1965 (probably at the hands of the Black Muslims), was preaching in behalf of his own version of Black Power. A more persuasive and moderate case for Black Power was made by a new group of leaders, of whom the most effective was Stokely Carmichael, National Chairman of the Student Non-violent Coordinating Committee and a veteran of many battles for Negro rights. The emergence of violent non-violence and of even moderate extremism on the part of Negroes alarmed large segments of the white community and doubtless contributed to the defeat of the 1966 Civil Rights Bill.*

One of the tragedies of the struggle against racism is that up to now there has been no national organization which could speak to the growing militancy of young black people in the urban ghetto. There has been only a civil rights movement, whose tone of voice was adapted to an audience of liberal whites. It served as a sort of buffer zone between them and angry young blacks. None of its so-called leaders could go into a rioting community and be listened to. In a sense, I blame ourselves—together with the mass media—for what has happened in Watts, Harlem, Chicago, Cleveland, Omaha. Each time the people in those cities saw Martin Luther King get slapped, they became angry; when they saw four little black girls bombed to death, they were angrier; and when nothing happened, they were steaming. We had nothing to offer that they could see, except to go out and be beaten again. We helped to build their frustration.

For too many years, black Americans marched and had their heads broken and got shot. They were saying to the country, "Look, you guys are supposed to be nice guys and we are only going to do what we are supposed to do—why do you beat us up, why don't you give us what we ask, why don't you straighten yourselves out?" After years of this, we are at almost the same point—because we demonstrated from a position of weakness. We cannot be expected any longer to march and have our heads broken in order to say to whites: come on, you're nice guys. For you are not nice guys. We have found you out.

An organization which claims to speak for the needs of a community—as does the Student Nonviolent Coordinating Committee—must speak in the tone of that community, not as somebody else's buffer zone. This is the significance of black power as a slogan. For once, black people are going to use the words they want to use—not just the words whites want to hear. And they will do this no matter how often the press tries to stop the use of the slogan by equating it with racism or separatism. . . .

Black power can be clearly defined for those who do not attach the fears of white America to their questions about it. We should begin with the basic fact that black Americans have two problems: they are poor and they are black. All other problems arise from this two-sided reality: lack of education, the so-called apathy of black men. Any program to end racism must address itself to that double reality.

Almost from its beginning, SNCC sought to address itself to both conditions with a program aimed at winning political power for impoverished Southern blacks. We had to begin with politics because black Americans are a propertyless people in a country where property is valued above all. We had to work for power, because this country does not function by morality, love, and nonviolence, but by power. Thus we determined to win political power, with the idea of moving on from there into activity that would have economic effects. With power, the masses could *make or participate in making* the decisions which govern their destinies, and thus create basic change in their day-to-day lives.

But if political power seemed to be the key to self-determination, it was also obvious that the key had been thrown down a deep well many years earlier. Disenfranchisement, maintained by racist terror, makes it impossible to talk about organizing for political power in 1960. The right to vote had to be won, and SNCC workers devoted their energies to this from 1961 to 1965. They set up voter registration drives in the Deep South. They created pressure for the vote by holding mock elections in Mississippi in 1963 and by helping to establish the Mississippi Freedom Democratic Party (MFDP) in 1964. That struggle was eased, though not won, with the passage of the 1965 Voting Rights Act. SNCC workers could then address themselves to the question: "Who can we vote for, to have our needs met—how do we make our vote meaningful?"

SNCC had already gone to Atlantic City for recognition of the Mississippi Freedom Democratic Party by the Democratic convention and been rejected; it had gone with the Mississippi Freedom Democratic Party to Washington for recognition by Congress and been rejected. In Arkansas, SNCC helped thirty Negroes to run for School Board elections; all but one were defeated, and there was evidence of fraud and intimidation sufficient to cause their defeat.

In Atlanta, Julian Bond ran for the state legislature and was elected —twice—and unseated—twice. In several states, black farmers ran in elections for agricultural committees which make crucial decisions concerning land use, loans, etc. Although they won places on a number of committees, they never gained the majorities needed to control them.

All of the efforts were attempts to win black power. Then, in Alabama, the opportunity came to see how blacks could be organized on an independent party basis. An unusual Alabama law provides that any group of citizens can nominate candidates for county office and, if they win 20 per cent of the vote, may be recognized as a county political party. The same then applies on a state level. SNCC went to organize in several counties such as Lowndes, where black people—who form 80 per cent of the population and have an average annual income of $943—felt they could accomplish nothing within the framework of the Alabama Democratic Party because of its racism and because the qualifying fee for this year's elections was raised from $50 to $500 in order to prevent most Negroes from becoming candidates. On May 3, five new county "freedom organizations" convened and nominated candidates for the offices of sheriff, tax assessor, members of the school boards. These men and women are up for election in November—if they live until then. Their ballot symbol is the black panther: a bold, beautiful animal, representing the strength and dignity of black demands today. A man needs a black panther on his side when he and his family must endure—as hundreds of Alabamians have endured—loss of job, eviction, starvation, and sometimes death, for political activity. He may also need a gun and SNCC reaffirms the right of black men everywhere to defend themselves when threatened or attacked. As for initiating the use of violence, we hope that such programs as ours will make that unnecessary; but it is not for us to tell black communities whether they can or cannot use any particular form of action to resolve their problems. Responsibility for the use of violence by black men, whether in self defense or initiated by them, lies with the white community.

This is the specific historical experience from which SNCC's call for "black power" emerged on the Mississippi march last July. But the concept of "black power" is not a recent or isolated phenomenon: It has grown out of the ferment of agitation and activity by different people and organizations in many black communities over the years. Our last year of work in Alabama added a new concrete possibility. In Lowndes county, for example, black power will mean that if a Negro is elected sheriff, he can end police brutality. If a black man is elected tax assessor, he can collect and channel funds for the building of better roads and schools serving black people—thus advancing the move from political power into the economic arena. In such areas as Lowndes, where black men have a majority, they will attempt to use it to exercise control. This is what they seek: control. Where Negroes lack a majority, black power means proper representation and sharing of control. It means the creation of power bases from which black people can work to change statewide or nationwide patterns of oppression through pressure from strength—instead of weakness. Politically, black power means what it has always meant to SNCC: the coming-together of black people to elect representatives and *to force those representatives to speak to their needs.* It does not mean merely putting black faces into office. A man or woman who is black and from the slums cannot be automatically expected to speak to the needs of black people. Most of the black politicians we see around the country today are not what SNCC means by black power. The power must be that of a community, and emanate from there. . . .

Ultimately, the economic foundations of this country must be shaken if black people are to control their lives. The colonies of the United States—and this includes the black ghettoes within its borders, north and south—must be liberated. For a century, this nation has been like an octopus of exploitation, its tentacles stretching from Mississippi and Harlem to South America, the Middle East, southern Africa, and Vietnam; the form of exploitation varies from area to area but the essential result has been the same—a powerful few have been maintained and enriched at the expense of the poor and voiceless colored masses. This pattern must be broken. As its grip loosens here and there around the world, the hopes of black Americans become more realistic. For racism to die, a totally different America must be born.

This is what the white society does not wish to face; this is why that society prefers to talk about integration. But integration speaks not at all to the problem of poverty, only to the problem of blackness. Integration today means the man who "makes it," leaving his black brothers behind in the ghetto as fast as his new sports car will take him. It has no relevance to the Harlem wino or to the cottonpicker making three dollars a day. As a lady I know in Alabama once said, "the food that Ralph Bunche eats doesn't fill my stomach."

Integration, moreover, speaks to the problem of blackness in a despicable way. As a goal, it has been based on complete acceptance of the fact that *in order to have* a decent house or education, blacks must move into a white neighborhood or send their children to a white school. This reinforces, among both black and white, the idea that "white" is automatically better and "black" is by definition inferior. This is why integration is a subterfuge for the maintenance of white supremacy. It allows the nation to focus on a handful of Southern children who get into white schools, at great price, and to ignore the 94 per cent who are left behind in unimproved all-black schools. Such situations will not change until black people have power—to control their own school boards, in this case. Then Negroes become equal in a way that means something, and integration ceases to be a one-way street. Then integration doesn't mean draining skills and energies from the ghetto into white neighborhoods; then it can mean white people moving from Beverly Hills into Watts, white people joining the Lowndes County Freedom Organization. Then integration becomes relevant. . . .

To most whites, black power seems to mean that the Mau Mau are coming to the suburbs at night. The Mau Mau are coming, and whites must stop them. Articles appear about plots to "get Whitey," creating an atmosphere in which "law and order must be maintained." Once again, responsibility is shifted from the oppressor to the oppressed. Other whites chide, "Don't forget—you're only 10 per cent of the population; if you get too smart, we'll wipe you out." If they are liberals, they complain, "what about me?—don't you want my help any more?" These are people supposedly concerned about black Americans, but today they think first of themselves, of their feelings of rejection. Or they admonish, "you can't get anywhere without coalitions," when there is in fact no group at present with whom to form a coalition in which blacks will not be absorbed and betrayed. Or they accuse us of "polarizing the races" by our calls for black unity, when the true responsibility for polarization lies with whites who will not accept their responsibility as the majority power for making the democratic process work.

White America will not face the problem of color, the reality of it. The well-intended say: "We're all human, everybody is really decent, we must forget color." But color cannot be "forgotten" until its weight is recognized and dealt with. White America will not acknowledge that the ways in which this country sees itself are contradicted by being black—and always have been. Whereas most of the people who settled this country came here for freedom or for economic opportunity, blacks were brought here to be slaves. When the Lowndes County Freedom Organization chose the black panther as its symbol, it was christened by the press "the Black Panther Party"—but the Alabama Democratic Party, whose symbol is a rooster, has never been called the White Cock Party. No one ever talked about "white power" because power in this country *is* white. All this adds up to more than merely identifying a group phenomenon by some catchy name or adjective. The furor over that black panther reveals the problems that white America has with color and sex; the furor over "black power" reveals how deep racism runs and the great fear which is attached to it.

From birth, black people are told a set of lies about themselves. We are told that we are lazy—yet I drive through the Delta area of Mississippi and watch black people picking cotton in the hot sun for fourteen hours. We are told, "If you work hard, you'll succeed"—but if that were true, black people would own this country. We are oppressed because we are black—not because we are ignorant, not because we are lazy, not because we're stupid (and got good rhythm), but because we're black.

I remember that when I was a boy, I used to go to see Tarzan movies on Saturday. White Tarzan used to beat up the black natives. I would sit there yelling, "Kill the beasts, kill the savages, kill 'em!" I was saying: Kill *me*. It was as if a Jewish boy watched Nazis taking Jews off to concentration camps and cheered them on. Today, I want the chief to beat hell out of Tarzan and send him back to Europe. But it takes time to become free of the lies and their shaming effect on black minds. It takes time to reject the most important lie: that black people inherently can't do the same things white people can do, unless white people help them.

The need for psychological equality is the reason why SNCC today believes that blacks must organize in the black community. Only black people can convey the revolutionary idea that black people are able to do things themselves. Only they can help create in the community an aroused and continuing black consciousness that will provide the basis for political strength. In the past, white allies have furthered white supremacy without the whites involved realizing it—or wanting it, I think. Black people must do things for themselves; they must get poverty money they will control and spend themselves, they must conduct tutorial programs themselves so that black children can identify with black people. This is one reason Africa has such importance: The reality of black men ruling their own natives gives blacks elsewhere a sense of possibility, of power, which they do not now have.

This does not mean we don't welcome help, or friends. But we want the right to decide whether anyone is, in fact, our friend. In the past, black Americans have been almost the only people whom everybody and his momma could jump up and call their friends. We have been tokens, symbols, objects—as I was in high school to many young whites, who liked having "a Negro friend." We want to decide who is our friend, and we will not accept someone who comes to us and says: "If you do X, Y, and Z, then I'll help you." We will not be told whom we should choose as allies. We will not be isolated from any group or nation except by our own choice. We cannot have the oppressors telling the oppressed how to rid themselves of the oppressor.

I have said that most liberal whites react to "black power" with the question, What about me?, rather than saying: Tell me what you want me to do and I'll see if I can do it. There are answers to the right question. One of the most disturbing things about almost all white supporters of the movement has been that they are afraid to go into their own communities—which is where the racism exists—and work to get rid of it. They want to run from Berkeley to tell us what to do in Mississippi; let them look instead at

Berkeley. They admonish blacks to be nonviolent; let them preach nonviolence in the white community. They come to teach me Negro history; let them go to the suburbs and open up freedom schools for whites. Let them work to stop America's racist foreign policy; let them press this government to cease supporting the economy of South Africa.

There is a vital job to be done among poor whites. We hope to see, eventually, a coalition between poor blacks and poor whites. That is the only coalition which seems acceptable to us, and we see such a coalition as the major internal instrument of change in American society. SNCC has tried several times to organize poor whites; we are trying again now, with an initial training program in Tennessee. It is purely academic today to talk about bringing poor blacks and whites together, but the job of creating a poor-white power bloc must be attempted. The main responsibility for it falls upon whites. Black and white can work together in the white community where possible; it is not possible, however, to go into a poor Southern town and talk about integration. Poor whites everywhere are becoming more hostile—not less—because they see the nation's attention focused on black poverty and nobody coming to them. Too many young middle-class Americans, like some sort of Pepsi generation, have wanted to come alive through the black community; they've wanted to be where the action is—and the action has been in the black community.

Black people do not want to "take over" this country. They don't want to "get whitey"; they just want to get him off their backs, as the saying goes. It was for example the exploitation by Jewish landlords and merchants which first created black resentment toward Jews—not Judaism. The white man is irrelevant to blacks, except as an oppressive force. Blacks want to be in his place, yes, but not in order to terrorize and lynch and starve him. They want to be in his place because that is where a decent life can be had.

But our vision is not merely of a society in which all black men have enough to buy the good things of life. When we urge that black money go into black pockets, we mean the communal pocket. We want to see money go back into the community and used to benefit it. We want to see the cooperative concept applied in business and banking. We want to see black ghetto residents demand that an exploiting store keeper sell them, at minimal cost, a building or a shop that they will own and improve cooperatively; they can back their demand with a rent strike, or a boycott, and a community so unified behind them that no one else will move into the building or buy at the store. The society we seek to build among black people, then, is not a capitalist one. It is a society in which the spirit of community and humanistic love prevail. The word love is suspect; black expectations of what it might produce have been betrayed too often. But those were expectations of a response from the white community, which failed us. The love we seek to encourage is within the black community, the only American community where men call each other "brother" when they meet. We can build a community of love only where we have the ability and power to do so: among blacks.

As for white America, perhaps it can stop crying out against "black supremacy," "black nationalism," "racism in reverse," and begin facing reality. The reality is that this nation, from top to bottom, is racist; that racism is not primarily a problem of "human relations" but of an exploitation maintained—either actively or through silence—by the society as a whole. Camus and Sartre have asked, can a man condemn himself? Can whites, particularly liberal whites, condemn themselves? Can they stop blaming us, and blame their own system? Are they capable of the shame which might become a revolutionary emotion?

We have found that they usually cannot condemn themselves, and so we have done it. But the rebuilding of this society, if at all possible, is basically the responsibility of whites—not blacks. We won't fight to save the present society, in Vietnam or anywhere else. We are just going to work, in the way *we* see fit, and on goals *we* define, not for civil rights but for all our human rights.

—STOKELY CARMICHAEL, "What We Want"

Revised June, 1967

harper torchbooks

HUMANITIES AND SOCIAL SCIENCES

American Studies: General

THOMAS C. COCHRAN: The Inner Revolution. *Essays on the Social Sciences in History* TB/1140
HENRY STEELE COMMAGER, Ed.: The Struggle for Racial Equality TB/1300
EDWARD S. CORWIN: American Constitutional History. *Essays edited by Alpheus T. Mason and Gerald Garvey* △ TB/1136
CARL N. DEGLER, Ed.: Pivotal Interpretations of American History TB/1240, TB/1241
A. HUNTER DUPREE: Science in the Federal Government: *A History of Policies and Activities to 1940* TB/573
A. S. EISENSTADT, Ed.: The Craft of American History: *Recent Essays in American Historical Writing* Vol. I TB/1255; Vol. II TB/1256
CHARLOTTE P. GILMAN: Women and Economics: *A Study of the Economic Relation between Men and Women as a Factor in Social Evolution. ‡ Ed. with an Introduction by Carl N. Degler* TB/3073
OSCAR HANDLIN, Ed.: This Was America: *As Recorded by European Travelers in the Eighteenth, Nineteenth and Twentieth Centuries. Illus.* TB/1119
MARCUS LEE HANSEN: The Atlantic Migration: 1607-1860. *Edited by Arthur M. Schlesinger* TB/1052
MARCUS LEE HANSEN: The Immigrant in American History. TB/1120
JOHN HIGHAM, Ed.: The Reconstruction of American History △ TB/1068
ROBERT H. JACKSON: The Supreme Court in the American System of Government TB/1106
JOHN F. KENNEDY: A Nation of Immigrants. △ *Illus.* TB/1118
LEONARD W. LEVY, Ed.: American Constitutional Law: *Historical Essays* TB/1285
LEONARD W. LEVY, Ed.: Judicial Review and the Supreme Court TB/1296
LEONARD W. LEVY: The Law of the Commonwealth and Chief Justice Shaw TB/1309
RALPH BARTON PERRY: Puritanism and Democracy TB/1138
ARNOLD ROSE: The Negro in America TB/3048
MAURICE R. STEIN: The Eclipse of Community. *An Interpretation of American Studies* TB/1128
W. LLOYD WARNER and Associates: Democracy in Jonesville: *A Study in Quality and Inequality* ¶ TB/1129
W. LLOYD WARNER: Social Class in America: *The Evaluation of Status* TB/1013

American Studies: Colonial

BERNARD BAILYN, Ed.: Apologia of Robert Keayne: *Self-Portrait of a Puritan Merchant* TB/1201
BERNARD BAILYN: The New England Merchants in the Seventeenth Century TB/1149
JOSEPH CHARLES: The Origins of the American Party System TB/1049
CHARLES GIBSON: Spain in America † TB/3077
LAWRENCE HENRY GIPSON: The Coming of the Revolution: 1763-1775. † *Illus.* TB/3007
LEONARD W. LEVY: Freedom of Speech and Press in Early American History: *Legacy of Suppression* TB/1109
PERRY MILLER: Errand Into the Wilderness TB/1139
PERRY MILLER & T. H. JOHNSON, Eds.: The Puritans: *A Sourcebook of Their Writings* Vol. I TB/1093; Vol. II TB/1094
EDMUND S. MORGAN, Ed.: The Diary of Michael Wigglesworth, 1653-1657: *The Conscience of a Puritan* TB/1228
EDMUND S. MORGAN: The Puritan Family: *Religion and Domestic Relations in Seventeenth-Century New England* TB/1227
RICHARD B. MORRIS: Government and Labor in Early America TB/1244
KENNETH B. MURDOCK: Literature and Theology in Colonial New England TB/99
WALLACE NOTESTEIN: The English People on the Eve of Colonization: 1603-1630. † *Illus.* TB/3006
JOHN P. ROCHE: Origins of American Political Thought: *Selected Readings* TB/1301
JOHN SMITH: Captain John Smith's America: *Selections from His Writings. Ed. with Intro. by John Lankford* TB/3078
LOUIS B. WRIGHT: The Cultural Life of the American Colonies: 1607-1763. † *Illus.* TB/3005

American Studies: From the Revolution to 1860

JOHN R. ALDEN: The American Revolution: 1775-1783. † *Illus.* TB/3011
MAX BELOFF, Ed.: The Debate on the American Revolution, 1761-1783: *A Sourcebook* △ TB/1225
RAY A. BILLINGTON: The Far Western Frontier: 1830-1860. † *Illus.* TB/3012
EDMUND BURKE: On the American Revolution: *Selected Speeches and Letters. ‡ Edited by Elliott Robert Barkan* TB/3068
WHITNEY R. CROSS: The Burned-Over District: *The Social and Intellectual History of Enthusiastic Religion in Western New York, 1800-1850* △ TB/1242
GEORGE DANGERFIELD: The Awakening of American Nationalism: 1815-1828. † *Illus.* TB/3061
CLEMENT EATON: The Freedom-of-Thought Struggle in the Old South. *Revised and Enlarged. Illus.* TB/1150
CLEMENT EATON: The Growth of Southern Civilization: 1790-1860. † *Illus.* TB/3040

† The New American Nation Series, edited by Henry Steele Commager and Richard B. Morris.
‡ American Perspectives series, edited by Bernard Wishy and William E. Leuchtenburg.
* The Rise of Modern Europe series, edited by William L. Langer.
** History of Europe series, edited by J. H. Plumb.
¶ Researches in the Social, Cultural and Behavioral Sciences, edited by Benjamin Nelson.
§ The Library of Religion and Culture, edited by Benjamin Nelson.
Σ Harper Modern Science Series, edited by James R. Newman.
° Not for sale in Canada.
△ Not for sale in the U. K.

LOUIS FILLER: The Crusade Against Slavery: 1830-1860. † *Illus.* TB/3029
DIXON RYAN FOX: The Decline of Aristocracy in the Politics of New York: 1801-1840. ‡ *Edited by Robert V. Remini* TB/3064
WILLIAM W. FREEHLING, Ed.: The Nullification Era: *A Documentary Record* ‡ TB/3079
FELIX GILBERT: The Beginnings of American Foreign Policy: *To the Farewell Address* TB/1200
FRANCIS GRIERSON: The Valley of Shadows: *The Coming of the Civil War in Lincoln's Midwest: A Contemporary Account* TB/1246
FRANCIS J. GRUND: Aristocracy in America: *Social Class in the Formative Years of the New Nation* TB/1001
ALEXANDER HAMILTON: The Reports of Alexander Hamilton. ‡ *Edited by Jacob E. Cooke* TB/3060
THOMAS JEFFERSON: Notes on the State of Virginia. ‡ *Edited by Thomas P. Abernethy* TB/3052
JAMES MADISON: The Forging of American Federalism: *Selected Writings of James Madison. Edited by Saul K. Padover* TB/1226
BERNARD MAYO: Myths and Men: *Patrick Henry, George Washington, Thomas Jefferson* TB/1108
JOHN C. MILLER: Alexander Hamilton and the Growth of the New Nation TB/3057
RICHARD B. MORRIS, Ed.: The Era of the American Revolution TB/1180
R. B. NYE: The Cultural Life of the New Nation: 1776-1801. † *Illus.* TB/3026
FRANCIS S. PHILBRICK: The Rise of the West, 1754-1830. † *Illus.* TB/3067
TIMOTHY L. SMITH: Revivalism and Social Reform: *American Protestantism on the Eve of the Civil War* TB/1229
FRANK THISTLETHWAITE: America and the Atlantic Community: *Anglo-American Aspects, 1790-1850* TB/1107
ALBION W. TOURGÉE: A Fool's Errand. ‡ *Ed. by George Fredrickson* TB/3074
A. F. TYLER: Freedom's Ferment: *Phases of American Social History from the Revolution to the Outbreak of the Civil War. 31 illus.* TB/1074
GLYNDON G. VAN DEUSEN: The Jacksonian Era: 1828-1848. † *Illus.* TB/3028
LOUIS B. WRIGHT: Culture on the Moving Frontier TB/1053

American Studies: The Civil War to 1900

W. R. BROCK: An American Crisis: Congress and Reconstruction, 1865-67 ° △ TB/1283
THOMAS C. COCHRAN & WILLIAM MILLER: The Age of Enterprise: *A Social History of Industrial America* TB/1054
W. A. DUNNING: Essays on the Civil War and Reconstruction. *Introduction by David Donald* TB/1181
W. A. DUNNING: Reconstruction, Political and Economic: 1865-1877 TB/1073
HAROLD U. FAULKNER: Politics, Reform and Expansion: 1890-1900. † *Illus.* TB/3020
HELEN HUNT JACKSON: A Century of Dishonor: *The Early Crusade for Indian Reform.* ‡ *Edited by Andrew F. Rolle* TB/3063
ALBERT D. KIRWAN: Revolt of the Rednecks: *Mississippi Politics, 1876-1925* TB/1199
ROBERT GREEN MC CLOSKEY: American Conservatism in the Age of Enterprise: 1865-1910 TB/1137
ARTHUR MANN: Yankee Reformers in the Urban Age: *Social Reform in Boston, 1880-1900* TB/1247
WHITELAW REID: After the War: *A Tour of the Southern States, 1865-1866.* ‡ *Edited by C. Vann Woodward* TB/3066
CHARLES H. SHINN: Mining Camps: *A Study in American Frontier Government.* ‡ *Edited by Rodman W. Paul* TB/3062
VERNON LANE WHARTON: The Negro in Mississippi: 1865-1890 TB/1178

American Studies: 1900 to the Present

RAY STANNARD BAKER: Following the Color Line: *American Negro Citizenship in Progressive Era.* ‡ *Illus. Edited by Dewey W. Grantham, Jr.* TB/3053
RANDOLPH S. BOURNE: War and the Intellectuals: *Collected Essays, 1915-1919.* ‡ *Edited by Carl Resek* TB/3043
A. RUSSELL BUCHANAN: The United States and World War II. † *Illus.* Vol. I TB/3044; Vol. II TB/3045
ABRAHAM CAHAN: The Rise of David Levinsky: *a documentary novel of social mobility in early twentieth century America. Intro. by John Higham* TB/1028
THOMAS C. COCHRAN: The American Business System: *A Historical Perspective, 1900-1955* TB/1080
FOSTER RHEA DULLES: America's Rise to World Power: 1898-1954. † *Illus.* TB/3021
JOHN D. HICKS: Republican Ascendancy: 1921-1933. † *Illus.* TB/3041
SIDNEY HOOK: Reason, Social Myths, and Democracy TB/1237
ROBERT HUNTER: Poverty: *Social Conscience in the Progressive Era.* ‡ *Edited by Peter d'A. Jones* TB/3065
WILLIAM L. LANGER & S. EVERETT GLEASON: The Challenge to Isolation: *The World Crisis of 1937-1940 and American Foreign Policy* Vol. I TB/3054; Vol. II TB/3055
WILLIAM E. LEUCHTENBURG: Franklin D. Roosevelt and the New Deal: 1932-1940. † *Illus.* TB/3025
ARTHUR S. LINK: Woodrow Wilson and the Progressive Era: 1910-1917. † *Illus.* TB/3023
GEORGE E. MOWRY: The Era of Theodore Roosevelt and the Birth of Modern America: 1900-1912. † *Illus.* TB/3022
RUSSEL B. NYE: Midwestern Progressive Politics: *A Historical Study of Its Origins and Development, 1870-1958* TB/1202
WILLIAM PRESTON, JR.: Aliens and Dissenters: *Federal Suppression of Radicals, 1903-1933* TB/1287
WALTER RAUSCHENBUSCH: Christianity and the Social Crisis. ‡ *Edited by Robert D. Cross* TB/3059
JACOB RIIS: The Making of an American. ‡ *Edited by Roy Lubove* TB/3070
PHILIP SELZNICK: TVA and the Grass Roots: *A Study in the Sociology of Formal Organization* TB/1230
IDA M. TARBELL: The History of the Standard Oil Company: *Briefer Version.* ‡ *Edited by David M. Chalmers* TB/3071
GEORGE B. TINDALL, Ed.: A Populist Reader ‡ TB/3069
TWELVE SOUTHERNERS: I'll Take My Stand: *The South and the Agrarian Tradition. Intro. by Louis D. Rubin, Jr., Biographical Essays by Virginia Rock* TB/1072
WALTER E. WEYL: The New Democracy: *An Essay on Certain Political Tendencies in the United States.* ‡ *Edited by Charles B. Forcey* TB/3042

Anthropology

JACQUES BARZUN: Race: *A Study in Superstition. Revised Edition* TB/1172
JOSEPH B. CASAGRANDE, Ed.: In the Company of Man: *Twenty Portraits of Anthropological Informants. Illus.* TB/3047
W. E. LE GROS CLARK: The Antecedents of Man: *Intro. to Evolution of the Primates.* ° △ *Illus.* TB/559
CORA DU BOIS: The People of Alor. *New Preface by the author. Illus.* Vol. I TB/1042; Vol. II TB/1043
RAYMOND FIRTH, Ed.: Man and Culture: *An Evaluation of the Work of Bronislaw Malinowski* ¶ ° △ TB/1133
DAVID LANDY: Tropical Childhood: *Cultural Transmission and Learning in a Puerto Rican Village* ¶ TB/1235
L. S. B. LEAKEY: Adam's Ancestors: *The Evolution of Man and His Culture.* △ *Illus.* TB/1019
ROBERT H. LOWIE: Primitive Society. *Introduction by Fred Eggan* TB/1056

EDWARD BURNETT TYLOR: The Origins of Culture. *Part I of "Primitive Culture." § Intro. by Paul Radin* TB/33
EDWARD BURNETT TYLOR: Religion in Primitive Culture. *Part II of "Primitive Culture." § Intro. by Paul Radin* TB/34
W. LLOYD WARNER: A Black Civilization: *A Study of an Australian Tribe. ¶ Illus.* TB/3056

Art and Art History

WALTER LOWRIE: Art in the Early Church. *Revised Edition. 452 illus.* TB/124
EMILE MÂLE: The Gothic Image: *Religious Art in France of the Thirteenth Century. § △ 190 illus.* TB/44
MILLARD MEISS: Painting in Florence and Siena after the Black Death: *The Arts, Religion and Society in the Mid-Fourteenth Century. 169 illus.* TB/1148
ERICH NEUMANN: The Archetypal World of Henry Moore. *△ 107 illus.* TB/2020
DORA & ERWIN PANOFSKY : Pandora's Box: *The Changing Aspects of a Mythical Symbol. Revised Edition. Illus.* TB/2021
ERWIN PANOFSKY: Studies in Iconology: *Humanistic Themes in the Art of the Renaissance. △ 180 illustrations* TB/1077
ALEXANDRE PIANKOFF: The Shrines of Tut-Ankh-Amon. *Edited by N. Rambova. 117 illus.* TB/2011
JEAN SEZNEC: The Survival of the Pagan Gods: *The Mythological Tradition and Its Place in Renaissance Humanism and Art. 108 illustrations* TB/2004
OTTO VON SIMSON: The Gothic Cathedral: *Origins of Gothic Architecture and the Medieval Concept of Order. △ 58 illus.* TB/2018
HEINRICH ZIMMER: Myth and Symbols in Indian Art and Civilization. *70 illustrations* TB/2005

Business, Economics & Economic History

REINHARD BENDIX: Work and Authority in Industry: *Ideologies of Management in the Course of Industrialization* TB/3035
GILBERT BURCK & EDITORS OF FORTUNE: The Computer Age: *And Its Potential for Management* TB/1179
THOMAS C. COCHRAN: The American Business System: *A Historical Perspective, 1900-1955* TB/1080
THOMAS C. COCHRAN: The Inner Revolution: *Essays on the Social Sciences in History △* TB/1140
THOMAS C. COCHRAN & WILLIAM MILLER: The Age of Enterprise: *A Social History of Industrial America* TB/1054
ROBERT DAHL & CHARLES E. LINDBLOM: Politics, Economics, and Welfare: *Planning and Politico-Economic Systems Resolved into Basic Social Processes* TB/3037
PETER F. DRUCKER: The New Society: *The Anatomy of Industrial Order △* TB/1082
EDITORS OF FORTUNE: America in the Sixties: *The Economy and the Society* TB/1015
ROBERT L. HEILBRONER: The Great Ascent: *The Struggle for Economic Development in Our Time* TB/3030
ROBERT L. HEILBRONER: The Limits of American Capitalism TB/1305
FRANK H. KNIGHT: The Economic Organization TB/1214
FRANK H. KNIGHT: Risk, Uncertainty and Profit TB/1215
ABBA P. LERNER: Everybody's Business: *Current Assumptions in Economics and Public Policy* TB/3051
ROBERT GREEN MC CLOSKEY: American Conservatism in the Age of Enterprise, 1865-1910 △ TB/1137
PAUL MANTOUX: The Industrial Revolution in the Eighteenth Century: *The Beginnings of the Modern Factory System in England ° △* TB/1079
WILLIAM MILLER, Ed.: Men in Business: *Essays on the Historical Role of the Entrepreneur* TB/1081
RICHARD B. MORRIS: Government and Labor in Early America △ TB/1244
HERBERT SIMON: The Shape of Automation: *For Men and Management* TB/1245
PERRIN STRYKER: The Character of the Executive: *Eleven Studies in Managerial Qualities* TB/1041
PIERRE URI: Partnership for Progress: *A Program for Transatlantic Action* TB/3036

Education

JACQUES BARZUN: The House of Intellect △ TB/1051
RICHARD M. JONES, Ed.: Contemporary Educational Psychology: *Selected Readings* TB/1292
CLARK KERR: The Uses of the University TB/1264
JOHN U. NEF: Cultural Foundations of Industrial Civilization △ TB/1024
NATHAN M. PUSEY: The Age of the Scholar: *Observations on Education in a Troubled Decade* TB/1157
PAUL VALÉRY: The Outlook for Intelligence △ TB/2016

Historiography & Philosophy of History

JACOB BURCKHARDT: On History and Historians. *△ Introduction by H. R. Trevor-Roper* TB/1216
WILHELM DILTHEY: Pattern and Meaning in History: *Thoughts on History and Society. ° △ Edited with an Introduction by H. P. Rickman* TB/1075
J. H. HEXTER: Reappraisals in History: *New Views on History & Society in Early Modern Europe △* TB/1100
H. STUART HUGHES: History as Art and as Science: *Twin Vistas on the Past* TB/1207
RAYMOND KLIBANSKY & H. J. PATON, Eds.: Philosophy and History: *The Ernst Cassirer Festschrift. Illus.* TB/1115
ARNALDO MOMIGLIANO: Studies in Historiography ° △ TB/1288
GEORGE H. NADEL, Ed.: Studies in the Philosophy of History: *Selected Essays from* History and Theory TB/1208
JOSE ORTEGA Y GASSET: The Modern Theme. *Introduction by Jose Ferrater Mora* TB/1038
KARL R. POPPER: The Open Society and Its Enemies △
Vol. I: The Spell of Plato TB/1101
Vol. II: The High Tide of Prophecy: Hegel, Marx and the Aftermath TB/1102
KARL R. POPPER: The Poverty of Historicism ° △ TB/1126
G. J. RENIER: History: Its Purpose and Method △ TB/1209
W. H. WALSH: Philosophy of History: *An Introduction △* TB/1020

History: General

L. CARRINGTON GOODRICH: A Short History of the Chinese People. *△ Illus.* TB/3015
DAN N. JACOBS & HANS H. BAERWALD: Chinese Communism: *Selected Documents* TB/3031
BERNARD LEWIS: The Arabs in History △ TB/1029
BERNARD LEWIS: The Middle East and the West ° △ TB/1274

History: Ancient

A. ANDREWES: The Greek Tyrants △ TB/1103
ADOLF ERMAN, Ed. The Ancient Egyptians: *A Sourcebook of Their Writings. New material and Introduction by William Kelly Simpson* TB/1233
MICHAEL GRANT: Ancient History ° △ TB/1190
SAMUEL NOAH KRAMER: Sumerian Mythology TB/1055
NAPHTALI LEWIS & MEYER REINHOLD, Eds.: Roman Civilization. *Sourcebook I: The Republic* TB/1231
NAPHTALI LEWIS & MEYER REINHOLD, Eds.: Roman Civilization. *Sourcebook II: The Empire* TB/1232

History: Medieval

P. BOISSONNADE: Life and Work in Medieval Europe: *The Evolution of the Medieval Economy, the 5th to the 15th Century. ° △ Preface by Lynn White, Jr.* TB/1141
HELEN CAM: England before Elizabeth △ TB/1026
NORMAN COHN: The Pursuit of the Millennium: *Revolutionary Messianism in Medieval and Reformation Europe △* TB/1037

G. G. COULTON: Medieval Village, Manor, and Monastery TB/1022

CHRISTOPHER DAWSON, Ed.: Mission to Asia: *Narratives and Letters of the Franciscan Missionaries in Mongolia and China in the 13th and 14 Centuries* △ TB/315

HEINRICH FICHTENAU: The Carolingian Empire: *The Age of Charlemagne* △ TB/1142

GALBERT OF BRUGES: The Murder of Charles the Good. *Trans. with Intro. by James Bruce Ross* TB/1311

F. L. GANSHOF: Feudalism △ TB/1058

DENO GEANAKOPLOS: Byzantine East and Latin West: *Two Worlds of Christendom in the Middle Ages and Renaissance* TB/1265

EDWARD GIBBON: The Triumph of Christendom in the Roman Empire *(Chaps. XV-XX of "Decline and Fall," J. B. Bury edition).* § △ *Illus.* TB/46

W. O. HASSALL, Ed.: Medieval England: *As Viewed by Contemporaries* △ TB/1205

DENYS HAY: Europe: The Emergence of an Idea TB/1275

DENYS HAY: The Medieval Centuries ° △ TB/1192

J. M. HUSSEY: The Byzantine World △ TB/1057

ROBERT LATOUCHE: The Birth of Western Economy: *Economic Aspects of the Dark Ages.* ° △ *Intro. by Philip Grierson* TB/1290

FERDINAND LOT: The End of the Ancient World and the Beginnings of the Middle Ages. *Introduction by Glanville Downey* TB/1044

MARSILIUS OF PADUA: The Defender of the Peace. *Trans. with Intro. by Alan Gewirth* TB/1310

G. MOLLAT: The Popes at Avignon: 1305-1378 △ TB/308

CHARLES PETIT-DUTAILLIS: The Feudal Monarchy in France and England: *From the Tenth to the Thirteenth Century* ° △ TB/1165

HENRI PIRENNE: Early Democracies in the Low Countries: *Urban Society and Political Conflict in the Middle Ages and the Renaissance. Introduction by John H. Mundy* TB/1110

STEVEN RUNCIMAN: A History of the Crusades. △
Volume I: *The First Crusade and the Foundation of the Kingdom of Jerusalem. Illus.* TB/1143
Volume II: *The Kingdom of Jerusalem and the Frankish East, 1100-1187. Illus.* TB/1243
Volume III: *The Kingdom of Acre and the Later Crusades* TB/1298

FERDINAND SCHEVILL: Siena: *The History of a Medieval Commune. Intro. by William M. Bowsky* TB/1164

SULPICIUS SEVERUS et al.: The Western Fathers: *Being the Lives of Martin of Tours, Ambrose, Augustine of Hippo, Honoratus of Arles and Germanus of Auxerre.* △ *Edited and trans. by F. O. Hoare* TB/309

HENRY OSBORN TAYLOR: The Classical Heritage of the Middle Ages. *Foreword and Biblio. by Kenneth M. Setton* TB/1117

F. VAN DER MEER: Augustine The Bishop: *Church and Society at the Dawn of the Middle Ages* △ TB/304

J. M. WALLACE-HADRILL: The Barbarian West: *The Early Middle Ages, A.D. 400-1000* △ TB/1061

History: Renaissance & Reformation

JACOB BURCKHARDT: The Civilization of the Renaissance in Italy. △ *Intro. by Benjamin Nelson & Charles Trinkaus. Illus.* Vol. I TB/40; Vol. II TB/41

JOHN CALVIN & JACOPO SADOLETO: A Reformation Debate. *Edited by John C. Olin* TB/1239

ERNST CASSIRER: The Individual and the Cosmos in Renaissance Philosophy. △ *Translated with an Introduction by Mario Domandi* TB/1097

FEDERICO CHABOD: Machiavelli and the Renaissance △ TB/1193

EDWARD P. CHEYNEY: The Dawn of a New Era, 1250-1453. * *Illus.* TB/3002

G. CONSTANT: The Reformation in England: *The English Schism, Henry VIII, 1509-1547* △ TB/314

R. TREVOR DAVIES: The Golden Century of Spain, 1501-1621 ° △ TB/1194

G. R. ELTON: Reformation Europe, 1517-1559 ** ° △ TB/1270

DESIDERIUS ERASMUS: Christian Humanism and the Reformation: *Selected Writings. Edited and translated by John C. Olin* TB/1166

WALLACE K. FERGUSON et al.: Facets of the Renaissance TB/1098

WALLACE K. FERGUSON et al.: The Renaissance: *Six Essays. Illus.* TB/1084

JOHN NEVILLE FIGGIS: The Divine Right of Kings. *Introduction by G. R. Elton* TB/1191

JOHN NEVILLE FIGGIS: Political Thought from Gerson to Grotius: 1414-1625: *Seven Studies. Introduction by Garrett Mattingly* TB/1032

MYRON P. GILMORE: The World of Humanism, 1453-1517. * *Illus.* TB/3003

FRANCESCO GUICCIARDINI: Maxims and Reflections of a Renaissance Statesman *(Ricordi). Trans. by Mario Domandi. Intro. by Nicolai Rubinstein* TB/1160

J. H. HEXTER: More's Utopia: *The Biography of an Idea. New Epilogue by the Author* TB/1195

HAJO HOLBORN: Ulrich von Hutten and the German Reformation TB/1238

JOHAN HUIZINGA: Erasmus and the Age of Reformation. △ *Illus.* TB/19

JOEL HURSTFIELD, Ed.: The Reformation Crisis △ TB/1267

ULRICH VON HUTTEN et al.: On the Eve of the Reformation: *"Letters of Obscure Men." Introduction by Hajo Holborn* TB/1124

PAUL O. KRISTELLER: Renaissance Thought: *The Classic, Scholastic, and Humanist Strains* TB/1048

PAUL O. KRISTELLER: Renaissance Thought II: *Papers on Humanism and the Arts* TB/1163

NICCOLÒ MACHIAVELLI: History of Florence and of the Affairs of Italy: *from the earliest times to the death of Lorenzo the Magnificent.* △ *Introduction by Felix Gilbert* TB/1027

ALFRED VON MARTIN: Sociology of the Renaissance. *Introduction by Wallace K. Ferguson* TB/1099

GARRETT MATTINGLY et al.: Renaissance Profiles. △ *Edited by J. H. Plumb* TB/1162

MILLARD MEISS: Painting in Florence and Siena after the Black Death: *The Arts, Religion and Society in the Mid-Fourteenth Century.* △ *169 illus.* TB/1148

J. E. NEALE: The Age of Catherine de Medici ° △ TB/1085

ERWIN PANOFSKY: Studies in Iconology: *Humanistic Themes in the Art of the Renaissance.* △ *180 illustrations* TB/1077

J. H. PARRY: The Establishment of the European Hegemony: 1415-1715: *Trade and Exploration in the Age of the Renaissance* △ TB/1045

J. H. PLUMB: The Italian Renaissance: *A Concise Survey of Its History and Culture* △ TB/1161

A. F. POLLARD: Henry VIII. ° △ *Introduction by A. G. Dickens* TB/1249

A. F. POLLARD: Wolsey. ° △ *Introduction by A. G. Dickens* TB/1248

CECIL ROTH: The Jews in the Renaissance. *Illus.* TB/834

A. L. ROWSE: The Expansion of Elizabethan England. ° △ *Illus.* TB/1220

GORDON RUPP: Luther's Progress to the Diet of Worms ° △ TB/120

FERDINAND SCHEVILL: The Medici. *Illus.* TB/1010

FERDINAND SCHEVILL: Medieval and Renaissance Florence. *Illus.* Volume I: *Medieval Florence* TB/1090
Volume II: *The Coming of Humanism and the Age of the Medici* TB/1091

G. M. TREVELYN: England in the Age of Wycliffe, 1368-1520 ° △ TB/1112

VESPASIANO: Renaissance Princes, Popes, and Prelates: *The Vespasiano Memoirs: Lives of Illustrious Men of the XVth Century. Intro. by Myron P. Gilmore* TB/1111

History: Modern European

FREDERICK B. ARTZ: Reaction and Revolution, 1815-1832. * *Illus.* TB/3034

MAX BELOFF: The Age of Absolutism, 1660-1815 △ TB/1062

ROBERT C. BINKLEY: Realism and Nationalism, 1852-1871. * *Illus.* TB/3038

ASA BRIGGS: The Making of Modern England, 1784-1867: *The Age of Improvement* ° △ TB/1203

CRANE BRINTON: A Decade of Revolution, 1789-1799. * *Illus.* TB/3018

D. W. BROGAN: The Development of Modern France. ° △ Volume I: *From the Fall of the Empire to the Dreyfus Affair* TB/1184
Volume II: *The Shadow of War, World War I, Between the Two Wars. New Introduction by the Author* TB/1185

J. BRONOWSKI & BRUCE MAZLISH: The Western Intellectual Tradition: *From Leonardo to Hegel* △ TB/3001

GEOFFREY BRUUN: Europe and the French Imperium, 1799-1814. * Illus. TB/3033

ALAN BULLOCK: Hitler, A Study in Tyranny. ° △ *Illus.* TB/1123

E. H. CARR: German-Soviet Relations Between the Two World Wars, 1919-1939 TB/1278

E. H. CARR: International Relations Between the Two World Wars, 1919-1939 ° △ TB/1279

E. H. CARR: The Twenty Years' Crisis, 1919-1939: *An Introduction to the Study of International Relations* ° △ TB/1122

GORDON A. CRAIG: From Bismarck to Adenauer: *Aspects of German Statecraft. Revised Edition* TB/1171

DENIS DIDEROT: The Encyclopedia: *Selections. Ed. and trans. by Stephen Gendzier* TB/1299

WALTER L. DORN: Competition for Empire, 1740-1763. * *Illus.* TB/3032

FRANKLIN L. FORD: Robe and Sword: *The Regrouping of the French Aristocracy after Louis XIV* TB/1217

CARL J. FRIEDRICH: The Age of the Baroque, 1610-1660. * *Illus.* TB/3004

RENÉ FUELOEP-MILLER: The Mind and Face of Bolshevism: *An Examination of Cultural Life in Soviet Russia. New Epilogue by the Author* TB/1188

M. DOROTHY GEORGE: London Life in the Eighteenth Century △ TB/1182

LEO GERSHOY: From Despotism to Revolution, 1763-1789. * *Illus.* TB/3017

C. C. GILLISPIE: Genesis and Geology: *The Decades before Darwin* § TB/51

ALBERT GOODWIN: The French Revolution △ TB/1064

ALBERT GUÉRARD: France in the Classical Age: *The Life and Death of an Ideal* △ TB/1183

CARLTON J. H. HAYES: A Generation of Materialism, 1871-1900. * *Illus.* TB/3039

J. H. HEXTER: Reappraisals in History: *New Views on History and Society in Early Modern Europe* △ TB/1100

STANLEY HOFFMANN et al.: In Search of France: *The Economy, Society and Political System in the Twentieth Century* TB/1219

A. R. HUMPHREYS: The Augustan World: *Society, Thought, & Letters in 18th Century England* ° △ TB/1105

DAN N. JACOBS, Ed.: The New Communist Manifesto *and Related Documents. Third edition, revised* TB/1078

LIONEL KOCHAN: The Struggle for Germany: *1914-45* TB/1304

HANS KOHN: The Mind of Germany: *The Education of a Nation* △ TB/1204

HANS KOHN, Ed.: The Mind of Modern Russia: *Historical and Political Thought of Russia's Great Age* TB/1065

WALTER LAQUEUR & GEORGE L. MOSSE, Eds.: International Fascism, 1920-1945. ° △ *Volume I* of Journal of Contemporary History TB/1276

WALTER LAQUEUR & GEORGE L. MOSSE, Eds.: The Left-Wing Intellectuals between the Wars 1919-1939. ° △ *Volume 2* of Journal of Contemporary History TB/1286

WALTER LAQUEUR & GEORGE L. MOSSE, Eds.: 1914: *The Coming of the First World War.* ° △ *Volume 3* of Journal of Contemporary History TB/1306

FRANK E. MANUEL: The Prophets of Paris: *Turgot, Condorcet, Saint-Simon, Fourier, and Comte* TB/1218

KINGSLEY MARTIN: French Liberal Thought in the Eighteenth Century: *A Study of Political Ideas from Bayle to Condorcet* TB/1114

L. B. NAMIER: Facing East: *Essays on Germany, the Balkans, and Russia in the 20th Century* △ TB/1280

L. B. NAMIER: Personalities and Powers: *Selected Essays* △ TB/1186

L. B. NAMIER: Vanished Supremacies: *Essays on European History, 1812-1918* ° TB/1088

JOHN U. NEF: Western Civilization Since the Renaissance: *Peace, War, Industry, and the Arts* TB/1113

FRANZ NEUMANN: Behemoth: *The Structure and Practice of National Socialism, 1933-1944* TB/1289

FREDERICK L. NUSSBAUM: The Triumph of Science and Reason, 1660-1685. * *Illus.* TB/3009

DAVID OGG: Europe of the Ancien Régime, 1715-1783 ** ° △ TB/1271

JOHN PLAMENATZ: German Marxism and Russian Communism. ° △ *New Preface by the Author* TB/1189

RAYMOND W. POSTGATE, Ed.: Revolution from 1789 to 1906: *Selected Documents* TB/1063

PENFIELD ROBERTS: The Quest for Security, 1715-1740. * *Illus.* TB/3016

PRISCILLA ROBERTSON: Revolutions of 1848: *A Social History* TB/1025

GEORGE RUDÉ: Revolutionary Europe, 1783-1815 ** ° △ TB/1272

LOUIS, DUC DE SAINT-SIMON: Versailles, The Court, and Louis XIV. ° △ *Introductory Note by Peter Gay* TB/1250

ALBERT SOREL: Europe Under the Old Regime. *Translated by Francis H. Herrick* TB/1121

N. N. SUKHANOV: The Russian Revolution, 1917: *Eyewitness Account.* △ *Edited by Joel Carmichael* Vol. I TB/1066; Vol. II TB/1067

A. J. P. TAYLOR: From Napoleon to Lenin: *Historical Essays* ° △ TB/1268

A. J. P. TAYLOR: The Habsburg Monarchy, 1809-1918: *A History of the Austrian Empire and Austria-Hungary* ° △ TB/1187

G. M. TREVELYAN: British History in the Nineteenth Century and After: *1782-1919.* ° △ *Second Edition* TB/1251

H. R. TREVOR-ROPER: Historical Essays ° △ TB/1269

ELIZABETH WISKEMANN: Europe of the Dictators, 1919-1945 ** ° △ TB/1273

JOHN B. WOLF: The Emergence of the Great Powers, 1685-1715. * *Illus.* TB/3010

JOHN B. WOLF: France: 1814-1919: *The Rise of a Liberal-Democratic Society* TB/3019

Intellectual History & History of Ideas

HERSCHEL BAKER: The Image of Man: *A Study of the Idea of Human Dignity in Classical Antiquity, the Middle Ages, and the Renaissance* TB/1047

R. R. BOLGAR: The Classical Heritage and Its Beneficiaries: *From the Carolingian Age to the End of the Renaissance* △ TB/1125

RANDOLPH S. BOURNE: War and the Intellectuals: *Collected Essays, 1915-1919.* △ ‡ *Edited by Carl Resek* TB/3043

J. BRONOWSKI & BRUCE MAZLISH: The Western Intellectual Tradition: *From Leonardo to Hegel* △ TB/3001

ERNST CASSIRER: The Individual and the Cosmos in Renaissance Philosophy. △ *Translated with an Introduction by Mario Domandi* TB/1097

NORMAN COHN: The Pursuit of the Millennium: *Revolutionary Messianism in Medieval and Reformation Europe* △ TB/1037

C. C. GILLISPIE: Genesis and Geology: *The Decades before Darwin* § TB/51

G. RACHEL LEVY: Religious Conceptions of the Stone Age and Their Influence upon European Thought. △ *Illus. Introduction by Henri Frankfort* TB/106

ARTHUR O. LOVEJOY: The Great Chain of Being: *A Study of the History of an Idea* TB/1009

FRANK E. MANUEL: The Prophets of Paris: *Turgot, Condorcet, Saint-Simon, Fourier, and Comte* △ TB/1218

PERRY MILLER & T. H. JOHNSON, Editors: The Puritans: *A Sourcebook of Their Writings* Vol. I TB/1093; Vol. II TB/1094

MILTON C. NAHM: Genius and Creativity: *An Essay in the History of Ideas* TB/1196

ROBERT PAYNE: Hubris: *A Study of Pride. Foreword by Sir Herbert Read* TB/1031

RALPH BARTON PERRY: The Thought and Character of William James: *Briefer Version* TB/1156

GEORG SIMMEL et al.: Essays on Sociology, Philosophy, and Aesthetics. ¶ *Edited by Kurt H. Wolff* TB/1234

BRUNO SNELL: The Discovery of the Mind: *The Greek Origins of European Thought* △ TB/1018

PAGET TOYNBEE: Dante Alighieri: *His Life and Works. Edited with Intro. by Charles S. Singleton* △ TB/1206

ERNEST LEE TUVESON: Millennium and Utopia: *A Study in the Background of the Idea of Progress. ¶ New Preface by the Author* TB/1134

PAUL VALÉRY: The Outlook for Intelligence △ TB/2016

W. WARREN WAGAR, Ed.: European Intellectual History since Darwin and Marx TB/1297

PHILIP P. WIENER: Evolution and the Founders of Pragmatism. △ *Foreword by John Dewey* TB/1212

BASIL WILLEY: Nineteenth Century Studies: *Coleridge to Matthew Arnold* ° △ TB/1261

BASIL WILLEY: More Nineteenth Century Studies: *A Group of Honest Doubters* ° △ TB/1262

Law

EDWARD S. CORWIN: American Constitutional History: *Essays edited by Alpheus T. Mason & Gerald Garvey* TB/1136

ROBERT H. JACKSON: The Supreme Court in the American System of Government TB/1106

LEONARD W. LEVY, Ed.: American Constitutional Law: *Historical Essays* TB/1285

LEONARD W. LEVY: Freedom of Speech and Press in Early American History: *Legacy of Suppression* TB/1109

LEONARD W. LEVY, Ed.: Judicial Review and the Supreme Court TB/1296

LEONARD W. LEVY: The Law of the Commonwealth and Chief Justice Shaw TB/1309

Literature, Poetry, The Novel & Criticism

JAMES BAIRD: Ishmael: *The Art of Melville in the Contexts of International Primitivism* TB/1023

JACQUES BARZUN: The House of Intellect △ TB/1051

W. J. BATE: From Classic to Romantic: *Premises of Taste in Eighteenth Century England* TB/1036

RACHEL BESPALOFF: On the Iliad TB/2006

R. P. BLACKMUR et al.: Lectures in Criticism. *Introduction by Huntington Cairns* TB/2003

JAMES BOSWELL: The Life of Dr. Johnson & The Journal of a Tour to the Hebrides with Samuel Johnson LL.D.: *Selections.* ° △ *Edited by F. V. Morley. Illus. by Ernest Shepard* TB/1254

ABRAHAM CAHAN: The Rise of David Levinsky: *a documentary novel of social mobility in early twentieth century America. Intro. by John Higham* TB/1028

ERNST R. CURTIUS: European Literature and the Latin Middle Ages △ TB/2015

ADOLF ERMAN, Ed.: The Ancient Egyptians: *A Sourcebook of Their Writings. New Material and Introduction by William Kelly Simpson* TB/1233

ÉTIENNE GILSON: Dante and Philosophy TB/1089

ALFRED HARBAGE: As They Liked It: *A Study of Shakespeare's Moral Artistry* TB/1035

STANLEY R. HOPPER, Ed.: Spiritual Problems in Contemporary Literature § TB/21

A. R. HUMPHREYS: The Augustan World: *Society, Thought and Letters in 18th Century England* ° △ TB/1105

ALDOUS HUXLEY: Antic Hay & The Giaconda Smile. ° △ *Introduction by Martin Green* TB/3503

ARNOLD KETTLE: An Introduction to the English Novel. △
Volume I: *Defoe to George Eliot* TB/1011
Volume II: *Henry James to the Present* TB/1012

RICHMOND LATTIMORE: The Poetry of Greek Tragedy △ TB/1257

J. B. LEISHMAN: The Monarch of Wit: *An Analytical and Comparative Study of the Poetry of John Donne* ° △ TB/1258

J. B. LEISHMAN: Themes and Variations in Shakespeare's Sonnets ° △ TB/1259

ROGER SHERMAN LOOMIS: The Development of Arthurian Romance △ TB/1167

JOHN STUART MILL: On Bentham and Coleridge. △ *Introduction by F. R. Leavis* TB/1070

KENNETH B. MURDOCK: Literature and Theology in Colonial New England TB/99

SAMUEL PEPYS: The Diary of Samuel Pepys. ° *Edited by O. F. Morshead. Illus. by Ernest Shepard* TB/1007

ST.-JOHN PERSE: Seamarks TB/2002

V. DE S. PINTO: Crisis in English Poetry, 1880-1940 ° TB/1260

ROBERT PREYER, Ed.: Victorian Literature TB/1302

GEORGE SANTAYANA: Interpretations of Poetry and Religion § TB/9

C. K. STEAD: The New Poetic: *Yeats to Eliot* △ TB/1263

HEINRICH STRAUMANN: American Literature in the Twentieth Century. △ *Third Edition, Revised* TB/1168

PAGET TOYNBEE: Dante Alighieri: *His Life and Works. Edited with Intro. by Charles S. Singleton* TB/1206

DOROTHY VAN GHENT: The English Novel: *Form and Function* TB/1050

E. B. WHITE: One Man's Meat. *Introduction by Walter Blair* TB/3505

BASIL WILLEY: Nineteenth Century Studies: *Coleridge to Matthew Arnold* △ TB/1261

BASIL WILLEY: More Nineteenth Century Studies: *A Group of Honest Doubters* ° △ TB/1262

RAYMOND WILLIAMS: Culture and Society, 1780-1950 ° △ TB/1252

RAYMOND WILLIAMS: The Long Revolution. ° △ *Revised Edition* TB/1253

MORTON DAUWEN ZABEL, Editor: Literary Opinion in America Vol. I TB/3013; Vol. II TB/3014

Myth, Symbol & Folklore

JOSEPH CAMPBELL, Editor: Pagan and Christian Mysteries *Illus.* TB/2013

MIRCEA ELIADE: Cosmos and History: *The Myth of the Eternal Return* § △ TB/2050

MIRCEA ELIADE: Rites and Symbols of Initiation: *The Mysteries of Birth and Rebirth* § △ TB/1236

THEODOR H. GASTER: Thespis: *Ritual, Myth and Drama in the Ancient Near East* △ TB/1281

C. G. JUNG & C. KERÉNYI: Essays on a Science of Mythology: *The Myths of the Divine Child and the Divine Maiden* TB/2014

DORA & ERWIN PANOFSKY: Pandora's Box: *The Changing Aspects of a Mythical Symbol.* △ *Revised edition. Illus.* TB/2021

ERWIN PANOFSKY: Studies in Iconology: *Humanistic Themes in the Art of the Renaissance.* △ *180 illustrations* TB/1077

JEAN SEZNEC: The Survival of the Pagan Gods: *The Mythological Tradition and its Place in Renaissance Humanism and Art.* △ *108 illustrations* TB/2004

HELLMUT WILHELM: Change: *Eight Lectures on the I Ching* △ TB/2019

HEINRICH ZIMMER: Myths and Symbols in Indian Art and Civilization. △ *70 illustrations* TB/2005

Philosophy

G. E. M. ANSCOMBE: An Introduction to Wittgenstein's Tractatus. ° △ *Second Edition, Revised* TB/1210

HENRI BERGSON: Time and Free Will: *An Essay on the Immediate Data of Consciousness* ° △ TB/1021

H. J. BLACKHAM: Six Existentialist Thinkers: *Kierkegaard, Nietzsche, Jaspers, Marcel, Heidegger, Sartre* ° △ TB/1002

CRANE BRINTON: Nietzsche. *New Preface, Bibliography and Epilogue by the Author* TB/1197

MARTIN BUBER: The Knowledge of Man. △ *Ed. with an Intro. by Maurice Friedman. Trans. by Maurice Friedman and Ronald Gregor Smith* TB/135

ERNST CASSIRER: The Individual and the Cosmos in Renaissance Philosophy. △ *Translated with an Introduction by Mario Domandi* TB/1097

ERNST CASSIRER: Rousseau, Kant and Goethe. *Introduction by Peter Gay* TB/1092

FREDERICK COPLESTON: Medieval Philosophy ° △ TB/376

F. M. CORNFORD: Principium Sapientiae: *A Study of the Origins of Greek Philosophical Thought. Edited by W. K. C. Guthrie* TB/1213

F. M. CORNFORD: From Religion to Philosophy: *A Study in the Origins of Western Speculation* § TB/20

WILFRID DESAN: The Tragic Finale: *An Essay on the Philosophy of Jean-Paul Sartre* TB/1030

A. P. D'ENTRÈVES: Natural Law: *An Historical Survey* △ TB/1223

MARVIN FARBER: The Aims of Phenomenology: *The Motives, Methods, and Impact of Husserl's Thought* TB/1291

MARVIN FARBER: Phenomenology and Existence: *Towards a Philosophy within Nature* TB/1295

HERBERT FINGARETTE: The Self in Transformation: *Psychoanalysis, Philosophy and the Life of the Spirit* ¶ TB/1177

PAUL FRIEDLÄNDER: Plato: *An Introduction* △ TB/2017

ÉTIENNE GILSON: Dante and Philosophy TB/1089

J. GLENN GRAY: The Warriors: *Reflections on Men in Battle. Intro. by Hannah Arendt* TB/1294

WILLIAM CHASE GREENE: Moira: *Fate, Good, and Evil in Greek Thought* TB/1104

W. K. C. GUTHRIE: The Greek Philosophers: *From Thales to Aristotle* ° △ TB/1008

G. W. F. HEGEL: The Phenomenology of Mind ° △ TB/1303

F. H. HEINEMANN: Existentialism and the Modern Predicament △ TB/28

ISAAC HUSIK: A History of Medieval Jewish Philosophy JP/3

EDMUND HUSSERL: Phenomenology and the Crisis of Philosophy. *Translated with an Introduction by Quentin Lauer* TB/1170

IMMANUEL KANT: The Doctrine of Virtue, *being Part II of the* Metaphysic of Morals. *Trans. with Notes & Intro. by Mary J. Gregor. Foreword by H. J. Paton* TB/110

IMMANUEL KANT: Groundwork of the Metaphysic of Morals. *Trans. & analyzed by H. J. Paton* TB/1159

IMMANUEL KANT: Lectures on Ethics. § △ *Introduction by Lewis W. Beck* TB/105

IMMANUEL KANT: Religion Within the Limits of Reason Alone. § *Intro. by T. M. Greene & J. Silber* TB/67

QUENTIN LAUER: Phenomenology: *Its Genesis and Prospect* TB/1169

GABRIEL MARCEL: Being and Having: *An Existential Diary.* △ *Intro. by James Collins* TB/310

GEORGE A. MORGAN: What Nietzsche Means TB/1198

PHILO, SAADYA GAON, & JEHUDA HALEVI: Three Jewish Philosophers. *Ed. by Hans Lewy, Alexander Altmann, & Isaak Heinemann* TB/813

MICHAEL POLANYI: Personal Knowledge: *Towards a Post-Critical Philosophy* △ TB/1158

WILLARD VAN ORMAN QUINE: Elementary Logic: *Revised Edition* TB/577

WILLARD VAN ORMAN QUINE: From a Logical Point of View: *Logico-Philosophical Essays* TB/566

BERTRAND RUSSELL et al.: The Philosophy of Bertrand Russell. *Edited by Paul Arthur Schilpp* Vol. I TB/1095; Vol. II TB/1096

L. S. STEBBING: A Modern Introduction to Logic △ TB/538

ALFRED NORTH WHITEHEAD: Process and Reality: *An Essay in Cosmology* △ TB/1033

PHILIP P. WIENER: Evolution and the Founders of Pragmatism. *Foreword by John Dewey* TB/1212

WILHELM WINDELBAND: A History of Philosophy
Vol. I: *Greek, Roman, Medieval* TB/38
Vol. II: *Renaissance, Enlightenment, Modern* TB/39

LUDWIG WITTGENSTEIN: The Blue and Brown Books ° TB/1211

Political Science & Government

JEREMY BENTHAM: The Handbook of Political Fallacies: *Introduction by Crane Brinton* TB/1069

KENNETH E. BOULDING: Conflict and Defense: *A General Theory* TB/3024

CRANE BRINTON: English Political Thought in the Nineteenth Century TB/1071

ROBERT CONQUEST: Power and Policy in the USSR: *The Study of Soviet Dynastics* △ TB/1307

EDWARD S. CORWIN: American Constitutional History: *Essays edited by Alpheus T. Mason and Gerald Garvey* TB/1136

ROBERT DAHL & CHARLES E. LINDBLOM: Politics, Economics, and Welfare: *Planning and Politico-Economic Systems Resolved into Basic Social Processes* TB/3037

JOHN NEVILLE FIGGIS: The Divine Right of Kings. *Introduction by G. R. Elton* TB/1191

JOHN NEVILLE FIGGIS: Political Thought from Gerson to Grotius: 1414-1625: *Seven Studies. Introduction by Garrett Mattingly* TB/1032

F. L. GANSHOF: Feudalism △ TB/1058

G. P. GOOCH: English Democratic Ideas in the Seventeenth Century TB/1006

J. H. HEXTER: More's Utopia: *The Biography of an Idea. New Epilogue by the Author* TB/1195

SIDNEY HOOK: Reason, Social Myths and Democracy △ TB/1237

ROBERT H. JACKSON: The Supreme Court in the American System of Government △ TB/1106

DAN N. JACOBS, Ed.: The New Communist Manifesto *and Related Documents. Third Edition, Revised* TB/1078

DAN N. JACOBS & HANS BAERWALD, Eds.: Chinese Communism: *Selected Documents* TB/3031

HANS KOHN: Political Ideologies of the 20th Century TB/1277

ROBERT GREEN MC CLOSKEY: American Conservatism in the Age of Enterprise, 1865-1910 TB/1137

KINGSLEY MARTIN: French Liberal Thought in the Eighteenth Century: *Political Ideas from Bayle to Condorcet* △ TB/1114

ROBERTO MICHELS: First Lectures in Political Sociology. *Edited by Alfred de Grazia* ¶ ° TB/1224

JOHN STUART MILL: On Bentham and Coleridge. △ *Introduction by F. R. Leavis* TB/1070

BARRINGTON MOORE, JR.: Political Power and Social Theory: *Seven Studies* ¶ TB/1221

BARRINGTON MOORE, JR.: Soviet Politics—The Dilemma of Power: *The Role of Ideas in Social Change* ¶ TB/1222

BARRINGTON MOORE, JR.: Terror and Progress—USSR: *Some Sources of Change and Stability in the Soviet Dictatorship* ¶ TB/1266

JOHN B. MORRALL: Political Thought in Medieval Times △ TB/1076

JOHN PLAMENATZ: German Marxism and Russian Communism. ° △ *New Preface by the Author* TB/1189

KARL R. POPPER: The Open Society and Its Enemies △
Vol. I: *The Spell of Plato* TB/1101
Vol. II: *The High Tide of Prophecy: Hegel, Marx and the Aftermath* TB/1102

HENRI DE SAINT-SIMON: Social Organization, The Science of Man, and Other Writings. *Edited and Translated by Felix Markham* TB/1152

JOSEPH A. SCHUMPETER: Capitalism, Socialism and Democracy △ TB/3008

BENJAMIN I. SCHWARTZ: Chinese Communism and the Rise of Mao TB/1308

CHARLES H. SHINN: Mining Camps: *A Study in American Frontier Government.* ‡ *Edited by Rodman W. Paul* TB/3062

PETER WOLL, Ed.: Public Administration and Policy: *Selected Essays* TB/1284

Psychology

ALFRED ADLER: The Individual Psychology of Alfred Adler. △ *Edited by Heinz L. and Rowena R. Ansbacher* TB/1154

ALFRED ADLER: Problems of Neurosis. *Introduction by Heinz L. Ansbacher* TB/1145

ANTON T. BOISEN: The Exploration of the Inner World: *A Study of Mental Disorder and Religious Experience* TB/87

ARTHUR BURTON & ROBERT E. HARRIS, Eds.: Clinical Studies of Personality
Vol. I TB/3075; Vol. II TB/3076

HADLEY CANTRIL: The Invasion from Mars: *A Study in the Psychology of Panic* ¶ TB/1282

HERBERT FINGARETTE: The Self in Transformation: *Psychoanalysis, Philosophy and the Life of the Spirit* ¶ TB/1177

SIGMUND FREUD: On Creativity and the Unconscious: *Papers on the Psychology of Art, Literature, Love, Religion.* § △ *Intro. by Benjamin Nelson* TB/45

C. JUDSON HERRICK: The Evolution of Human Nature TB/545

WILLIAM JAMES: Psychology: *The Briefer Course. Edited with an Intro. by Gordon Allport* TB/1034

C. G. JUNG: Psychological Reflections △ TB/2001

C. G. JUNG: Symbols of Transformation: *An Analysis of the Prelude to a Case of Schizophrenia.* △ *Illus.*
Vol. I TB/2009; Vol. II TB/2010

C. G. JUNG & C. KERÉNYI: Essays on a Science of Mythology: *The Myths of the Divine Child and the Divine Maiden* TB/2014

JOHN T. MC NEILL: A History of the Cure of Souls TB/126

KARL MENNINGER: Theory of Psychoanalytic Technique TB/1144

ERICH NEUMANN: Amor and Psyche: *The Psychic Development of the Feminine* △ TB/2012

ERICH NEUMANN: The Archetypal World of Henry Moore. △ *107 illus.* TB/2020

ERICH NEUMANN : The Origins and History of Consciousness △ Vol. I *Illus.* TB/2007; Vol. II TB/2008

C. P. OBERNDORF: A History of Psychoanalysis in America TB/1147

RALPH BARTON PERRY: The Thought and Character of William James: *Briefer Version* TB/1156

JEAN PIAGET, BÄRBEL INHELDER, & ALINA SZEMINSKA: The Child's Conception of Geometry ° △ TB/1146

JOHN H. SCHAAR: Escape from Authority: *The Perspectives of Erich Fromm* TB/1155

MUZAFER SHERIF: The Psychology of Social Norms TB/3072

Sociology

JACQUES BARZUN: Race: *A Study in Superstition. Revised Edition* TB/1172

BERNARD BERELSON, Ed.: The Behavioral Sciences Today TB/1127

ABRAHAM CAHAN: The Rise of David Levinsky: *A documentary novel of social mobility in early twentieth century America. Intro. by John Higham* TB/1028

THOMAS C. COCHRAN: The Inner Revolution: *Essays on the Social Sciences in History* TB/1140

LEWIS A. COSER, Ed.: Political Sociology TB/1293

ALLISON DAVIS & JOHN DOLLARD: Children of Bondage: *The Personality Development of Negro Youth in the Urban South* ¶ TB/3049

ST. CLAIR DRAKE & HORACE R. CAYTON: Black Metropolis: *A Study of Negro Life in a Northern City.* △ *Revised and Enlarged. Intro. by Everett C. Hughes*
Vol. I TB/1086; Vol. II TB/1087

EMILE DURKHEIM et al.: Essays on Sociology and Philosophy: *With Analyses of Durkheim's Life and Work.* ¶ *Edited by Kurt H. Wolff* TB/1151

LEON FESTINGER, HENRY W. RIECKEN & STANLEY SCHACHTER: When Prophecy Fails: *A Social and Psychological Account of a Modern Group that Predicted the Destruction of the World* ¶ TB/1132

ALVIN W. GOULDNER: Wildcat Strike: *A Study in Worker-Management Relationships* ¶ TB/1176

FRANCIS J. GRUND: Aristocracy in America: *Social Class in the Formative Years of the New Nation* △ TB/1001

KURT LEWIN: Field Theory in Social Science: *Selected Theoretical Papers.* ¶ △ *Edited with a Foreword by Dorwin Cartwright* TB/1135

R. M. MAC IVER: Social Causation TB/1153

ROBERT K. MERTON, LEONARD BROOM, LEONARD S. COTTRELL, JR., Editors: Sociology Today: *Problems and Prospects* ¶ Vol. I TB/1173; Vol. II TB/1174

ROBERTO MICHELS: First Lectures in Political Sociology. *Edited by Alfred de Grazia* ¶ ° TB/1224

BARRINGTON MOORE, JR.: Political Power and Social Theory: *Seven Studies* ¶ TB/1221

BARRINGTON MOORE, JR.: Soviet Politics—The Dilemma of Power: *The Role of Ideas in Social Change* ¶ TB/1222

TALCOTT PARSONS & EDWARD A. SHILS, Editors: Toward a General Theory of Action: *Theoretical Foundations for the Social Sciences* TB/1083

JOHN H. ROHRER & MUNRO S. EDMONDSON, Eds.: The Eighth Generation Grows Up: *Cultures and Personalities of New Orleans Negroes* ¶ TB/3050

ARNOLD ROSE: The Negro in America: *The Condensed Version of Gunnar Myrdal's* An American Dilemma TB/3048

KURT SAMUELSSON: Religion and Economic Action: *A Critique of Max Weber's* The Protestant Ethic and the Spirit of Capitalism. ¶ ° *Trans. by E. G. French. Ed. with Intro. by D. C. Coleman* TB/1131

PHILIP SELZNICK: TVA and the Grass Roots: *A Study in the Sociology of Formal Organization* TB/1230

GEORG SIMMEL et al.: Essays on Sociology, Philosophy, and Aesthetics. ¶ *Edited by Kurt H. Wolff* TB/1234

HERBERT SIMON: The Shape of Automation: *For Men and Management* △ TB/1245

PITIRIM A. SOROKIN: Contemporary Sociological Theories. *Through the First Quarter of the 20th Century* TB/3046

MAURICE R. STEIN: The Eclipse of Community: *An Interpretation of American Studies* TB/1128

FERDINAND TÖNNIES: Community and Society: *Gemeinschaft und Gesellschaft. Translated and edited by Charles P. Loomis* TB/1116

W. LLOYD WARNER & Associates: Democracy in Jonesville: *A Study in Quality and Inequality* TB/1129

W. LLOYD WARNER: Social Class in America: *The Evaluation of Status* TB/1013

RELIGION

Ancient & Classical

J. H. BREASTED: Development of Religion and Thought in Ancient Egypt. *Intro. by John A. Wilson* TB/57
HENRI FRANKFORT: Ancient Egyptian Religion: *An Interpretation* TB/77
G. RACHEL LEVY: Religious Conceptions of the Stone Age *and their Influence upon European Thought.* △ *Illus. Introduction by Henri Frankfort* TB/106
MARTIN P. NILSSON: Greek Folk Religion. *Foreword by Arthur Darby Nock* TB/78
ALEXANDRE PIANKOFF: The Shrines of Tut-Ankh-Amon. △ *Edited by N. Rambova. 117 illus.* TB/2011
ERWIN ROHDE: Psyche: *The Cult of Souls and Belief in Immortality Among the Greeks.* △ *Intro. by W. K. C. Guthrie* Vol. I TB/140; Vol. II TB/141
H. J. ROSE: Religion in Greece and Rome △ TB/55

Biblical Thought & Literature

W. F. ALBRIGHT: The Biblical Period from Abraham to Ezra TB/102
C. K. BARRETT, Ed.: The New Testament Background: *Selected Documents* △ TB/86
C. H. DODD: The Authority of the Bible △ TB/43
M. S. ENSLIN: Christian Beginnings △ TB/5
M. S. ENSLIN: The Literature of the Christian Movement △ TB/6
JOHN GRAY: Archaeology and the Old Testament World. △ *Illus.* TB/127
JAMES MUILENBURG: The Way of Israel: *Biblical Faith and Ethics* △ TB/133
H. H. ROWLEY: The Growth of the Old Testament △ TB/107
GEORGE ADAM SMITH: The Historical Geography of the Holy Land. ° △ *Revised and reset* TB/138
D. WINTON THOMAS, Ed.: Documents from Old Testament Times △ TB/85
WALTHER ZIMMERLI: The Law and the Prophets: *A Study of the Meaning of the Old Testament* △ TB/144

The Judaic Tradition

LEO BAECK: Judaism and Christianity. *Trans. with Intro. by Walter Kaufmann* TB/823
SALO W. BARON: Modern Nationalism and Religion JP/18
MARTIN BUBER: Eclipse of God: *Studies in the Relation Between Religion and Philosophy* △ TB/12
MARTIN BUBER: For the Sake of Heaven TB/801
MARTIN BUBER: Hasidism and Modern Man. △ *Ed. and Trans. by Maurice Friedman* TB/839
MARTIN BUBER: The Knowledge of Man. △ *Edited with an Introduction by Maurice Friedman. Translated by Maurice Friedman and Ronald Gregor Smith* TB/135
MARTIN BUBER: Moses: *The Revelation and the Covenant* △ TB/837
MARTIN BUBER: The Origin and Meaning of Hasidism △ TB/835
MARTIN BUBER: Pointing the Way. △ *Introduction by Maurice S. Friedman* TB/103
MARTIN BUBER: The Prophetic Faith TB/73
MARTIN BUBER: Two Types of Faith: *the interpenetration of Judaism and Christianity* ° △ TB/75
ERNST LUDWIG EHRLICH: A Concise History of Israel: *From the Earliest Times to the Destruction of the Temple in A.D. 70* ° △ TB/128
MAURICE S. FRIEDMAN: Martin Buber: *The Life of Dialogue* △ TB/64
GENESIS: *The NJV Translation* TB/836
SOLOMON GRAYZEL: A History of the Contemporary Jews TB/816
WILL HERBERG: Judaism and Modern Man TB/810
ARTHUR HERTZBERG: The Zionist Idea TB/817
ABRAHAM J. HESCHEL: God in Search of Man: *A Philosophy of Judaism* TB/807
ISAAC HUSIK: A History of Medieval Jewish Philosophy TB/803
FLAVIUS JOSEPHUS: The Great Roman-Jewish War, *with* The Life of Josephus. *Introduction by William R. Farmer* TB/74
JACOB R. MARCUS: The Jew in the Medieval World TB/814
MAX L. MARGOLIS & ALEXANDER MARX: A History of the Jewish People TB/806
T. J. MEEK: Hebrew Origins TB/69
JAMES PARKES: The Conflict of the Church and the Synagogue: *The Jews and Early Christianity* JP/21
PHILO, SAADYA GAON, & JEHUDA HALEVI: Three Jewish Philosophers. *Ed. by Hans Lewey, Alexander Altmann, & Isaak Heinemann* TB/813
CECIL ROTH: A History of the Marranos TB/812
CECIL ROTH: The Jews in the Renaissance. *Illus.* TB/834
HERMAN L. STRACK: Introduction to the Talmud and Midrash TB/808
JOSHUA TRACHTENBERG: The Devil and the Jews: *The Medieval Conception of the Jew and its Relation to Modern Anti-Semitism* TB/822

Christianity: General

ROLAND H. BAINTON: Christendom: *A Short History of Christianity and its Impact on Western Civilization.* △ *Illus.* Vol. I TB/131; Vol. II TB/132

Christianity: Origins & Early Development

AUGUSTINE: An Augustine Synthesis. △ *Edited by Erich Przywara* TB/335
ADOLF DEISSMANN: Paul: *A Study in Social and Religious History* TB/15
EDWARD GIBBON: The Triumph of Christendom in the Roman Empire *(Chaps. XV-XX of "Decline and Fall," J. B. Bury edition).* § △ *Illus.* TB/46
MAURICE GOGUEL: Jesus and the Origins of Christianity. ° △ *Introduction by C. Leslie Mitton*
Volume I: *Prolegomena to the Life of Jesus* TB/65
Volume II: *The Life of Jesus* TB/66
EDGAR J. GOODSPEED: A Life of Jesus TB/1
ROBERT M. GRANT: Gnosticism and Early Christianity. △ *Revised Edition* TB/136
ADOLF HARNACK: The Mission and Expansion of Christianity in the First Three Centuries. *Introduction by Jaroslav Pelikan* TB/92
R. K. HARRISON: The Dead Sea Scrolls : *An Introduction* ° △ TB/84
EDWIN HATCH: The Influence of Greek Ideas on Christianity. § △ *Introduction and Bibliography by Frederick C. Grant* TB/18
ARTHUR DARBY NOCK: Early Gentile Christianity and Its Hellenistic Background TB/111
ARTHUR DARBY NOCK: St. Paul ° △ TB/104
ORIGEN: On First Principles. △ *Edited by G. W. Butterworth. Introduction by Henri de Lubac* TB/311
JAMES PARKES: The Conflict of the Church and the Synagogue: *The Jews and Early Christianity* JP/21
SULPICIUS SEVERUS et al.: The Western Fathers: *Being the Lives of Martin of Tours, Ambrose, Augustine of Hippo, Honoratus of Arles and Germanus of Auxerre.* △ *Edited and translated by F. R. Hoare* TB/309
F. VAN DER MEER: Augustine the Bishop: *Church and Society at the Dawn of the Middle Ages* △ TB/304
JOHANNES WEISS: Earliest Christianity: *A History of the Period A.D. 30-150. Introduction and Bibliography by Frederick C. Grant* Volume I TB/53
Volume II TB/54

Christianity: The Middle Ages and The Reformation

ANSELM OF CANTERBURY: Truth, Freedom and Evil: *Three Philosophical Dialogues. Ed., trans., and Intro. by Jasper Hopkins & Herbert Richardson* TB/317

JOHN CALVIN & JACOPO SADOLETO: A Reformation Debate. *Edited by John C. Olin* TB/1239

G. CONSTANT: The Reformation in England: *The English Schism, Henry VIII, 1509-1547* △ TB/314

CHRISTOPHER DAWSON, Ed.: Mission to Asia: *Narratives and Letters of the Franciscan Missionaries in Mongolia and China in the 13th and 14th Centuries* △ TB/315

JOHANNES ECKHART: Meister Eckhart: *A Modern Translation by R. B. Blakney* TB/8

DESIDERIUS ERASMUS: Christian Humanism and the Reformation: *Selected Writings. Edited and translated by John C. Olin* TB/1166

ÉTIENNE GILSON: Dante and Philosophy △ TB/1089

WILLIAM HALLER: The Rise of Puritanism △ TB/22

HAJO HOLBORN: Ulrich von Hutten and the German Reformation TB/1238

JOHAN HUIZINGA: Erasmus and the Age of Reformation. △ *Illus.* TB/19

A. C. MC GIFFERT: Protestant Thought Before Kant △ *Preface by Jaroslav Pelikan* TB/93

JOHN T. MC NEILL: Makers of the Christian Tradition: *From Alfred the Great to Schleiermacher* △ TB/121

G. MOLLAT: The Popes at Avignon, 1305-1378 △ TB/308

GORDON RUPP: Luther's Progress to the Diet of Worms ° △ TB/120

Christianity: The Protestant Tradition

KARL BARTH: Church Dogmatics: *A Selection* △ TB/95

KARL BARTH: Dogmatics in Outline △ TB/56

KARL BARTH: The Word of God and the Word of Man TB/13

RUDOLF BULTMANN et al: Translating Theology into the Modern Age: *Historical, Systematic and Pastoral Reflections on Theology and the Church in the Contemporary Situation. Volume 2 of* Journal for Theology and the Church, *edited by Robert W. Funk in association with Gerhard Ebeling* TB/252

WHITNEY R. CROSS: The Burned-Over District: *The Social and Intellectual History of Enthusiastic Religion in Western New York, 1800-1850* △ TB/1242

WINTHROP HUDSON: The Great Tradition of the American Churches TB/98

SOREN KIERKEGAARD: On Authority and Revelation: *The Book on Adler. Translated by Walter Lowrie. Intro. by Frederick Sontag* TB/139

SOREN KIERKEGAARD: Crisis in the Life of an Actress *and Other Essays on Drama.* △ *Trans. with Intro. by Stephen D. Crites* TB/145

SOREN KIERKEGAARD: Edifying Discourses. *Edited with an Introduction by Paul Holmer* TB/32

SOREN KIERKEGAARD: The Journals of Kierkegaard. ° △ *Ed. with Intro. by Alexander Dru* TB/52

SOREN KIERKEGAARD: The Point of View for My Work as an Author: *A Report to History.* § *Preface by Benjamin Nelson* TB/88

SOREN KIERKEGAARD: The Present Age. § △ *Translated and edited by Alexander Dru. Introduction by Walter Kaufmann* TB/94

SOREN KIERKEGAARD: Purity of Heart △ TB/4

SOREN KIERKEGAARD: Repetition: *An Essay in Experimental Psychology.* △ *Translated with Introduction & Notes by Walter Lowrie* TB/117

SOREN KIERKEGAARD: Works of Love: *Some Christian Reflections in the Form of Discourses* △ TB/122

WALTER LOWRIE: Kierkegaard: *A Life* Vol. I TB/89
Vol. II TB/90

JOHN MACQUARRIE: The Scope of Demythologizing: *Bultmann and His Critics* △ TB/134

PERRY MILLER & T. H. JOHNSON, Editors: The Puritans: *A Sourcebook of Their Writings* Vol. I TB/1093
Vol. II TB/1094

JAMES M. ROBINSON et al.: The Bultmann School of Biblical Interpretation: New Directions? *Volume 1 of* Journal for Theology and the Church, *edited by Robert W. Funk in association with Gerhard Ebeling* TB/251

F. SCHLEIERMACHER: The Christian Faith. △ *Introduction by Richard R. Niebuhr* Vol. I TB/108
Vol. II TB/109

F. SCHLEIERMACHER: On Religion: *Speeches to Its Cultured Despisers. Intro. by Rudolf Otto* TB/36

TIMOTHY L. SMITH: Revivalism and Social Reform: *American Protestantism on the Eve of the Civil War* TB/1229

PAUL TILLICH: Dynamics of Faith △ TB/42

PAUL TILLICH: Morality and Beyond TB/142

EVELYN UNDERHILL: Worship △ TB/10

Christianity: The Roman and Eastern Traditions

DOM CUTHBERT BUTLER: Western Mysticism: *The Teaching of Augustine, Gregory and Bernard on Contemplation and the Contemplative Life* § ° △ TB/312

A. ROBERT CAPONIGRI, Ed.: Modern Catholic Thinkers I: *God and Man* △ TB/306

A. ROBERT CAPONIGRI, Ed.: Modern Catholic Thinkers II: *The Church and the Political Order*△ TB/307

THOMAS CORBISHLEY, S.J.: Roman Catholicism △ TB/112

CHRISTOPHER DAWSON: The Historic Reality of Christian Culture TB/305

G. P. FEDOTOV: The Russian Religious Mind: *Kievan Christianity, the 10th to the 13th centuries* TB/370

G. P. FEDOTOV, Ed.: A Treasury of Russian Spirituality TB/303

ÉTIENNE GILSON: The Spirit of Thomism TB/313

DAVID KNOWLES: The English Mystical Tradition △ TB/302

GABRIEL MARCEL: Being and Having: *An Existential Diary.* △ *Introduction by James Collins* TB/310

GABRIEL MARCEL: Homo Viator: *Introduction to a Metaphysic of Hope* TB/397

FRANCIS DE SALES: Introduction to the Devout Life. *Trans. by John K. Ryan* TB/316

GUSTAVE WEIGEL, S. J.: Catholic Theology in Dialogue TB/301

Oriental Religions: Far Eastern, Near Eastern

TOR ANDRAE: Mohammed: *The Man and His Faith* △ TB/62

EDWARD CONZE: Buddhism: *Its Essence and Development.* ° △ *Foreword by Arthur Waley* TB/58

EDWARD CONZE et al., Editors: Buddhist Texts Through the Ages △ TB/113

ANANDA COOMARASWAMY: Buddha and the Gospel of Buddhism. △ *Illus.* TB/119

H. G. CREEL: Confucius and the Chinese Way TB/63

FRANKLIN EDGERTON, Trans. & Ed.: The Bhagavad Gita TB/115

SWAMI NIKHILANANDA, Trans. & Ed.: The Upanishads: *A One-Volume Abridgment* △ TB/114

HELLMUT WILHELM: Change: *Eight Lectures on the I Ching* △ TB/2019

Philosophy of Religion

NICOLAS BERDYAEV: The Beginning and the End § △ TB/14

NICOLAS BERDYAEV: Christian Existentialism: *A Berdyaev Synthesis.* △ *Ed. by Donald A. Lowrie* TB/130

NICOLAS BERDYAEV: The Destiny of Man △ TB/61

RUDOLF BULTMANN: History and Eschatology: *The Presence of Eternity* ° TB/91

RUDOLF BULTMANN AND FIVE CRITICS: Kerygma and Myth: *A Theological Debate* △ TB/80

RUDOLF BULTMANN and KARL KUNDSIN: Form Criticism: *Two Essays on New Testament Research.* △ *Translated by Frederick C. Grant* TB/96

MIRCEA ELIADE: The Sacred and the Profane TB/81
LUDWIG FEUERBACH: The Essence of Christianity. § *Introduction by Karl Barth. Foreword by H. Richard Niebuhr* TB/11
ÉTIENNE GILSON: The Spirit of Thomism TB/313
ADOLF HARNACK: What is Christianity? § △ *Introduction by Rudolf Bultmann* TB/17
FRIEDRICH HEGEL: On Christianity: *Early Theological Writings. Ed. by R. Kroner and T. M. Knox* TB/79
KARL HEIM: Christian Faith and Natural Science △ TB/16
IMMANUEL KANT: Religion Within the Limits of Reason Alone. § *Intro. by T. M. Greene & J. Silber* TB/67
K. E. KIRK: The Vision of God: *The Christian Doctrine of the Summum Bonum* § △ TB/137
JOHN MACQUARRIE: An Existentialist Theology: *A Comparison of Heidegger and Bultmann.* ° △ *Preface by Rudolf Bultmann* TB/125
PAUL RAMSEY, Ed.: Faith and Ethics: *The Theology of H. Richard Niebuhr* TB/129
EUGEN ROSENSTOCK-HUESSY: The Christian Future *or the Modern Mind Outrun. Intro. by Harold Stahmer* TB/143
PIERRE TEILHARD DE CHARDIN: The Divine Milieu ° △ TB/384
PIERRE TEILHARD DE CHARDIN: The Phenomenon of Man ° △ TB/383

Religion, Culture & Society

JOSEPH L. BLAU, Ed.: Cornerstones of Religious Freedom in America: *Selected Basic Documents, Court Decisions and Public Statements. Revised and Enlarged Edition* TB/118
C. C. GILLISPIE: Genesis and Geology: *The Decades before Darwin* § TB/51
KYLE HASELDEN: The Racial Problem in Christian Perspective TB/116
WALTER KAUFMANN, Ed.: Religion from Tolstoy to Camus: *Basic Writings on Religious Truth and Morals. Enlarged Edition* TB/123
JOHN T. MC NEILL: A History of the Cure of Souls TB/126
KENNETH B. MURDOCK: Literature and Theology in Colonial New England TB/99
H. RICHARD NIEBUHR: Christ and Culture △ TB/3
H. RICHARD NIEBUHR: The Kingdom of God in America TB/49
R. B. PERRY: Puritanism and Democracy TB/1138
PAUL PFUETZE: Self, Society, Existence: *Human Nature and Dialogue in the Thought of George Herbert Mead and Martin Buber* TB/1059
WALTER RAUSCHENBUSCH: Christianity and the Social Crisis. ‡ *Edited by Robert D. Cross* TB/3059
KURT SAMUELSSON: Religion and Economic Action: *A Critique of Max Weber's* The Protestant Ethic and the Spirit of Capitalism ¶ ° △ *Trans. by E. G. French. Ed. with Intro. by D. C. Coleman* TB/1131
TIMOTHY L. SMITH: Revivalism and Social Reform: *American Protestantism on the Eve of the Civil War* △ TB/1229
ERNST TROELTSCH: The Social Teaching of the Christian Churches ° △ Vol. I TB/71; Vol. II TB/72

NATURAL SCIENCES AND MATHEMATICS

Biological Sciences

CHARLOTTE AUERBACH: The Science of Genetics Σ △ TB/568
MARSTON BATES: The Natural History of Mosquitoes. *Illus.* TB/578
A. BELLAIRS: Reptiles: *Life History, Evolution, and Structure.* △ *Illus.* TB/520
LUDWIG VON BERTALANFFY: Modern Theories of Development: *An Introduction to Theoretical Biology* TB/554
LUDWIG VON BERTALANFFY: Problems of Life: *An Evaluation of Modern Biological and Scientific Thought* △ TB/521
HAROLD F. BLUM: Time's Arrow and Evolution TB/555
JOHN TYLER BONNER: The Ideas of Biology. Σ △ *Illus.* TB/570
A. J. CAIN: Animal Species and their Evolution. △ *Illus.* TB/519
WALTER B. CANNON: Bodily Changes in Pain, Hunger, Fear and Rage. *Illus.* TB/562
W. E. LE GROS CLARK: The Antecedents of Man: *An Introduction to Evolution of the Primates.* ° △ *Illus.* TB/559
W. H. DOWDESWELL: Animal Ecology. △ *Illus.* TB/543
W. H. DOWDESWELL: The Mechanism of Evolution. △ *Illus.* TB/527
R. W. GERARD: Unresting Cells. *Illus.* TB/541
DAVID LACK: Darwin's Finches. △ *Illus.* TB/544
ADOLF PORTMANN: Animals as Social Beings. ° △ *Illus.* TB/572
O. W. RICHARDS: The Social Insects. △ *Illus.* TB/542
P. M. SHEPPARD: Natural Selection and Heredity. △ *Illus.* TB/528
EDMUND W. SINNOTT: Cell and Psyche: *The Biology of Purpose* TB/546
C. H. WADDINGTON: How Animals Develop. △ *Illus.* TB/553
C. H. WADDINGTON: The Nature of Life: *The Main Problems and Trends in Modern Biology* △ TB/580

Chemistry

J. R. PARTINGTON: A Short History of Chemistry. △ *Illus.* TB/522

Communication Theory

J. R. PIERCE: Symbols, Signals and Noise: *The Nature and Process of Communication* △ TB/574

Geography

R. E. COKER: This Great and Wide Sea: *An Introduction to Oceanography and Marine Biology. Illus.* TB/551
F. K. HARE: The Restless Atmosphere △ TB/560

History of Science

MARIE BOAS: The Scientific Renaissance, 1450-1630 ° △ TB/583
W. DAMPIER, Ed.: Readings in the Literature of Science. *Illus.* TB/512
A. HUNTER DUPREE: Science in the Federal Government. *A History of Policies and Activities to 1940* △ TB/573
ALEXANDRE KOYRÉ: From the Closed World to the Infinite Universe: *Copernicus, Kepler, Galileo, Newton, etc.* △ TB/31
A. G. VAN MELSEN: From Atomos to Atom: *A History of the Concept* Atom TB/517
O. NEUGEBAUER: The Exact Sciences in Antiquity TB/552
HANS THIRRING: Energy for Man: *From Windmills to Nuclear Power* △ TB/556
STEPHEN TOULMIN & JUNE GOODFIELD: The Architecture of Matter: *Physics, Chemistry & Physiology of Matter, Both Animate & Inanimate, As it Evolved Since the Beginning of Science* ° △ TB/584
STEPHEN TOULMIN & JUNE GOODFIELD: The Discovery of Time ° △ TB/585
LANCELOT LAW WHYTE: Essay on Atomism: *From Democritus to 1960* △ TB/565

Mathematics

E. W. BETH: The Foundations of Mathematics: *A Study in the Philosophy of Science* △ TB/581
H. DAVENPORT: The Higher Arithmetic: *An Introduction to the Theory of Numbers* △ TB/526

H. G. FORDER: Geometry: *An Introduction* △ TB/548

S. KÖRNER: The Philosophy of Mathematics: *An Introduction* △ TB/547

D. E. LITTLEWOOD: Skeleton Key of Mathematics: *A Simple Account of Complex Algebraic Problems* △ TB/525

GEORGE E. OWEN: Fundamentals of Scientific Mathematics TB/569

WILLARD VAN ORMAN QUINE: Mathematical Logic TB/558

O. G. SUTTON: Mathematics in Action. ° △ *Foreword by James R. Newman. Illus.* TB/518

FREDERICK WAISMANN: Introduction to Mathematical Thinking. *Foreword by Karl Menger* TB/511

Philosophy of Science

R. B. BRAITHWAITE: Scientific Explanation TB/515

J. BRONOWSKI: Science and Human Values. △ *Revised and Enlarged Edition* TB/505

ALBERT EINSTEIN et al.: Albert Einstein: Philosopher-Scientist. *Edited by Paul A. Schilpp* Vol. I TB/502 Vol. II TB/503

WERNER HEISENBERG: Physics and Philosophy: *The Revolution in Modern Science* △ TB/549

JOHN MAYNARD KEYNES: A Treatise on Probability. ° △ *Introduction by N. R. Hanson* TB/557

KARL R. POPPER: Logic of Scientific Discovery △ TB/576

STEPHEN TOULMIN: Foresight and Understanding: *An Enquiry into the Aims of Science.* △ *Foreword by Jacques Barzun* TB/564

STEPHEN TOULMIN: The Philosophy of Science: *An Introduction* △ TB/513

G. J. WHITROW: The Natural Philosophy of Time ° △ TB/563

Physics and Cosmology

JOHN E. ALLEN: Aerodynamics: *A Space Age Survey* △ TB/582

STEPHEN TOULMIN & JUNE GOODFIELD: The Fabric of the Heavens: *The Development of Astronomy and Dynamics.* △ *Illus.* TB/579

DAVID BOHM: Causality and Chance in Modern Physics. △ *Foreword by Louis de Broglie* TB/536

P. W. BRIDGMAN: Nature of Thermodynamics TB/537

P. W. BRIDGMAN: A Sophisticate's Primer of Relativity △ TB/575

A. C. CROMBIE, Ed.: Turning Point in Physics TB/535

C. V. DURELL: Readable Relativity. △ *Foreword by Freeman J. Dyson* TB/530

ARTHUR EDDINGTON: Space, Time and Gravitation: *An Outline of the General Relativity Theory* TB/510

GEORGE GAMOW: Biography of Physics Σ △ TB/567

MAX JAMMER: Concepts of Force: *A Study in the Foundation of Dynamics* TB/550

MAX JAMMER: Concepts of Mass *in Classical and Modern Physics* TB/571

MAX JAMMER: Concepts of Space: *The History of Theories of Space in Physics. Foreword by Albert Einstein* TB/533

G. J. WHITROW: The Structure and Evolution of the Universe: *An Introduction to Cosmology.* △ *Illus.* TB/504

Code to Torchbook Libraries:

TB/1+	: The Cloister Library
TB/301+	: The Cathedral Library
TB/501+	: The Science Library
TB/801+	: The Temple Library
TB/1001+	: The Academy Library
TB/2001+	: The Bollingen Library
TB/3001+	: The University Library
JP/1+	: Jewish Publication Society Series